T0196553

# Blueprint for Immortality

# Blueprint for Immortality

Julian Valderrama

| Library of Congress Control Number: | | 2016915041 |
|---|---|---|
| ISBN: | Hardcover | 978-1-5245-4237-5 |
| | Softcover | 978-1-5245-4236-8 |
| | eBook | 978-1-5245-4235-1 |

Print information available on the last page.

Rev. date: 12/26/2019

**To order additional copies of this book, contact:**
Xlibris
1-888-795-4274
www.Xlibris.com
Orders@Xlibris.com
746213

# CONTENTS

Chapter 1   Evidence and the Importance of Communicating
Results.................................................................................1
Moses: A Sort of Scientist...............................................1
Please Question Everything and Everyone!......................3
Please Do Not Kill the Messenger!...................................5
Moses Uses the Scientific Method to Observe Facts.......5
The Real Reason We Do Not Have Success....................8

Chapter 2   The Importance of Empirical Evidence
and Background Research: Science................................11
What Quantum Mechanics Has Revealed....................13
Scientific Concept 1: Everything in the Universe
Is Energy, Frequency, and Vibration............................14
Scientific Concept 2: The Double-Slit
Experiment Proves That Everything in the
Universe Exists in a Paradoxical Duality......................15
Scientific Concept 3: Quantum Entanglement ...........17
Scientific Principle 4: The Uncertainty Principle
and Quantum Tunneling...............................................18
Scientific Concept 5: Our Brain Is a Transmitter
and Receiver of Energy, Frequency, or Vibration..........20
Scientific Concept 6: Laws of Magnetic
Attraction, Friction, and String Theory.......................22
Tying It All Together: The Four Principles of Science......25

Chapter 3   The Importance of Empirical Evidence and
Background Research: Spirit Science............................28
Spiritual Principle 1: Everything Is Light, Energy,
Frequency, and Vibration..............................................31
The Triad of Knowledge................................................35
Scientific Potentiality 1: Water Is Wine......................37

Scientific Potentiality 2: Two Fishes and Five
Loaves Feed over Five Thousand ..................................38
Scientific Potentiality 3: Christ's Consciousness
Can Use Brain Transmission to Change the
Channel on Illness and Disease...............................39
Accepting Future Realities by Traveling to the Past ......41
Spiritual Principle 2: The Law of Magnetic Attraction.... 42
Your Powerful Thoughts ...............................................43
Practical Application.....................................................45

Chapter 4    Law of the Universe: Our Moral Obligation to
Obtain Our Desires ......................................................47
Law of the Universe: Achieving Biological Eternity......55
The Bright Future of Humankind: For Every
Action, There Is an Equal and Opposite Reaction........60
The Matrix of the Universe ...........................................66
The Ether and the Matrix of Reality.............................68

Chapter 5    "We Must Become Like a Tree Planted by
Streams of Water" ........................................................75
The Basics of Input and Output...................................79
A System That Builds Us Firmly Toward Higher
Realms of Reality.........................................................82
Books, Audio, Meetings, Relationships, and
Recognition .................................................................84
Group Meetings and Relationships: Power of the
Master Mind ...............................................................85
Sharpening Your Ax: Do We "Know" or Just
"Know About"? ...........................................................88
The Teachability Index: Quoting Kevin Trudeau..........92
The Power of Books and Audio.....................................95
The Power of Recognition.............................................99

Chapter 6    The Power of Giving: Exercising Our Mental
Faculties with the Power of Faith...............................104
Self-Awareness and the Present Moment: The
Power of Contentment and Discontentment .............105

Contentment and the Power of Feeling Good............108
Always Be Rejoicing, Give Thanks For Everything.....110
We Must Be at Cause and in Control .......................111
Being At Cause Over Negative Feelings Or Events.....115
The Power Of Perseverance And Asking For
What We Want......................................................118
The Other Side Of The Coin Of Faith: Works..........123
Difference Between Knowing The Path And
Walking The Path .................................................125
The Successful Failure.............................................128
Life As We Think We Know It Is Impossible;
Therefore We Must Focus .........................................132
The Best Energy We Can Give to Achieve
Financial Wealth...................................................135

Chapter 7   The Unfathomable Power of A Master Mind.............140
The Eight-Step Pattern For Success.........................141
Step 1: Clearly Define Your Dream And Get A
Burning Desire For Its Achievement .........................142
Step 2: Make Some Commitments ...........................148
Step 3: Be A Product Of What You Are Giving..........152
Steps 4 And 5: Find A Prospect And Share The
Program................................................................156
Step 6: Answering Questions And Overcoming
Objections, Following Up, And Following Through..... 158
Steps 7 And 8: Start Them Right By Plugging
Them Into The System.............................................159
Skipping All the Nitty-Gritty Work ..........................161

Chapter 8   The Alchemy of the Universe ................................ 162
What Happens After Making A Decision ..................163
The Irony: The Universe Convinces You That It
Is Impossible.........................................................164
The Nature of the First Set of PCES:
"Being at the right place at the right time"................164
The nature of the second set of PCES:
"Have we been convinced that it is impossible?" ........164

The Nature of the Third Set of PCES: "A taste of
success" .................................................................................167
The Nature of the Fourth Set of PCES: "The
green light to failure" .................................................168
The Nature of the Fifth Set of PCES: "We Win!".......169
How To Unfold Your Own Personal Legend.............173
Letting Go of All Decision Making .........................176
Your Personal Legend .............................................180
Activating Your Own Personal Legend......................184
Gideon and His Three Hundred Men.......................187
An Introduction to Part II of Blueprint for
Biological Immortality.............................................193

Chapter 9    Blueprint for Immortality: Part I............................. 195
The First Key to the Door to Immortality.................197
The Foundational Laws of Immortality.....................198
The Second Key to the Door to Immortality.............202
The Third Key to the Door to Immortality ...............209

Chapter 10   Blueprint For Immortality: Part II............................ 215
Plenipotentiary of Christ Consciousness?..................216
Ambassador and Minister Under Christ
Consciousness? .......................................................219
The first and final set of inexorable agents; the
error of our quintessence.........................................225
Are we our body?....................................................226
In conclusion: We are our spirit (probably)...............232
Sin and Imperfection ..............................................236
The True Definition of Sin and Imperfection............238
Hear What the Spirit Says to the Congregations........242
Prime Minister; Administers Life .............................244
Our Inheritance; A Debt Sentence...........................245
Legal Disclosure for Loss of Property........................248
The Final Axiom: The Reengineering of our
DNA Genome.........................................................251
Tying it all together ................................................254

Chapter 11  Identifying Christ's Consciousness
           And The True; 'New World Order' ...........................255
           The "Triad Of Knowledge" ......................................257
           Foundational Law for Immortality 1:.......................258
           Foundational Law for Immortally 2:........................258
           1st Principle...............................................................259
           2nd Principle............................................................261
           3rd Principle.............................................................264
           4th Principle.............................................................267
           Modern Day Egypt; As Above, So Below ..................269
           The Issue of Our Sovereignty Settled .......................276
           Tying it all together ..................................................277
           Recommended References ........................................293

           Index ........................................................................295

# DEDICATION

To whom should this knowledge be dedicated? What purpose will this instruction play in our lives? When and where do we see the physical evidence that this insight plays a role in the lives of every individual as much as we see the law of gravity affect our personal lives?

Can instruction, knowledge, understanding just be relevant to each individual conscious being? Is it just really "to each its own"? Can we readily find that there are principles and rules in life that, when applied, affect and effect every aspect of our reality regardless of background, race, birthright, and origin? We can certainly admit to the fact that no matter who you are, you obey and respect the law of gravity. We enjoy its discernible benefits, as well as its immediate dire consequences if we break this most basic law. People will jump off tall buildings to their deaths to escape their painful present realities, while others will jump off from much higher altitudes to experience the exhilaration of falling from an airplane with the safety of a parachute. The law of gravity plays its role all the same.

With that being said, the probability is that your life is at effect. Consider the word *effect*. A definition says that it is "a change that is a result or consequence of an action or other cause" Its verb form means "to cause (something) to happen" or "to bring about." Isaac Newton described through the laws of physics that for every action, there is an equal and opposite reaction. Cause and effect. In simpler terms, it has also been described as "you reap what you sow," and "what goes around comes around." People at times feel like their lives are the result and at the mercy of "outside" influences beyond their control. This may be true to a certain extent, but do we realize that these laws of physics work in our lives whether we consciously know about them or not?

Therefore in the simplest form, this book was designed and dedicated for everyone who is currently reading this page as a result of whatever people, circumstances, or events had to take place in order for you to be here in this instant in time, now, reading this exact sentence. Everyone who is at cause or at effect. You.

## Disclaimer

Before reading this book, please check with your professional advisors; psychologist, psychiatrist, rabbi, priest, pastor, church leader, politician of preference—anyone whose guidance and opinion you feel are better than yours. For that matter, you are certainly encouraged to pray to your choice of deity and ask permission to read this book.

You must know simply that everything I say in this book is simply my opinion in written form, and there are many people who may strongly disagree with these statements. No one has a monopoly over knowledge and or information; so under the first amendment or moral law, my free speech is being expressed naturally. Doing anything written in this book without the supervision of those who you have given your approval to supervise your actions, you will do so at your own risk. The publisher and the author, the distributors and bookstores, present this information for educational purposes only and for your entertainment. I am not prescribing medical treatment or offering financial advice or legal advice, for I do not hold the proper titles or licenses to do so.

So this book is only my opinions, my thoughts, and my conclusions. Again, it is for educational purposes only, and you and only you are responsible if you choose to do anything based on what you read in this book.

Julian Valderrama

# An Introduction to Part I of *Blueprint for Immortality*

> *If I have seen further than others, it is by standing upon the shoulders of giants.*
>
> —Isaac Newton

To preface the content of this book would be to write a book as big as the Bible. To try to read it may excite some, but it would most likely turn off most. In essence, what we want as humans, who just love instant gratification, is to find instant answers. The shortest, quickest way from point A to point B. Or we may just want to enjoy the scenery. Which means that getting from point A to point B is getting from where we are not doing what we want to the point where we are doing exactly what we want, enjoying the scenery. But we want it *now*! As such is the case, it will be briefly described in simple and ready-to-use terms, without going on a long-winded explanation, why the principles described in the content of this book will absolutely get us from our point A to point B. They are exactly what we need to know and not just know about.

It may be said that being impatient is a weakness, but have we considered that it could be a strong point that we all have? Technology may be a witness, a testament to that reality. We are learning and experiencing faster than ever before, and it continues to add discernible value to our immediate present reality. We can now instantly contact anybody on the other side of the globe, while just over 150 years ago, it would have taken weeks or months or even years for information to arrive at its destination. So maybe it is our mission to impatiently create better lives so we can just enjoy life more patiently and plainly. Or is it the other way around? Do we patiently create better lives so we can impatiently live more fully? Maybe both are true—I'll let you decide.

The point is that we want to improve every facet of our lives instantly. In this instant, our desires are obviously relevant only to each its own. While one person may desire a simple life in the woods in a log cabin where nature is more accessible, another may readily jump at the excitement of competing against themselves or others, to attain a fast-paced life in a major city full of life. A person may want a little of both worlds, and there is nothing wrong with that. Whatever experience we desire to attain to now, we generally want more of that—physical, emotional, and mental, as well as spiritual wealth. Through the quantum physical definition, I believe, it tells us that we just want more "energy intensified."

Science has plainly described to us that the deeper we observe the universe, whether outwardly or inwardly, whether we are observing the macrocosmos or the microcosmos, that our power of observation is teaching us that the we are only observing the infinite universe of infinite energy. There may be debate in the concept that the universe may or may not be infinite. I personally believe there is more evidence of the reality of an infinite universe. But we can all agree that the current understanding is that everything in the universe is energy, vibration, or frequency.

In the same manner that we may desire to build something as tangible as a house, we know we need its most basic components. Wood, metal, nails, etc. Then we must readily accept that if we *know* by definition,  not just know about the most basic components of all matter in our physical universe, then we'll be able to build better and more consistently. Consider the field of science as it relates to health care. During the 1800s, we learned that doctors were going into surgery with unwashed hands and using medical tools that were not proper cleaned and sanitized. The mortality rate in the delivery room was catastrophic. Women had a higher chance of survival when giving birth at home than trying to deliver in the hospital. It was discovered that doctors were going into the delivery room with contaminated hands, carrying agents causing fatal disease. How? After teaching a postmortem examination in class, they would fail to clean their hands. The so-called doctors were careless about their practice, and trusting mothers that had to pay with their lives. Even after providing evidence of the positive results of scrubbing one's hands before every procedure and clearly showing the mortality rate become zero, the medical establishment "proceeded to vilify, ostracize, and finally have him discharged from this prestigious positions in maternity hospitals. Haunted by the fact that hundreds of thousands of women continued to die, Dr. Semmelweis eventually died of insanity in 1865" (from *Let's Cure Humanity* by Robert Barefoot). This was a gross result of injustice, prejudice, and pride, as well as abuse of authority. A consequence of willful ignorance. This is but one example among many cases of injustice.

Since this was the case, the real heresy is the continuous idea that insists on permeating people's minds: believing that "we know all there is to know." Obviously there is the idea that the more we know, the more we realize how much we don't know. The status quo keeps on being challenged. Those who are, in essence, on top of the status quo will not accept resistance and many times will persecute those who threaten their current power, even if it means overstepping on other people's rights and free will. Albert Einstein was quoted as saying, "Great sprits have always encountered violent opposition from mediocre minds." I personally believe this to be a sad reality seen throughout history.

> *What we know is a drop, what we don't know is an ocean.*

> —Isaac Newton

Newton's principle of success helps us to be fully aware that our present knowledge, whether individual or collective, is but a fraction of what it could potentially become. It helps us keep a keen observation on those who may have achieved more success so as to have contrast contextually to our present growth. We should always consider that our personal or collective status quo of knowledge is what we "know" so far. We must understand this law as individuals and as a collective society if we are to progress. And when we experience a different opinion or understanding, we must never shut our eyes to the possibility of others discernment, points of view, or frame of minds. Therefore, the scientific method—that of taking a question, doing background research and taking every possible piece of data without bias, constructing a hypothesis, then testing it through honest experimentation, analyzing the results to form a conclusion—is indispensable, for this process is of utmost importance when taking and establishing new knowledge.

This method has allowed us to go out into outer space and create powerful methods of enhancing our immediate experience. Therefore, if we feel that our beliefs are being challenged, we should consider the possibility that most likely we don't have the whole truth or the only truth. Considering other points of view may enforce what we feel we already know and therefore give us more conviction of our personal or general understanding of what makes our world work or not work. It can help us discern what creates success or does not create success based on tangible, real-life results. And if we find that our current understanding is not working, we must toss the idea and be open to a better one for our own good and that of others. This is the logical scientific method that can propel us positively forward without judgment or willful ignorance. This takes us to our immediate present life, for in connection with this thought, we must fully integrate honesty in our personal lives. Do we have the evidence that our life is better and improving every day, or are we regressing?

But as we sit back and observe our personal circumstances that surround our immediate lives, do we feel appreciation and gratitude? When we reflect back on our lives as we grew up to this personal point in our lives, do we feel strong, powerful recognition because we had every advantage given to us to achieve the great success we have now achieved? Do we feel empowered now in this instant in time as we observe our immediate reality? Are we where we want to be?

Did you know that there is a war being waged against you and your mind, just so they can profit from you and your loved ones' negative emotional outputs? Did you also know that it is by making you mentally sick and incapable that powerful forces in this world are prospering beyond belief all in the name of personal gain and advantage? Did you know that like trash or disposable property, human beings are no longer being born to life but are grown to become just another form of resource?

For those few who acknowledge and recognize their life as blessed, you must be congratulated for you have harnessed powerful thinking patterns that will continue to enrich your life. But most likely for you personally, as you are reading this book, you may feel less than gratitude and appreciation for your personal circumstances. You may feel that there is much to be wanted in your life. Feelings of despondency and dissatisfaction might overwhelm us at times, making us depressed and stressed because our lives have less-than-desirable outcomes. Maybe we look at our finances, and feelings and thoughts of anxiety and hopelessness are triggered. Maybe as we look at our personal relationships, we wonder how we could improve such emotional rides. Also, maybe as we go through our day, we continue to examine that our feelings are consistently negative because every day we realize our lives are not getting better. Or it could also be that we have more that we could ever need and realize that we have privileged lives but can't help to continue to feel unfulfilled and generally unhappy.

It is all designed to blind us from one powerful truth. This truth is so empowering to the individual, that comprehension of it has made them use exorbitant amounts of money and resources to maintain this demented, finely orchestrated illusion just to keep us convinced otherwise. Throughout this book, it will be explained with scientific data why the general population is being oppressed and suppressed. The problem is that people are not aware who the enemy is nor how to fight against it. This system's inner workings are so complex that it has convince the entire world that we are free and happy, even though we are enslaved. Before revealing this personal truth that will empower us, we must be aware of a specific mental attitude and avert it.

Instead of feeling like victims of circumstances beyond our control, we must decide to be at cause over it. The great thing about taking control is that not a single literal blow of violence will have to be taken. There will be no need for unnecessary coups or mass protests or the use of any sort of violence. In reality, our real power comes from our own blueprint for immortality. It is a powerful force that will drive us to infinite progress. It is the laws of quantum physics that have aptly helped us to demonstrate it simply, and they have proven that this power is hidden in every individual, including yourself.

We must exercise the mental attitude that a colorful speech by General S. Patton successfully bred into the minds of literal soldiers of war before going into battle: "No bastard ever won a war by dying for his country. He won it by making the other poor dumb bastard die for his country." Our determination is mainly acknowledging that we must drive the force of our thoughts to win this war by taking back our individual sovereignties. People readily admire heroes for their ability to persevere under pressure and win. We must not be afraid to show courage, for it is our moral obligation to accept the sting of battle and love it. We must develop the mental ability to decide to win this war, for our lives and the lives of our loved ones have suffered because of our ignorant inaction. We have stood in neutrality for far too long, and our very physical health and emotional well-being have been paying the price. We must readily understand who the enemy is and make them die for their cause in life. Patton expressed, "We're going to cut out their living guts and use them to grease the treads of our tanks."

And when in battle, "we may chicken out." But the second "you put your hand into a bunch of goo that a moment before was your best friend's face, you'll know what to do." Obviously these phrases here in these sentences are metaphorical, but it may be very literal, for it is the quality of our lives that continues to pay the price. This is a real-life war, and we must harness our own resources and weapons and learn how and when to use them because it is our personal lives and of those whom we love the most that have been enslaved. We must understand the basic truths of our most powerful innate abilities. The symbol portrayed on the cover of this book represents the following concepts and will serve as a reminder of the unfathomable power and ability that we personally carry. Our potential is truly infinite. The axioms for this personal potential will be referred as the following:

# The "Triad of Knowledge"

*If the genius of invention were to reveal tomorrow the secret of immortality, of eternal beauty and youth, for which all humanity is aching, the same inexorable agents which prevent a mass from changing suddenly its velocity would likewise resist the force of the new knowledge until time gradually modifies human thought.*

—Nikola Tesla

*For truly I say to you, if you have faith the size of a mustard grain, you will say to this mountain, "Move from here to there," and it will move, and nothing will be impossible for you.*

—Jesus Christ, Matthew 17:20

*Whatever the mind of man can conceive and believe, it can achieve.*

—Napoleon Hill

Throughout the pages of this book, you will examine data from three of the most fundamentally accepted sources of information: science, spirituality, and success philosophy. Although incongruences may be found within and between the sources of information, it is through common denominators which are found within these sources that we will observe and prove how we can harness these truisms. From the field of quantum physics, classical physics, DNA biology, archeology, cosmology, and from spiritual and philosophical sources such as the Bible and other publications that have been accredited for our benefit.

In this book, we focus more on the world of quantum physics and spirituality to examine what creates success and what does not create success. We will also examine how general spiritual beliefs and other philosophical teachings perfectly parallel new lessons in the field of quantum physics. All three fields are suggesting, according to its findings, that these fields of knowledge are essentially giving light to powerful common denominators of practical data. They are lessons about the universe just taken from a different frame of mind. They are different sets of filters of perception describing our reality. Since these ideas will be observed throughout this book, they will be examined from the simplest form of understanding in connection to success and then explained how it relates to a few quantum experiments and then brought back to the principle. Quantum physics is now proving and describing what has been known as "true" spiritual beliefs. These fields of knowledge have revealed that they are also, in essence, "laws of the physical universe."

Certain individuals have integrated these abilities and principles into their life to create mind-blowing lifestyles; thus, for some, it has been their absolute desire to share their discoveries. Andrew Carnegie is one of the foremost examples of financial success, for his ability to acquire wealth and financial prosperity was remarkable. It will be proven undoubtedly how you can use the same laws and principles he used, so you can personally apply them toward your own personal desires and endeavors in life, whatever they may be.

Universal principles will be expounded upon through common denominators, as they are defined through these windows of knowledge or different frames of mind. They are all mental perceptions ultimately looking at the same thing. The scientific method is required through observational experimentation to establish real-life empirical evidence to establish infallible understandings. We will prove how certain knowledge and understandings have been hidden and purposefully mystified to obscure people's minds of the ultimate truth in their personal lives. It has to do with the true definition of free will and freedom; it is the place where we make the rules and our personal outcome as we decide it must happen. It is the understanding that we are our own genie that can grant us our every wish.

JULIAN VALDERRAMA

To build a foundation, in chapter 1 we will examine a very well-known but mystified story in the scripture. We will show how Moses was sort of a scientist looking to acquire physical evidence as proof of empirical evidence.

Whether you believe in this story or not, there are valid principles we can derive as easily as a public speaker or teacher uses allegories or illustrations to make a point. In the biblical reference, the record of Moses and the Red Sea is accepted by many as historical. If you don't personally believe it to be, please keep an open mind to at least just some of the lessons we will take in and how the scientific method is relevant to the entire story. Keep in mind, the book will examine all forms of authority, from experts in the field of science to experts in the field of spirituality and philosophy. We may want to strongly consider that both concepts of spirituality and philosophy have virtually always been the study and understanding of energy and how it relates to our immediate experience or reality. This is true since we all accept that the universe is nothing but energy, vibration, or frequency.     In essence, everything is energy vibrating at different frequencies.

A list of authoritative references will be made in this book that the reader may have the free will to examine through his own cognitive reference and point of view. In this book, every effort has been made to point the reader to someone who has real-life evidence to highlight what is being described thereof is true. Which brings us to the point that also studying those who may have empirical evidence in the field of finances or money will derive us incredible benefit. Isaac Newton's quote at the start of this preface, in essence, testifies to that truth. To what end?

In that together we come to the cognition and discovery, the awareness, the realization, and the truth about ourselves: "that we have awesome power." The following statements were quoted a long time ago, but as mentioned before, they have been and will continually to be scientifically proven as the truth about us humankind.

## The Triad of Knowledge

"If the genius of invention were to reveal tomorrow the secret of immortality, of eternal beauty and youth, for which all humanity is aching, the same inexorable agents which prevent a mass from changing suddenly its velocity would likewise resist the force of the new knowledge until time gradually modifies human thought." Nikola Tesla

"For truly I say to you that if you have faith the size of a mustard grain you will say to this mountain; 'Move from here to there,' and it will move, and NOTHING WILL BE IMPOSSIBLE FOR YOU." Christ's Consciousness

"Whatever the mind of man can conceive, and believe, it can achieve." Napoleon Hill

Obviously these authorities of knowledge are not the only ones who have been quoted as saying something of the like. But as previously stated, this book is going to prove with hard scientific evidence that what the biblical accounts, as well as other true philosophical teachings have been describing all along, are easily more discernible by the field of quantum physics. This emphasizes plainly that the field of quantum mechanics is giving light to spiritual phenomena or events described as miracles. Scientists are now theorizing the possibilities of instant transmissions of large masses from one place to another. Other reliable sources are testifying that this is already being done. They are also believing the possibility of being able to walk through walls and communicating instantly with other dimensions. It will be plainly shown how all of it relates to our own personal success, whatever we choose that to be. Now back to the story of Moses . . .

# CHAPTER 1

# Evidence and the Importance of Communicating Results

B ASED ON THE scientific method, the last and final step is for the one experimenting to honestly report on the findings, to properly describe the data and the cold, hard facts. It must be shown and described precisely from step 1, the question, to the hypothesis, and finally, to the conclusion what was happening and being observed. What does the scientific method have anything to do with the account of Moses? Also, what does the story of Moses have anything to do with the field of quantum physics and our personal success and that which we desire? It is of utmost importance that we realize that it has everything to do with everything.

## Moses: A Sort of Scientist

Let's briefly consider a small part of what is described as a very powerful moment in Moses' life. I would strongly encourage you to stop reading in this point in time and go and read it in the Book of Exodus, specifically the third and fourth chapter in their entirety.

At this moment, hopefully you have read it. Either way, let's briefly state the circumstances in which Moses is approached by the god of the Hebrews. Moses had ran away from Egypt, leaving prestige and position because he had committed murder. An Egyptian guard had abused a Hebrew slave, and Moses felt the need to avenge the abused man. Moses had grown up under the protection of royalty while watching his nation of Israel being oppressed by the Egyptians. The situation had gotten the best of him and made him react to this one act of oppression, thus Moses ended up killing the Egyptian guard. Obviously he fled as a criminal and a murderer under Egyptian rulership and therefore avoided prosecution. The morality of the situation will not be discussed, and it will be left up to the reader. Murder is obviously wrong. The facts are just being stated for posterity.

## From Whom Is This Information Coming From?

Moses, the convicted felon, had fled to a region where he was taken by a man named Jethro, who lived in the land of Midian with his seven daughters. There, Moses married one of Jethro's daughters and became a shepherd. After some forty years, he went to Horeb, which is referred to as the mountain of the true God. There he was approached by Jehovah, the god of the Hebrews, through an angelic representative. This is the interesting part. Moses listened attentively to the command from God to go free the Hebrews from another powerful god: Pharaoh, the king of Egypt. To the Hebrews and the Egyptians, it was obvious that Pharaoh's kingship was also supported by other more powerful gods than Pharaoh himself. Moses, in full honesty, asked this amazing question: "Who am I, that I should go to Pharaoh and bring the Israelites out of Egypt?

Let's consider the importance of this question. Here is a convicted felon, an old man, a lowly shepherd in the land of Midian, who had ran away to avoid conviction from that most powerful nation of that known world. Also, according to God, who is denoting to the fact that his so -called chosen people are enslaved under another god, is promising to deliver them from slavery!

Certainly Moses' confidence in his god and in himself was at an all-time low. This is incredibly relevant to our present day. Consider that we live in the information age. We are constantly bombarded with information that promise success and prosperity of all types. The ultimate advice on relationships comes from so -called experts in the fields of psychology, psychiatry, and medicine, as well as life coaches, etc. The ultimate advice on how to make money comes from as many sources or more. Just Google "How to be rich," "how to be wealthy," "how to be happy," "how to be healthy," or "how to (fill in the blank)." We are then taken to hundreds of pages showing so-called reliable sources. Go to a library or a bookstore. There are massive and awe-inspiring amounts of books, magazines, reports, and different written or audio materials promising the same things. We are certainly not bashing anybody in particular, but it is important that we consider that getting exact information has become hard work which takes enormous amount of time and effort.

There are so many different opinions from so many different places about how to achieve success that we easily become confused without knowing who to listen to and whose advice we should take to heart. The question is, why should you, the reader, continue to read this book, and why should you even consider finishing this book? Do I, the author, have the evidence and the physical manifestation in my physical world, and do I have the results as suggested by the scientific method? In essence, do I have what you want? Do I experience what you want to experience?

These are really important questions. Think about it. Every day we are fed information and given advice and opinions by virtually everybody, including our own uncontrolled, biased thoughts. We must ask the following questions from such sources: Do they all have the physical evidence for what they say is going to give us what we desire? This includes asking ourselves honestly: Do I give advice when I don't personally have the evidence that what I am saying works and gives results? Have I done it through the honest and proper experimentation of what it has been described as the truth about success from people who have done it? Do I give it to myself and others? Moses had it right. Who the heck was he to be taking on a task of that magnitude? I mean, really? A lowly shepherd taking away one of the most powerful economic forces under Pharaoh's control to his own detriment? Moses had every right to question God's decision of choosing him for such assignment. God let him ask his questions and gave him the freedom of speech.

Please Question Everything and Everyone!

This teaches us that since Moses questioned God's judgment, then how much more should we question every thought that comes out of people's mouths, whoever they are? Let's not suggest that we should be cynical and generally negative about information from others. There is plenty of instruction out there that we can access to get real-life results. But are we aware enough to do our due diligence, do research, and ask questions tactfully with insight and discernment. If we want to learn how to cook, are we learning from a master chef or low -wage line cook at a restaurant? If we want to learn how to operate a business, are we learning from a business school, or are we learning from someone who has a profitable business? In both scenarios, you can learn, but from whom, in reality, will you really learn the most and derive the most dividends? There is a saying that goes, "Be careful you are not taking weight loss advice from a fat person." A proverb by King Solomon says, "The one walking with the wise will become wise." Spiritual leader Paul wrote in 1 Corinthians 15:33: "Do not be misled. Bad associations spoil useful habits." Our parents always told us to not hang out with the wrong crowd because they were afraid we would turn out just like them.

This is why through this book, it will be examined why and how quantum physics relates to the workings and mechanics of our brains. We will examine that it teaches us that it is almost impossible to not be affected by others' negative or positive influence. This is good because through reverse osmosis, we can become successful. This means, then, that by having positive people around each one us, we can ultimately become just like them—successful. Aristotle Onassis, one of the richest men in the world, was quoted saying that if he ever became flat broke, he would just go and be in the presence of wealthy people; doing that in itself would restore his wealth.

By this point, we must readily admit that the advice is not only logical, reasonable, but also practical. We are also getting strong validation from people who are ultrasuccessful by definition. Everyone who is quoted in this book, has been or still is an authoritative and reliable source. They are people we may know in one way or another, and more importantly, we know they are people who have evidence in their lives—which proves that they know how to achieve successful results and not just know about, but also know by definition. Their information will be proven as timeless. Like the law of gravity, it always works.

So in all honesty, if we were to break it down, I would suggest that the best way to go about getting information to be successful is by this quote by a *New York Times* best seller:

> *Listen to people who have what you want, and have been where you are. Those who have the physical manifestations that what they are saying works.*

—Kevin Trudeau

## Please Do Not Kill the Messenger!

But let's go back to the question. Do I, the author, have the evidence that you wish to see? The answer is maybe. Why maybe? I can say I have great measure of success in certain areas of my life, but not in others. I may suggest it is irrelevant and allow me to prove it to you, the reader, and explain why. First and foremost, I promise to quote and derive sources and material from people who have or have had ultrasuccess. Second, it is all based on foundational knowledge from experts in the field of quantum physics acquired through the scientific method. Therefore I am not pointing to my success as it stands right now, but that of others through empirical evidence. Third, there is the thought that even though a person may be financially ultrasuccessful, they may be miserable when it comes to their health, or happiness, or even their personal relationships. You could learn how to have a great golf game from Tiger Woods, but not necessarily how you can have tremendous success from his basketball skills. You would go to Kobe Bryant or Michael Jordan for that training. I only wish to portray information objectively. As we should all consider: "This is what the current understanding is by the most authoritative sources thus far."

So I would suggest that you continue reading and examine this book as a condensed form of about twenty years of research and personal study.

## Moses Uses the Scientific Method to Observe Facts

Going back to Moses. We should thank Moses for having the guts to be honest in front of God. Jehovah acknowledged Moses's apprehension and dignified him with an answer by assuring Moses that he would be with him. Moses had trust that God was powerful but was not sure if God was powerful enough to do what he said. Thus he asked, "Suppose I go to the Israelites and say to them, 'The God of your ancestors has sent me to you,' and they say to me, 'What is his name?' What should I say to them?"

*Wow! Another powerful question that is relevant to our day!* Now Moses was asking for direct evidence and assurance in connection to the thoughts he was supposed to convey to the Hebrew slaves in Egypt so that they would have confidence in their so-called messenger from God. Thus far, Moses was asking for confidence and conclusive observations to help the slaves comprehend why his promise had any validity, when seemingly there was none. Moses' observation of the physical manifestations as shown by the allowance of their oppression by the Egyptians to continue for hundreds of years, obviously showed the opposite. Moses's courage to present these questions to God was very honest and candid. He should be applauded.

This is also a powerful lesson for us. We have acknowledged thus far that there are people who may come to us as messengers from others who claim to have the evidence to teach us how to be successful. I may suggest that, as the author of this book, I fall in this category. But we should learn from Moses's honesty again. He did not want to just run off excitedly telling people a sensational report about God right away. He demonstrated this when he asked another question. He asked, "But suppose they do not believe me and do not listen to my voice, for they will say, 'Jehovah did not appear to you.'" Moses deserves an outstanding ovation at this point. Still sticking to his guns, he asked the money question. "What evidence do you have that I can show them to prove, without question, your power and the authority that you claim?" Was he not in essence asking for empirical evidence, as the scientific method demands?

Thus we can acknowledge that it could happen; we may learn from people who claim to be messengers and truthfully have real-life information that will positively have an impact on our personal lives. But it is important that we know for sure that they, the messengers, have evidence from the authoritative sources they claim to represent. This is where our due diligence and powers of discernment must come into place and kick in like military training. Our lives, our livelihood, our success, and the success of those whom we love depend on it! *It is a matter of life and death!* I am not saying this as a hyperbole, but in the literal sense. People are dying prematurely every day because of the dissemination of wrong information to the masses. This point will absolutely, categorically be proven with scientific data as one of the main reasons we get sick and die.

At this moment, we may be thinking of times when we may have failed to heed this kind of advice in the past. Maybe we are still paying the consequences of such wrong decisions. I know I am.

So what physical manifestation did God provide that would help his messenger draw comfort and confidence in his god and himself to successfully accomplish what he was mandated to do? What physical manifestation did God provide that would convince the Hebrew slaves that their god was stronger than that of the Egyptian gods? What evidence would he show them that would prove that their god will accomplish what he promised? And what physical manifestations did God provide for Moses, so that the Egyptians would readily see and know that even though the Egyptians had the Hebrews under their command, they would come to the point of having no choice but to let the Hebrews go without resistance, thus acknowledging Jehovah's power as greater than that of their gods?

These are questions that are also relevant to our own personal circumstances. Take money, for example. Let's suppose a person makes $5,000 a month. He also desires to make a lot more. Then he meets three people who make more than him. The first one makes $20,000 a month. The second makes $100,000 a month. The third and final mentor makes $1,000,000 a month. The person does his due diligence, takes responsibility, and learns from all three. He finds that they do indeed acquire such incomes every month because he saw various bank statements, checked references, and examined their lifestyles that showed that they do indeed have the evidence of their financial success. We know for a fact that since they make more money than he does, the instruction that he will get from them will be of utmost relevance and value to him. But the one he is most likely get the most benefit from is the one who makes $1,000,000 a month. We could debate it, but the fact is that the financial records prove that he takes in $1,000,000 a month. Through the scientific method and the powers of observation, this is the truth and a fact, plain and simple.

Moses was told by Jehovah to throw his rod on the floor, and as he did, the rod turned into a snake. The account tells us that Moses kept fleeing from it but God assured him and commanded him to grab it. When Moses did, it turned back into a rod. Why was this significant? Without going into a long explanation, it was significant because the Egyptians worshipped reptiles, mainly the snake or cobra, as gods. This is known because pharaoh wore what is called a uraeus, which represented his kingship and authority or the divinity of their gods. Later in the account we read of a showdown between Moses' rod snake and the rod snake produced by Pharaoh's magic-practicing priests. Pharaoh's snake lost. The second physical manifestation was an act of healing. Moses was told by God to put his hand into his robe so that it became full of leprosy when he pulled it out. Then he put it back into his robe, and when he pulled his hand back out, it was completely healed. Both events are obvious physical manifestations for everyone to see. There could be no doubt or disbelief.

More physical manifestations were given. This was also obviously emphasized by the ten plagues and the parting of the Red Sea. To the majority of scientists who ridicule these stories, these "quantum miracles" sound more like allegories or myths. But the field of quantum physics alludes to the idea that these things are probable and plausible. This will be discussed thoroughly in the pages of this book, with practical application for immediate real-life results to help the reader improve and achieve desired results. In essence, this will help you get the physical manifestation in your world. Consider the following quote:

> *None are more hopelessly enslaved than those who falsely believe they are free.*
>
> —Johann Wolfgang von Goethe

## The Real Reason We Do Not Have Success

There is yet another lesson we can derive from Moses's conversation with God. Moses expressed apprehension in the form of self-doubt. He said, "Pardon me, Jehovah, but I have never been a fluent speaker, neither in the past nor since you have spoken to your servant, for I am slow of speech and slow of tongue." At which point, God offered training, emphasizing that it was him that could allow him to become better in his speaking ability. How would you feel if you were offered personal training from such authority? Yet Moses still showed self-doubt. "Pardon me, Jehovah, please send anyone whom you want to send."

We all deal with various forms of self-doubt and fear. This may cause us to lose out on fantastic opportunities to create what we want. We may have beliefs about ourselves that we are not good enough.

This may completely take away all desire to continue learning. So even though we may acquire powerful information and training from perfect, trustworthy, and reliable sources, we still will not do anything and would rather hide than experience something better. Our fears, many times, will overpower our own desires. We may want something and know exactly how to get it, but we will come up with every possible excuse and cling to it like a life jacket anchored to the seafloor.

We may also truly believe that we have real limitations. But through the field of quantum physics and other reliable sources, we will prove without question that they are truly just that—excuses based on fear. We will also show how fear is literally killing you and your loved ones. There is scientific evidence that this is true. But alas, have no fear, through the pages of this book, we will learn how we can progressively overcome fear.

Napoleon Hill has been quoted as saying: "Whatever the mind of man can conceive and bring itself to believe, it can achieve." His statement has tremendous weight since he is known as a powerful and reliable source of information that creates real-life success. And it is no wonder, since he had personal mentorship from Andrew Carnegie, one of the biggest business tycoons of his time. It is estimated that Mr. Andrew Carnegie, toward the end of his life, accumulated a net worth of almost three hundred billion dollars calculated to today's market! It could almost be said that Napoleon Hill was Moses and Andrew Carnegie his god. Obviously the previous statement is just to illustrate the importance of learning from people who themselves had a mentor, someone with more evidence than the immediate source.

On a side note, to this day, I continue to meet people who are ultrasuccessful who suggest I read Napoleon Hill's works, mainly *Think and Grow Rich*. As a real life example, the last person who told me to read and reread that specific book drives what it seemed to be a brand-new Rolls Royce, or maybe it was Bentley. Please really think about that idea. You will notice that certain common denominators begin to arise as you learn from people who have exponentially more success than the average person. We will examine with scientific background research in a later chapter why physical manifestations that we can see and touch are undeniable evidence of proper personal scientific experimentation.

## Tying It All Together

We discussed that even though many of these stories found in the scriptures may not be widely accepted as true, there are strong moral lessons in them that we can apply for ourselves. We can examine these stories through the scientific method and test the results that are promised within the lessons. We may be surprised that like expert scientists using the scientific method, we will experience and see real-life benefits. Our unbiased experimentation will propel us forward, as long as we do not prejudge without giving this process true justice.

So, like Moses, let's dedicate our lives to realize exactly where we stand in relation to our current knowledge and maybe admit that since we have so much to learn, we may need mentorship. Looking for people who have powerful evidence that we can see and touch and experience with our full senses will let us know what we may be doing wrong if we are experiencing frustration with our goals. We do not attribute all success to material things, but to the ability for us to be able to see in real life the ability of people to create physical manifestations of their original thoughts. There is background research in the scientific arena that proves that this procedure is exactly what happens when people achieve goals and desires. It is precisely what is required to achieve success, and these concepts are what will progressively be developed through the pages of this book.

Now let's move on to revealing the scientific empirical evidence of what we are talking about . . .

# CHAPTER 2

# The Importance of Empirical Evidence and Background Research: Science

*If you want to find the secrets of the universe, think in terms of energy, frequency and vibration.*

— Nikola Tesla

A S PREVIOUSLY STATED, whether we personally take biblical accounts as valuable sources of real data and facts or not, it is irrelevant. People often create stories and other myths to illustrate real-life lessons, which is practical in helping drive valuable points to those who are listening. For example, we all know of the dangers of lying or practical jokes from the story of the boy who cried wolf. It is the author's intention, however, to portray to the reader of this book to consider the Bible as a true and viable source of information.

Either way, know that this is not my opinion, or maybe it is, but it is also Albert Einstein's opinion. He was quoted saying that he was more inclined toward believing in a god who reveals himself through the "orderly of harmony of what exists." This I must agree with 100 percent as well. Romans 1:20 explains: "For his invisible qualities are clearly seen from the world's creation onward, because they are perceived by the things made."

Please also know that it is not stated that there is absolutely no difference of opinion between expert references and what it is being portrayed here. That would be a form of ignorance. What is merely suggested is that there is more than enough parallels of information to give credence to the observation of background research—mainly science and spirituality—and those who have absolute evidence and physical manifestations in one way or form, including people who may have what we want.

The fields of spirituality, success philosophy, and observable success are points of reference that have strong foundation as observable phenomena that prove they have a basis on quantum physics or on the currently known quintessential laws of the universe. It will be strongly suggested to the reader that all three aspects are points of view or frames of mind looking at the same thing. To also prove this, the reader will be given a list of references from experts to encourage you to explore freely without bias or prejudgment. You are encouraged to come to your own conclusions and opinions. It is known that as we study and consider information, we may find that there may be fundamental contradictions, but we also realize that this is the excitement of life and variety. It is great to consider other points of view talking about the same thing so that we may be able to integrate knowledge more fully. I believe this is a form of true education.

This chapter will specifically lay out the groundwork in the reader's mind that the Bible reference is a book of powerful science way ahead of its time. This will be done first by learning about the basic concepts of quantum mechanics. In the next chapters, it will be revealed that there is absolutely no way that the people described in the Bible could have known of the ideas that we are now learning through the field of quantum mechanics. But as a matter of fact, many of them were readily able to use tools to do extraordinary things that have been beyond explanation until now. Thus it has been ignored and tossed aside as myth and nonsense. But how could people in the Bible and other so-called holy books describe experiences that only quantum mechanics is able to explain as plausible?

Unless we strongly consider that spirituality originates and has been influenced by other sources outside of planet Earth, we might lose out on a huge point of reference. The Bible reference, as well as other spiritual books, describe extraordinary people doing extraordinary things under extraordinary circumstances. These are people who knew and spoke of such things as if they were common knowledge, or as a matter of fact, an absolute reality in the physical world. They were physical manifestations that were easily observed, and thus were described in terms and references that only very simple-minded persons could hope to explain.

The Bible has described some as angels from heaven, demons, the sons of God, and spirits, among other descriptive terms such as "ones who look like the sons of man." Today we may call them aliens from outer space, or interdimensional beings, or even superbeings from other, higher-vibrational dimensions. Could they all be one and the same, just descriptions of the same thing from different points of view? The same could be said about miracles, for, in essence, they are just the result of powerful technologies that are beyond our current understanding. We will explore these ideas in the next chapters.

## What Quantum Mechanics Has Revealed

We will now examine a list of accepted scientific concepts that have now paved the way for new technologies and discoveries that continue to shape and improve our lives. Think now about all the technology we take for granted, the ones we readily use, such as our TVs, our smartphones, tablets, video game consoles, computers, and laptops, among others. Can you sit back and explain to yourself or another person the exact mechanics of how every technological tool works to its most essential detail? Most likely the answer is no. Yet we don't debate their reality because we see their immediate affects in our immediate lives. We see them, play with them, and interact with them. They are real, physical things.

But have we considered that there are basic laws of the physical universe that we can use to apply to build these things, such as a house or a car? What about knowing or understanding the basic laws of the universe that will allow us to create our own success, whatever we choose that to be? Describing these laws is what will be our focus for the remainder of this chapter.

> *If the genius of invention were to reveal tomorrow the secret of immortality, of eternal beauty and youth, for which all humanity is aching, the same inexorable agents which prevent a mass from changing suddenly its velocity would likewise resist the force of the new knowledge until time gradually modifies human thought. . . . If you want to*

*find the secrets of the universe, think in terms of energy, frequency and vibration.*

—Nikola Tesla

Scientific Concept 1: Everything in the Universe
Is Energy, Frequency, and Vibration

In school, it has been ingrained in us that everything in the universe is made out of atoms. We learned in school and through empirical evidence that everything in the universe is made up of molecules which are made of atoms; electrons circulating around a nucleus; a collection of protons and neutrons. And that those individual particles, electrons, protons and neutrons are made of other smaller particles of energy. As they continue to observe, it is seen that particles become infinitely smaller. This is the process called quantization, thus the term *quantum physics*. It is the study of very basic components of what is known as matter. But thus far, it has been agreed on by the scientific community that the universe is made out of nothing but energy. It is unanimous.

We must also consider the facts about our visible spectrum of light. It is teaching us that our visible universe is tiny in comparison to the entire electromagnetic spectrum of energy. To illustrate, the tallest building in the world is the Burj Khalifa, standing at 160 stories tall or 2,716 feet tall. If we were to extend that building to one hundred times its height to represent the entire spectrum of energy, then we, our present observable reality as it stands, would only allow us to live and move around on the first six floors. This is also considering that each floor is about ten feet high. It is staggering to know and to realize how much energy we cannot possibly interpret with our basic senses. We need to create tools and gadgets to be able to measure the rest of the spectrum that is invisible to us. We must also strongly consider that there is even more that we can't possibly know yet.

Studies about the universe are finding that the entire light spectrum only makes up less than 5 percent of the entire universe. Dark energy and dark matter make up more than 95 percent of the universe, and we almost know nothing about these concepts. To illustrate: imagine stretching a tape measure from Orlando, Florida, to New York City.

The tape would stretch about 1,115 miles. Our entire existence would be limited to only about a six-feet span. Within those 72 inches lie our entire visible spectrum of light, including the billions of galaxies, the trillions of stars in each galaxy, and somewhere in there, we exist in our tiny planet Earth.

These facts aptly emphasize that there is just way too much that we don't know and that as we continue to expand our knowledge of the workings of the universe, we realize we are only seeing a fraction of the tip of a cosmic iceberg. The ocean of energy that these facts stipulate leave no room for dogmatic attitudes and thoughts. Nobody has a monopoly on knowledge and understanding, and when we individually and collectively accept the fact that we cannot know everything in this instant, then we must become better for it, for we will always be teachable.

Scientific Concept 2: The Double-Slit Experiment Proves That Everything in the Universe Exists in a Paradoxical Duality

Taking it a step further, let's examine a widely known experiment in the field of quantum physics known as the double-slit experiment. There are many scientific documentaries done by reliable sources putting it in simple terms through visual aids. One is in the movie *What the Bleep Do We Know!?* You are encouraged to watch not just that one, but multiple sources that explain this experiment as well so that the concept becomes clear in your mind. These explanations will do you more good than any amount of words I may be able to put down on this page. It certainly has done the same for myself and others.

Hopefully by this point, you have watched a documentary or a video explaining how the double-slit experiment is conducted. Simply put, the double-slit experiment's results and conclusion explains that particles of matter exist in a paradoxical existence. Particles of matter subsist as both particles defined in time and space and as waves of energy not relative to time and space. This is called "particle wave duality." And it is considered the foundational concept, the basics of all quantum mechanics.

In essence, what we must understand, is that the universe is all energy vibrating at different frequencies. To illustrate how this works, think of the visible space and all the stars and planets. The rays of the sun travel as photons in the form of waves. Research has shown that it takes eight minutes for the light of the sun to reach the surface of the Earth. Keep in mind that the speed of light travels at 186,282 miles per second. To illustrate how fast that is, consider that the circumference of the Earth is 24,901 miles. So if you were to run in a straight line around the globe and you ran at the speed of light, by the time one second has passed, you already would have run around the globe almost eight times.

We realize that the light of the sun is emitted in virtually all directions. Since the sun and all the stars in the universe are perfect spheres, then it is conclusive that their light travels in all possible directions and continues to travel unless there is resistance. We know this because we observe many stars or galaxies emitting their own collective vibrational frequency of light because it reaches us regardless of distance. Although there are many stars and galaxies we may not be able to see with our naked eyes, instrumentation helps us to see our neighboring stars and many more whose distance is unfathomable.

Consider that scientists are now explaining that an infinitesimally smaller quantum observation, the atoms in the stars are emitting frequencies all over the universe. This energy is permeating all time and space as readily as we observe the stars emit light in all directions throughout the universe, also permeating all time and space. We know this to be true because that is what the stars in fact do—they emit light in all directions, therefore their atoms at the smallest levels of energy are emitting a signal of energy in all directions. We are, in essence, observing the entire collective vibrational energy of the photons, or particles of energy that complement stars. Thus, we are observing what the most fundamental parts of the universe do. I would encourage you that you write and rewrite this paragraph on a separate sheet of paper. I would also encourage you to read and reread this paragraph. And I would certainly encourage you to watch and rewatch the experiment being explained for more clarity on this concept.

The point that everything in the universe, including everything in it, sends out a unique broadcast of frequency of vibration or energy must be stated plainly. This concept being continually comprehended is of utmost importance. Your material possessions, at a quantum level, transmit a frequency or vibration in all directions. Your body transmits a unique energy and frequency. And like the light of the sun that permeates all time and space, the transmission of your material possessions also permeate all time and space. This also proves that our own personal collective transmission also permeates all time and space. This is something that we should consider strongly. We must know it as a law of the universe, all the way to the quantum level in connection to matter.

So putting these concepts together, as far as the observations from the double-slit experiment has explained, you and I exist in the same manner as particles do: we exist in a paradoxical state, particle wave duality. We exist and operate in constant duality. We live and exist as a collection of particles defined in time and space or as a collective vibrational wave not relative to time and space. Just like the law of gravity is a constant, all individuals and everything else in the universe are constantly, twenty-four hours a day, seven days a week, vibrating their collective frequency into all space and time. This may be confusing at first, but it has been plainly stated by expert scientists that this is true.

The next scientific phenomena also reinforces the concept that energy is permeating all time and space.

Scientific Concept 3: Quantum Entanglement

Let's consider and plainly state what we said before. In essence, particles exist in duality. They are particles in time and space, but more importantly and significantly, they also exist as wave frequencies not relevant to space and time. It was described by the double-slit experiment, that when particles of energy are not being observed or measured, they are, in essence, waves of energy not defined by time or space. They are waves of energy of infinite possibility. Why or how? Scientists to this day don't know. But the double-slit experiment demonstrated with very clear, observable evidence that when the photon was shot toward the sheet of metal with two holes, it went through both holes on each side simultaneously and both holes individually at separate times. It went through the left slit, then the right slit, and then both at the same time. The photon did all three actions in the same instant. How and why can one particle of energy do three things in the same moment in time?

Again there is no explanation demonstrated as to the mechanics. But since the experiment showed that the photon was able to do all three movements—going in through each hole individually and going in through each hole at the same time—demonstrates that particles are, in essence, anywhere, everywhere, and nowhere. The conclusion then proves that electrons are omnipresent; everywhere at every instant in time and space. It also showed that they are only defined in time and space when chosen to be observed. Albert Einstein said that he didn't like the implications of quantum physics because he wanted to believe that the moon was still there even though he was not looking at it. They are particles of infinite possibility because they are defined in time and space when observed, but they are anywhere, nowhere, and everywhere at the same time when not observed.

This gives way to quantum entanglement. This describes that particles are in a symphony of immediate communication. It has been proven that a particle specifically defined in space and in time can affect another particle somewhere else, or anywhere else in time and space, in an instant, no matter the distance. They could be an inch away from each other, or they could be as far as away as the other side of the galaxy, or trillions of light-years away. This suggests that information seems to be able to travel instantaneously regardless of distance. And this is because one particle can be in one place and in an infinite amount of places at the same time. These particles of energy have been observed doing all kinds of things: from becoming invisible, from being in two places at the same time, and even traveling back in time and changing the past. This may sound bizarre, but the double-slit experiment does prove that, at a quantum level, the particles behave as such. This also suggests that we may be living in a holographic universe and that a solid universe is only an illusion.

> *If you want to find the secrets of the universe, think in terms of energy, frequency and vibration.*

> — Nikola Tesla

Scientific Principle 4: The Uncertainty
Principle and Quantum Tunneling

The uncertainty principle, plainly stated, is this: since particles of energy exist in a paradoxical duality, it is impossible to know exactly where a particle really is in time and space. This describes to us a strange paradox. We simply cannot know anything with absolute certainty. So because of the wavelike qualities of photons or particles of energy, they cannot be specifically located or pinpointed. Scientists can only say where the particle is most likely to be. Scientists are dealing in a paradox of just high and low probabilities of things existing, maybe, in space and time. The paradox is that things are visible with our eyes, felt with our touch, and completely defined in time and space. But at a quantum level, things are not really there.

Interestingly enough, scientists have experimented with this concept. They have taken particles and boxed them in, but the particles always seem to manage to generate enough energy to escape or break out of the box before its position and speed have been determined. This is mind-blowing. How can that be possible? Quoting a documentary on the uncertainty principle, scientists explain that "nature will not allow its fundamental elements to be boxed in." This makes quantum tunneling a reality.

Quoting the documentary again, English physicist Clifford Johnson says, "So because in the microscopic world particles will interact within an entire different set of rules . . . the uncertainty of the microscopic universe extends far beyond the location of particles. It applies to everything, including a particle's energy. This gives rise to an outstanding phenomena called quantum tunneling." An example given in this documentary by Frank Kuttner explains: "we all know that unless we give enough force to a moving object, let's say a ball hitting a wall, the ball will just bounce back. But if it is an electron against the wall and you do not throw it hard enough to go through the wall, it might go through anyway. We called that quantum tunneling." [The Universe: Microscopic Universe, (History)]. According to an explanation the particle is able to borrow energy "from the future," to go through the wall. This is because the particle in wave form is not defined in time and space, and therefore it is in both places at the same time. It is behind the wall, but it was also already on the other side of the wall or barrier. It is on both sides of the wall at the same time, just like it was observed that a photon will go through both slits of the wall at the same time.

These experiments and concepts may sound bizarre and unbelievable, and that is why it is strongly suggested to the reader to observe carefully the many illustrations readily available for a progressive comprehension. It has been known that the mind will gradually grasp concepts as long as the new knowledge is repeated through different time intervals.

A question then has risen among many scientists. Since we are made of particles, then can our collective vibration be in two or an infinite number of places at once and go through barriers if we choose to do so? Well, I have certainly heard of a historical teacher walk on water in the middle of a storm. He also dried up a fig tree at his command! He also fed thousands with just a few pieces of fish and bread. What does the biblical record and the one known as Christ have anything to do with the ability of energy particles to behave as previously discussed through the double-slit experiment? We will engage this question on another chapter. But let's move on to what your brain can do at a quantum physical level.

Scientific Concept 5: Our Brain Is a Transmitter and
Receiver of Energy, Frequency, or Vibration

We have examined that everything in the universe is energy and vibrates or resonates, or sends out frequencies simultaneously in all directions. We also learned that everything has its own unique rate of resonance or vibration, based on its collective particle accumulation. We also suggested therefore that we resonate or vibrate energy or frequencies and, as such, send out a unique frequency in all directions, permeating all time and space. We also examined that all of this crazy scientific principles are proven to be true thanks to the double-slit experiment, quantum entanglement, and quantum tunneling. These are the laws and rules of the crazy, mind-blowing world of quantum mechanics. It is almost a miracle in nature that we are able to learn and understand these concepts.

Considering all these concepts, we can conclude that our brain also has its own unique blueprint, a unique collective vibrational energy frequency. Let's also observe the idea that through our brains we think, we feel or emote, we see, we hear, we taste, we smell, we touch, and we move and operate. We live. We may have learned through science that since everything is energy, our brain just interprets inputs and outputs of vibrational energy. In essence, everything we experience is just electrical signals interpreted, translated, or decoded by our brain. It has been said by many reliable sources that "thoughts are things." It has also been expressed by them that "thoughts also become things."

Let's consider the point that now days there exists incredibly powerful instruments that can measure the resonance of thoughts. So like all things in the universe, thoughts can be measured or pinpointed in the different areas of the brain by picking up its frequencies; we can then conclude that thoughts are fundamentally things. And as such, they are like all things; they are also energy vibrating at different rates of frequency. We can also conclude that like photons, they are also in a state of duality. Thoughts exist in your brain but, like all things, in an infinite amount of places, just like photons. We can also conclude that like all particles that are entangled, effecting and affecting themselves and other particles simultaneously, then thoughts are also entangled and effect and affect themselves and other thoughts.

The next sentence is not only scientific, but also believed to be true by some of the wealthiest and most powerful people that exist and have ever existed. As stated before, everything that is written here encompasses science and spiritual knowledge. It is also validated by ultrasuccessful people who happen to have what you want in one way or another. So consider the next statement very carefully. "Your brain is a transmitter and receiver of energy, frequency, and vibration. And your brain transmission of energy or frequency is also picked up by other brains, And it affects physical matter." According to Kevin Trudeau, in the audio *Your Wish Is Your Command*, it has also been explained through observation that our brain can generate or create and broadcast any frequency we decide.

One of the best experiments ever done to prove this was done in Japan by a scientist named Masaru Emoto. If the reader has not watched the documentary *What the Bleep Do We Know!?*, I suggest you watch it after reading this entire chapter. In that documentary, it was explained that thoughts in themselves, as well as written words, affect the physical and molecular structure of water. Tanks of water were placed with specific words. Also, different types of music were played for the water. In another experiment, people were told to think certain thoughts or send out "prayers" to the water. The nature of the words, music, or prayers were either that of a positive nature or a negative nature. After drawing samples of the water, these were examined under a microscope, and it was found that once the water was frozen, the crystallization and molecular structure of the water changed. The positive outputs of energy made the crystals form beautifully, while the negative outputs of vibration made the water crystals jagged and deformed.

Here is the money question: Does this mean that our brain, or us as individual conscious beings, can not only influence, but create physical matter or photons? Does this mean that we can influence and create and expand the perceivable physical universe? I am personally inclined to say yes due to empirical evidence, although they are just theories. But I am more inclined to say yes because some of the most powerful people in the world to have ever existed testify and witness to the validity of the power that we hold. They include Thomas Edison, Albert Einstein, Andrew Carnegie, Napoleon Hill, and Nikola Tesla, among many more.

These previous statements will continue to be validated throughout the book with other viable sources of spiritual and scientific knowledge, which may be quoted directly or indirectly. This includes people who, although not scientists, do have real-life evidence and testify that this information is true. Maybe if you really think about it, they are scientists since they took this information and developed a question in the form of a desired result in their personal lives. People have formed hypotheses based on desires or goals, tested these hypotheses through experimentation and drawing conclusions, and got powerful real-life evidence. This is important because experiments have to be able to be replicated. Therefore, we can say success and results, based on conclusive evidence, can be and must be replicated.

Therefore, success, whatever you decide that to be in the observable universe and your own personal reality, is attainable scientifically. We can have what they have by doing what they did. We are coming to understand common denominators of success in connection to common denominators of action and reaction, for it is all based on laws of physics, specifically particle physics. Essentially, we can have be and do everything we want plain and simple—scientifically.

The next scientific principle is mostly validated by spiritual references and beliefs of people who testify to its existence, but it also has scientific evidence.

Scientific Concept 6: Laws of Magnetic
Attraction, Friction, and String Theory

Through the study of particle physics, quantum physics has been able to reveal that there are laws that govern the universe and everything in it. In essence, the previous five concepts we have considered are all based on physical laws that are in effect just like the law of gravity. They are all constants that are in effect in every moment of time and encompass all matter. Certainly, rules seem to apply differently or change once we decide to either measure or observe either the macroscopic universe or the microscopic universe of particle physics.

So what is string theory? Scientists are still debating it. And many times when we try to understand what they are saying, it can be confusing. They also acknowledge it could be wrong and that they could hit a wall and toss the theory. They do explain that it is based on viable mathematical equations. Thankfully though, many of them do try their best to give us illustrations on how these concepts work. The implications of string theory can be lengthy and complicated, so the material here will only focus on one aspect of the entire idea that is relevant to what is being conveyed—success in our personal lives. Not that everything else as it is explained in string theory is not relevant to the nature of our universe; what we want to make clear is that we only need to understand how the steering wheel works, how the gas pedal works, how the brake pedal works, and how the auto transmission works, as well as how to put gas in your car. We must only learn the basics to help ourselves learn how to drive and get from point A to point B. Everything else is just details.

If we were to go into greater detail of how the engine, the carburetor, the pistons, the internal electrical circuits work, how it was put together, etc., then we may start to believe that we can't learn to drive and apply these principles practically in your personal life. So as of now, we are helping ourselves to just understand enough of how our individuality works with the physical universe and how we can create what we desire in our personal lives.

Going back to string theory and the laws of magnetism. The concept of string theory has been explained by a renowned scientist as "a weird idea." But you will notice that it is as simple and obvious as the law of gravity and as pervasive as the air we breathe. In a NOVA documentary, scientist Brian Greene explains that the basis for string theory is that particles are in a constant form of communication, like two baseball players throwing a baseball back and forth. In this instance, the two players symbolize particles of energy in constant duality. The ball that is being thrown back and forth here represents a "particle of force." An example given is electromagnetism. Some forces are incredibly more powerful than others.

We can illustrate this by examining birds or an airplane. How is it that these things are able to defy the law of gravity? Obviously it is because much more powerful forces or laws are at work. These forces encompass the particles of a bird weighing just a few ounces or an airplane weighing tons. Certainly the law of gravity does not go away, but it is just superseded by a much stronger force, the law of lift. Think of a baby as he learns to lift himself up and defy the law of gravity as he grows to be a toddler. The baby, seemingly with ease, will learn to turn, then sit up, crawl, and then walk. Where is the law of gravity keeping this little person tied to the floor as it did the first few months? Also, think of a weight lifter bench-pressing two hundred pounds to exercise his body. We can see that they are all defying the law of gravity and applying much stronger forces.

"String theory explains that the more of these messenger particles or photons that are exchanged between the two baseball players, or particles, the stronger the magnetic attraction between particles. Scientists predicted that it is this exchange of messenger particles, photons between particles that create what we feel as force. Experiments confirm these predictions with the discovery of these messenger particles for electromagnetism, the strong force, and the weak force." [Brian Greene in; The Fabric of the Cosmos: Universe or Multiverse? (Nova, PBS)]

This gives ample circumstantial evidence proving that particles attract powerfully when they communicate and are drawn to each other the more they are alike and communicate. This is the law of magnetic attraction; similar frequencies of vibration or energy will attract because they are powerfully magnetized to each other. The opposite is true for a particle's magnetic force can repel powerfully. This is also suggested by the big bang theory. Considering that scientists are still hoping to observe the big bang, or another way of saying it, is that we have no clue as to what happen at such point which they call "singularity." Scientists have explained that sometime after the explosion of the singularity, the universe kept expanding outwardly and thus cooled off. A singularity has been defined as the point in space and time where all the energy that complements the universe, including all its physical laws, were concentrated and focused into a single point smaller than an atom. When the big bang occurred, particles began to lose energy and became more defined in time and space. At one point, particles of hydrogen were produced in mass quantities, with one electron revolving around one proton. It is the most basic composition of energy in our visible universe. This is known because the mass of all stars is made up of hydrogen. And stars are massive in comparison to our little planet Earth. So hydrogen attracts itself. Water also attracts itself. As we consider and think of water, we have learned that it is also one of the most basic known molecules in our known world. Water's polarity or magnetism is really strong. We can observe this when we take spilled water and see it move closer to other drops of water on a flat surface. Or think about this: we have all always wondered why when we have a full bladder and we are running water in a sink, we feel the strong urge to pee. Why is that? It is because of the strong magnetic force or polarity of the water molecules. They are drawn to each other. Like attracts like. In essence, there is an invisible force affecting your bladder. Of course I am just being facetious, but it is still true.

So to simplify this concept: frequencies of energy that are alike in nature are drawn to each other. Whatever frequencies are being put out, those same frequencies are being drawn to themselves. This has been explained before by many as very basic ideas, such as "You reap what you sow," "What comes around goes around," "What you put out comes back to you," and "There is more happiness in giving than receiving," among others.

Tying It All Together: The Four Principles of Science

So to emphasize, the known visible universe of particles are described and governed by the following foundational principles:

*Principle 1:* Everything is energy, frequency, or vibration. Everything in the known universe is a collection of energy vibrating at different frequencies. And each thing is collectively and individually putting out its own unique and distinct frequency. This is also true at every level of possible and known observation, from the macrocosmic observation to the microcosmic observation of the known universe.

*Principle 2:* Everything in the universe exists in a state of duality, also known as "particle wave duality." It is one of the basics of quantum physics. Energy exists as both; particles with particle-like qualities, defined in time and space, as well as wavelike frequencies, with wavelike properties *not* defined in time and space. Thus the conclusion is also that we, as people and human beings, also live in a state of vibrational duality. It is also explained that it is the observer that collapses the wave function of the particle, thus establishing the particle precisely in what "seems" to be a place in time and space. All this was explained by the double-slit experiment, quantum entanglement, the uncertainty principle, and quantum tunneling.

*Principle 3:* Since we also live in a state of particle wave duality, our brain also exists in a state of particle wave duality. Then it is conclusive that our brains transmit and receive energy, frequency, and vibration based on our command. Our transmission of energy is also picked up by other brains. Also, our brain's transmission of frequency affects physical matter. Simply put, we can create a transmission from what already exists, and we can create a frequency based on what has not come into existence. The previous statement will continue to be developed throughout.

*Principle 4:* Everything in the universe is governed by magnetic forces of attraction. Just like the law of gravity says, "What goes up must come down," as it is always a constant. Also, the law of magnetic attraction says that frequencies or vibrations that are alike or in communication attract and pull each other. Similar or same energy is attracted to itself. This is what string theory is based upon.

Before moving on, it is encouraged that the reader review this chapter so these concepts may align better with your understanding. A special phenomena will occur as we read, study, and think about concepts repeatedly on regular basis: neural pathways formed based on these concepts will be firmly established in our brains and progressively become more ingrained, which will enforce the benefit of our comprehension of the material.. Thus the previous laws of physics and principles that we just discussed will be made active and seemingly take on a life of their own. These laws will begin to permeate those neural pathways, and as such phenomena happens, we must begin to understand and acquire knowledge that will begin to validate what we have been discussing all along. You will absolutely begin to acquire more discoveries, cognition, and realizations that will unfold the unfathomable power that we personally have.

But let's ask some questions. How did people discern these basic truths in the past, since it is only now that we are able to explain them scientifically? What did they hear? Who spoke, and how did they listen? When have these things taken place? Why were they able to understand or comprehend and accomplish what seems to be impossible even with today's technology? How were nations of the past aware of such laws of the universe or principles of life, for they are one in the same with present spiritual beliefs? Is this evidence of the existence of known civilizations that seemed much more advanced than what others have made us believe? If so, are we truly more advanced, or did we just fall from what maybe is just supposed to be basic knowledge like 1 + 1 = 2 or ABC?

But before we examine such questions, let's see how and why something that has been considered to be by some in the scientific community and others as myth, superstition, stubbornness, foolishness, or plain useless nonsense is essentially of great value. Let's examine now through the foundation we have established, that the lenses known as science and empirical evidence, as well as spirituality and certain stories which have been considered as pure myth or impossibilities, are strongly rational and have basis in reality.

# CHAPTER 3

# The Importance of Empirical Evidence and Background Research: Spirit Science

*The day science begins to study nonphysical phenomena,*
*it will make more progress in one decade than in all the*
*previous centuries of its existence.*

—Nikola Tesla

THE LAST CHAPTER examined various basic concepts in quantum physics. These explain how the universe works at an infinitesimally smaller observation than the one we readily see with our basic senses. It was found that it is of utmost importance to be able to examine background research and empirical evidence in order to examine real-life scientific data, so we can come to integrated conclusions about life. This is so that we can carefully examine how our immediate universe affects each one of us. With this foundation, it is going to be plainly stated that the studies of what has been known as true religion or spirituality are essentially the same to what quantum mechanics has taught us about the nature of the universe and our innate abilities as humans beings.

The biblical reference will be examined carefully, proving that the spiritual principles described within have basis in quantum physics. This is not to say that other spiritual references such as the Jewish Talmud, Babylonian cuneiform, Egyptian hieroglyphics, the Vedas, and Western philosophies, among others, are not being considered. But what is being observed and considered, in essence, are common denominators of spiritual beliefs as they are found throughout these references. Many specific spiritual beliefs find parallels throughout all the known holy books. It is also acknowledged here that there are contradictions, whether subtle or obvious, within many of these sources. This is also stated in the spirit of knowing that it is all we know so far, based on latest discoveries in the field of archeology. It is also acknowledged that many principles described as spiritual beliefs or laws were only relevant to understandings in those societies and are not relevant in our day or the future. (Although some of these spiritual beliefs may be relevant to our times.)

It is emphasized that, in light of quantum mechanics and the scientific lenses of established empirical evidence, these common denominators found in spiritual references, mainly the Bible, will be shown in this book to have timeless benefit in our everyday life regardless of background, race, religion, beliefs, present understanding, and time. It is also strongly emphasized that we will examine philosophical teachings from experts through both the lenses of scientific and spiritual knowledge—experts or people known to have created incredible success, whether in their personal lives or by influencing the world and creating tangible positive changes in it. It is the desire of the author of this book to establish an unbiased and objective report of our personal power and ability in connection to our present reality. To what purpose? To help the reader establish a progressive understanding and realization that in fact:

> *If the genius of invention were to reveal tomorrow the secret of immortality, of eternal beauty and youth, for which all humanity is aching, the same inexorable agents which prevent a mass from changing suddenly its velocity would likewise resist the force of the new knowledge until time gradually modifies human thought. If you want to find the secrets of the universe, think in terms of energy, frequency and vibration.*
>
> —Nikola Tesla

> *For truly I say to you, if you have faith the size of a mustard grain, you will say to this mountain, "Move*

*from here to there," and it will move, and nothing will be impossible for you.*

—Jesus Christ, Matthew 17:20

*Whatever the mind of man can conceive and believe, it can achieve.*

—Napoleon Hill

All three quotes are placed here to give you the perspective and frame of mind that regardless of the lenses you wish to see from and that regardless of the point of observation that you pick, we are in actuality just observing the same rules under the same universe. With that in mind, let's consider what principles have been described in the Bible that emphasize the previous basic understandings of quantum mechanics.

## What the Field of Spirit Science Has Revealed

In the previous chapter, we established that science has paved the way for powerful discoveries and creations that have an immediate positive effect in our immediate lives. We realize that just because we can't describe how the various technological devices work to their essential detail, does not mean that we should reject their existence. Therefore, it would also make sense to not entirely reject, but just consider, the probability that the many of the outlandish observations in many of these spiritual books might have a basis in reality. What has been observed in these books may not be explained in detail by the people who witnessed and recorded such events, for as they experienced them in their personal lives, their perceptive abilities and points of reference were certainly limited. As a result, just like us who do not know the intricacies of how smartphones work, when we attempt to describe smartphones, wouldn't we just be describing miracles as well?

Certainly, if we brought someone from the past, say the early 1900s, to our time, this person would have no choice but to accept the present realities as factual. In the beginning, they may be confused about our current technologies, such as our cell phones or other devices, but at some point they will just accept them for what they are in the same way we know them. The opposite, though has a strange dichotomy. Let's say we are able to take any of these various devices, maybe a cell phone, and have it still access our current technological resources when we go to the past. Let's say we decide to go somewhere around the 1700s. The people of that time may readily condemn us and label us as the devil, sorcerers, evil beings, liars, the Antichrist, etc. Consider the same scenario with a different possible outcome. Let's say that we have incredible power and are able to influence a takeover of the few who are in power in that time and space. We then manage to establish a system of control. Once successful, we would be hailed as gods or angels from heaven who came here to bring salvation. As events unfold, the outcome can either prove disastrous or incredibly beneficial for that society. It could also be that they are just not ready for such revelations or miracles regardless of our desire to improve their lives.

By now, the idea should be firmly established in the reader's mind that it is all about different frames of mind, with different ways of looking at the same thing. A triad of knowledge: science, spirituality, and philosophy. With all these ideas in mind, let's examine spirituality considering quantum theory and philosophy.

Spiritual Principle 1: Everything Is Light,
Energy, Frequency, and Vibration.

"Then God said, 'Let there be light.' Then there was light." Interestingly enough, the creation account talks about a time where one of the first things to come about and be discerned in the universe was light. As we examined previously, light is nothing more than particles or waves in a paradoxical duality. Since everything is energy, frequency, and vibration, then we know for a fact that we can truly state that everything in the visible universe is light. Or more precisely; different forms of photons of light.

"I form light and create darkness" (Isaiah 45:7). Also consider this next passage: "For God is the one who said: 'Let the light shine out of the darkness'" (2 Corinthians 4:6). These texts and how they relate to light and darkness are an interesting parallel. Physicists are considering that darkness is just another form of energy. They are considering concepts such as antimatter, dark matter, and dark energy. It has been established that these different forms of energy essentially make up the majority of the known universe and that from these unobservable energies came what has been described as the 'visible spectrum of light.'

Although scientists admit that more is unknown than known about dark energy and dark matter, they do explain that roughly 68 percent of the universe is dark energy and that dark matter makes up about 27 percent. In addition, everything that is measurable or observable, including galaxies, stars, planets, and the entire light spectrum, precisely make up less than 5 percent of the universe. What is powerful about this is that Albert Einstein explained that empty space is not nothing, that it essentially has energetic properties, or that it contains its own energy. There is little to no evidence of the composition of dark matter or dark energy, but the observable phenomena suggest an interesting parallel between the following statement and these Bible texts:

"He stretches out the northern sky over empty space, suspending the earth upon nothing" (Job 26:7).

"You stretch out the heavens like a tent cloth" (Psalms 104:2).

"There is One who dwells above the 'circle' of the earth . . . He is stretching out the heaven like a fine gauze. And He spreads them out like a tent to dwell in" (Isaiah 40:22).

These descriptions of the heavens or the observable universe as we know it today are way ahead of their time. In a time where most people observed and readily accepted the Earth as flat, here in Isaiah it is being described as a circle or sphere and suspended upon nothing. It is estimated that the book of Psalms was finished or completed in 460 BCE and that the book of Isaiah was completed in 732 BCE. That is staggering, and mind-blowing.

But let's strongly consider what is being said about the heavens and that "Jehovah God stretches them out like a tent." In astrophysics, it has been described and it is accepted as scientific fact that the universe is expanding, that everything is moving across space. They are also observing that its expansion is accelerating. Considering that scientists still don't know what dark matter is or where it comes from and that they only know that it is a property of space, let's examine what the verses have described so far. Genesis 1:4 describes this strange phenomena: "After that God saw that the light was good, and God began to divide light from the darkness." This may suggest that dark matter existed before visible light, which is highly probable, considering that dark energy and dark matter make up most of the universe. Like a tree that is composed of mostly wood and leaves, after some time, it bears fruit or flowers. In this instance, light was its fruitage.

Let's also consider that it was mentioned in Isaiah that Jehovah creates darkness. Compare that to what Albert Einstein discovered: "It is possible for more space to come into existence" (NASA, *Dark Energy, Dark Matter*) The idea that dark matter can come from nothing is referred to as the "cosmological constant." In *Dark Energy, Dark Matter*, NASA says this about the "cosmological constant:

> *"[E]mpty space" can possess its own energy. Because this energy is a property of space itself, it would not be diluted as space expands. As more space comes into existence, more of this energy-of-space would appear. As a result, this form of energy would cause the Universe to expand faster and faster. Unfortunately, no one understands why the cosmological constant should even be there, much less why it would have exactly the right value to cause the observed acceleration of the Universe.*

In my opinion, there are strong parallels between quantum theory and the study of the cosmos and the observations written thousands of years ago by seemingly uneducated "mystics." Where did they receive this information? Did they meet aliens from outer space? Not necessarily, but let's think that it might have something to do with the concept that our brain not only transmits, but also *receives* energy, frequency, or vibration. Let's consider it as something to ponder.

Let's go back to the idea being developed within the scientific community: that the universe is expanding from nothing and that dark matter or energy seems to come from nowhere. Notice what this other passage in the Bible also says referring to the natural order of things.

"By faith we perceive that the systems of things were put in order by God's word, so that what is seen has come into existence from things that are not visible" (Hebrews 11:3).

I feel the two ideas described are strong parallels. Scientists are emphasizing that matter is created from nothing, as it has been observed.

The text in the Bible similarly is saying that everything we perceive with our senses has come from things unseen.

Matter is light. Darkness separated in creation from light is referred to as dark matter in the scientific community. It is known to be both empty space and not nothing in both references. In one, it is referred to as light shining out of darkness. In the other, it is described as its own form of energy, separate from light but allowing visible light to exist. Both references describe that the physical universe is expanding. Spirituality and science, lenses of perception looking at the same thing. All this evidence establishes a strong point: The Bible was way ahead of its time. It is almost like what is being described through advanced technological devices had to be simplified to its most basic description for those who are considered babies in the timeline of the progressive evolution of knowledge. A book from the future? Perhaps. A book written from a much higher point of view for the benefit of those from a much lower point of view? The reader can decide.

Please know that it is only suggested to consider these points of view.

Maybe you, as the reader of this book, has previously established in your own mind and take the Bible as an authority in information and practical knowledge.

Either way, even if you don't consider it as an authority and is not convinced as of yet, know that it is not the point here to force a change in your mind. It is here to help you consider a different point of view, where you are encouraged to take as your own mission to come to your own conclusions. It could mean your own personal success in life, whatever may that be. This book will only establish a few points to imprint a desire on the reader to come to personal cognition of reasoning. It is about developing your own personal discoveries out of your own free will.

Obviously, the experiments that prove what we discussed in chapter 2 could not have been done or replicated in biblical times, at least not on our own.

For emphasis, it teaches us that photons are only particles existing in what has already been established and known as particle wave duality. The question then arises: can many of the so -called miracles in the Bible be explained through quantum physics, as empirical evidence of what we know today? Again, the conclusion is up to the reader to decide.

Scientific Concepts 2, 3, 4, 5, and 6 in the previous chapter cannot be compared in the spiritual references since they could not be replicated by those who wrote the biblical reference. Thus these Scientific Concepts known as, 'The Double Slit Experiment: Everything in the Universe Exists in a Paradoxical Duality,' 'Quantum Entanglement,' 'The Uncertainty Principle & Quantum Tunneling,' 'Our Brain: A transmitter and receiver of energy, frequency and vibration, and finally 'String theory and the law of magnetic attraction' will not be discussed as we did now scientific concept 1. We will reestablish instead the principles described in connection to the universe at the end of chapter 2.

At this point, we want to imprint some points of reference for posterity. This will help the reader save patience as he reads. You will notice that as you continue to read, we will refer to the following references and its definitions. This will simplify the way this book is read and understood. So as we go on, we will refer to the following three quotes and points of reference as the "triad of knowledge." We will also refer to the six scientific concepts as they were simplified in the form of four principles of quantum physics. This is to help us understand the principles of science and how they relate to what is being observed in the Bible. So when we see these references, we should consider referring back to them so that we know exactly what are the points being established. They are the following:

The Triad of Knowledge

*If the genius of invention were to reveal tomorrow the secret of immortality, of eternal beauty and youth, for which all humanity is aching, the same inexorable agents which prevent a mass from changing suddenly its velocity would likewise resist the force of the new knowledge until time gradually modifies human thought. If you want to find the secrets of the universe, think in terms of energy, frequency and vibration.*

—Nikola Tesla

*For truly I say to you, if you have faith the size of a mustard grain, you will say to this mountain, "Move from here to there," and it will move, and nothing will be impossible for you.*

—Jesus Christ, Matthew 17:20

*Whatever the mind of man can conceive and believe, it can achieve.*

—Napoleon Hill

To emphasize, the known visible universe of particles are described and governed by the following principles:

*Principle 1*: Everything is energy, frequency, or vibration. Everything in the known universe is a collection of energy vibrating at different frequencies. And each thing is collectively and individually putting out its own unique and distinct frequency. This is also true at every level of possible and known observation, from the macrocosmic observation to the microcosmic observation of the universe.

*Principle 2*: Everything in the universe exists in a state of duality, also known as the "particle wave duality" It is one of the basics of quantum physics. Energy exists as both; particles with particle-like qualities, defined in time and space, as well as wavelike frequencies, with wavelike properties *not* defined in time and space. Thus the conclusion is also that we, as people and human beings, also live in a state of vibrational duality. It is also explained that it is the observer that collapses the wave function of the particle, thus establishing it precisely in what "seems" to be a specific place in time and space. All this was explained by the double-slit experiment, quantum entanglement, the uncertainty principle, and quantum tunneling. (Refer to chapter 2 for explanations of these concepts.)

*Principle 3*: Since we also live in a state of particle wave duality, our brain also exists in a state of particle wave duality. Then it is conclusive that our brain transmits and receives energy, frequency, and vibration at our command. Our transmission of energy is also picked up by other brains. Also, our brain's transmission of frequency affects physical matter.

Simply put, we can create a transmission from what already exists, and we create a frequency based on what has not come into existence. The previous statement will continue to be developed throughout.

*Principle 4*: Everything in the universe is governed by magnetic forces of attraction. Just like the law of gravity says, "What goes up must come down," as it is always constant. Also, the law of magnetic attraction says that frequencies or vibrations that are alike or communicate attract and pull each other. Similar or same energy is attracted to itself. This is what string theory is based upon.

Let's now also consider and observe how these scientific concepts and quotes from experts and their different points of reference relate to what the biblical account has described as miracles, or strange phenomena. This examination in the light of quantum mechanics can help us discern that these events are not as farfetched as some will have us believe.

Scientific Potentiality 1: Water Is Wine

Most people are aware of the time Jesus performed his first miracle. At a wedding reception, the people had ran out of wine, and Jesus decided to be the party saver by turning water into wine. This may sound as ludicrous as the lesson we learned about the particles of energy and what they are able to do at a quantum level, such as being in more than one place at the same time. Since this is true, is it a probable that the water particles of Jesus' story were also in a state of particle wave duality? Of course.

So can we ask, when those particles of water were not being observed, in essence those particles were connected to an infinite amount of places in time and space? We cannot deny what scientists have proven, so we have to say yes. We can conclude then that these particles were connected to wine particles in some place other than where the water was in that instant in time. If that is the case, then those particles were already potentially wine particles, as described by principle 2 How? Principles 1 and 2 explain that everything vibrates and is permeating all time and space. Therefore the water is connected to an infinite amount of possibilities in time and space. This is true because the experiment proved that all particles are really anywhere, everywhere, and nowhere.

It also proved that they are just relevant in space and in time based on the influence of the observer. That is why the wave function of particles collapses into a specific place in time and space, based on the decision of the observer.

(On a side note: We want to keep going back to the principles as they are being referred to. Please read and reread them.)

Could Jesus then, in command of his reality, have chosen to observe wine as opposed to water out of his own volition. Principle 3 explains this to be a certain probability in reality. Since reality is at our command, in this instance, Jesus' brain could have transmitted a frequency or vibration to affect the particles of matter found in the water. Maybe, like a computer programmer writes code, Jesus rewrote the code of the composition of the water. Or maybe he exchanged or replicated the particles of the wine already existing somewhere else in that instant in time. Teleportation is being discussed as a future probability within the scientific community, if it is not an already-hidden technological fact. Genius, famous inventor, and scientist Nikola Tesla was quoted saying that one day we would be teleported across space and time in an instant. He believed in antigravity airships, teleportation, and even time travel as a result of becoming aware of the particle wave duality concept. Nikola Tesla was probably the most powerful scientist of his time. How did Jesus perform this miracle? We don't know as of yet, but it seems that it is a probability in the realm of quantum mechanics through the power of our mind. But what we may yet to consider is that the real and best piece of technology is the human genome.

### Scientific Potentiality 2: Two Fishes and Five Loaves Feed over Five Thousand

Let's consider another quantum miracle by Jesus. We all may know, or at least heard of the few times where he was able to feed a crowd of possibly more than five thousand with only a couple of fishes and a few pieces of bread. Could he have taken the particle structure of each fish and piece of bread and just multiplied it through his power of observation? (Please refer to principle 2 and 3.) So maybe Jesus just chose to observe the particles in the fish and bread and decided to multiply them as needed. The triad of knowledge affirms the probability of Jesus choosing to match the frequency of the field of energy in space to his intention and desire to feed the crowd of thousands. In this instance, the fish and the bread particles are an infinite probability. It really denotes the idea that, the particles in the few fishes and bread as a wave function are irrelevant to amount or quantity. One fish is the same as one million. Two loaves of bread are the same as two million loaves of bread (principles 2 and 4).

We can illustrate the concept of infinity by the way we use our smartphone or computer to use the Internet. You could open one web page, but just because you opened that web page and it is in your immediate experience, it does not mean that someone else cannot open the same page. It also does not mean that you cannot open the same page a second time within the same window. Multiple pages within the same window are called tabs. You could virtually open an infinite amount of tabs in the same window or open an infinite amount of pages on the same computer screen. And thus, every person with a computer and Internet connection has the potential for an infinite amount information. Can we say that Jesus was able to do the same with the fish and bread and the water? According to the laws of quantum particle physics, this is a probability or reality and most likely possible in real life, according to the implications of time and space as defined by the particle wave duality. How did he do it, or what specific techniques did he use? We will discuss this in a later chapter. The triad of knowledge certainly gives us clues as to what we can personally use to change our immediate reality.

Scientific Potentiality 3: Christ's Consciousness Can Use Brain Transmission to Change the Channel on Illness and Disease

When you read the accounts of Matthew, Mark, Luke, and John, we find Jesus and his apostles performing powerful quantum miracles. We refer to them as quantum miracles because they are powerful changes that take place at a quantum level based on laws of physics. Consider that they affected the particle composition of people by changing it to what they commanded with their "speech" to happen. There is one account in the scripture found in Matthew 9 where Jesus is observed by a crowd of people commanding, or using his words, to make something that seemed impossible. While teaching a crowd, he was interrupted by some men bringing their friend on a stretcher. This friend was paralyzed from top to bottom. They wanted a cure. Jesus then used the words in the form of a command, or a transmission of frequency from his brain amplified by his vocal cords (principles 2, 3, and 4). He said, "Get up, pick up your stretcher, and go home." Plain and simple, he was telling the ill man to do something that was impossible for him to do, for he was paralyzed. But the crowd observed exactly what Jesus commanded: the man got up, picked up his stretcher, and went home. It was not a polite request, nor was it in the form of a question. So like an owner telling his dog to "Fetch! Sit! Lie down!" The paralyzed man had no choice but to do as Jesus said. But how?

We can consider the possibility of Jesus' command, in the form of vibration, affected the man's particles and added the particles needed to allow him to be a person who could walk and pick up things. Or maybe in the paralytic's state of particle wave duality, his energetic structure in wave form was also available as a completely healthy man. Thus through the law, a powerful magnetic force, the particles had to produce that which was called forth to happen. To illustrate, we can think of our TV remote and how it affects our TV at our command. The screen projects particles defined or not defined on the screen. We see it as static in some channels or as TV programs broadcasted that are picked up in the form of frequencies. All the channels may be static, but we can command them to be defined as TV programs with our remote. The frequencies of the channels are being constantly picked up by the receiver on your TV. They are always there, and all you have to do is choose to observe what we desire to watch by collapsing the wave function on the screen. We just press the button and we change the channel to our preference based on our transmitter, the remote controller. In this instance, Jesus, through his remote controller—his projected transmission commanded by his brain—affected the particles in duality of the paralyzed man. In essence, the TV station was changed to the health channel (principles 1, 2, 3, and 4). Interestingly the story is concluded like this:

"When the crowds saw this, they were struck with fear, and they glorified God, who gave such authority to men" (Matthew 9:8).

The text emphasized that such authority was given to "men." This is remarkable and needs to be strongly considered as a basic truth of life based on the triad of knowledge and the scientific principles here being described. We do indeed have the potential to replicate what Jesus or other biblical characters did to perform outstanding feats with their own power. We realize that this statement may sound like science fiction, but we need to consider that, just maybe, we are reading about experiences of a person using powerful technologies at his disposal.

Accepting Future Realities by Traveling to the Past

Reading these references in what has been considered as a spiritual book can help us realize that, in fact, we are just observing really advanced technology. We are seeing people who seemed to have come from the future, for as we observe these quantum miracles, we have traveled to the future, in essence, to experience what seems to be normal for others. For as we read these eyewitness accounts, we may be peering into what will be available to us in the near future. So then are we not forced to acknowledge these events as realities regardless of our understanding since we see them? Yes, the biblical account was written in the past, but in reality, those people were only observing advanced technology based on empirical evidence (principles 1, 2, 3, and 4). They had no choice but to report what they saw. So when we read these accounts, like the time traveler from the past, should we not readily accept them as probabilities of present realities in the light of scientific evidence? The choice to accept these as truths is really for the reader to decide, and it is your obligation to come up with your own conclusions. No one has a monopoly on knowledge and information. We wish to emphasize that these are just thoughts to consider as probabilities.

But now, let's think about what has been considered even more magical stories of technologies of unfathomable imagination. Going back to Moses, we may now realize or at least consider that they are no longer just myths based on unrealities. Consider the ten plagues. Turning the Nile into blood. The control of pests to torment the Egyptians like commanding trained dogs to attack criminals. Three days of darkness upon the Egyptians but not the Israelites at the same time in the same land. The seemingly easy victory of slaves in poor condition, defeating more powerful nations. The splitting of the Red Sea. Food falling from heaven to feed a camp of millions of men, women, and children.

Other accounts, such as that of the prophet Elijah, are good things to consider. He was able to outrun horses, escaping certain execution. He made a widow's remaining oil and flour last an entire drought. It is said that he was picked up by a fiery chariot with fiery horses and was taken into the sky. Maybe this was describing a spaceship of some sort and there was no other way to describe what his companion Elisha was seeing, since there was no reference point for this experience. But maybe it was truly a flying chariot with fire-breathing horses, thus we may consider them all to be true through the ramifications of the light spectrum and the principles of science described in this book. These principles all give way to high probabilities for these things to take place in our reality. There are many more so-called myths found not only throughout Bible, but also through many other sources. These and others will not be described, since only these few were described to prove the point that nothing is impossible. Through the lenses of quantum mechanics, we are certainly helped to consider these eyewitness accounts more strongly, for the many implications that allow for these things to take place unfortunately were done by seemingly uneducated people and civilizations. They are simple and inadequate descriptions, as allowed by their limited comprehension.

## Spiritual Principle 2: The Law of Magnetic Attraction

We want to digress just a little and firmly establish in our minds the ramifications and implications of spiritual principle 2. It is an examination of the application of the laws of magnetic attraction as it relates to string theory, in connection with spirituality. It has become, or it has always been, common knowledge among the populace that this law exists. The awareness is obviously at an all-time high nowadays unlike previous centuries.

But the Bible does describe the law of attraction and string theory through illustrations and some other parallels.

Let's consider the most basic known principle found in the Bible. "For whatever a person is sowing, this he will also reap" (Galatians 6:7). This has also been described as a form of karma in eastern philosophy. We constantly hear that what goes around comes around, or that whatever we give comes back to us manifold. Some call it causality—the principle that everything has a cause, that for every action, there is also an equal and opposite reaction. This is Newton's third law of motion. Many people, although not aware of it, may accept this reality at least at a near-subconscious level. We are aware that positive or negative actions and decisions have either negative or positive consequence.

## Your Powerful Thoughts

In *The Iron Lady*, which is a strongly recommended movie to watch, Meryl Streep, who plays Prime Minister Margaret Thatcher of England, says:

"Watch your thoughts, for they become your words. Watch your words, for they become your actions. Watch your actions, for they become your habits. Watch your habits, for they become your character, and watch your character, for it becomes your destiny. What we think, we become."

Earl Nightingale, creator of one of the oldest spoken-word records on personal development called *The Strangest Secret*, describes the same idea by saying that "we become what we think about most of the time." Interestingly Earl Nightingale developed his career through his personal study of the New Testament and Napoleon Hill's works, mainly *Think and Grow Rich*. But now lets' consider some more thoughts from the scriptures:

"For it is wind that they are sowing, and they will reap a storm wind" (Hosea 8:7).

"Whoever sows sparingly will also reap sparingly, and whoever sows bountifully will also reap bountifully" (2 Corinthians 9:6).

They are great illustrations that help us appreciate this powerful known universal principle or law. We readily see its effects on every conceivable aspect of our lives. As *The Iron Lady* pointed out, our thoughts, our words, our actions, our habits, our character, our destiny, each thought is a vibration of frequency in the form of wave. It permeates all time and space; it is all pervasive energies that affect every molecule that surrounds us. It defines us and drives us with powerful influence. It is a law.

People in the past have tried to fly in their psychosis, jumping off buildings to their death, not realizing that their collective vibration has to obey regardless of their childish and persistent thoughts. They have paid dearly with their lives.

We should consider that those forces permeate every thought that we formulate—from our words, all the way to our destiny. In essence, who we are and our lives are nothing but a result of what we have thought about or what we have been influenced to think up to this point. We have created our own destiny. *Destiny* here is defined as the collective vibrational frequency of what we are and who we are. This idea will be developed further in another chapter.

Therefore, as we continue to persist with our thoughts, whether of a positive nature or a negative nature, that is exactly what is being given to us through the natural response of the universe and its laws. At this point, many people wonder how could they have created so much misery or chaos in their lives themselves. We think that somehow we are just victims of people and circumstances beyond our control. This might be true to a certain extent, but it does not refute that these laws exist and affect and effect every conceivable thought and action of mind and body. We must reap what we have sown. Whatever frequency we generate and broadcast must come back instantly to us.

Consider what Jesus made very clear to those who were considered as unlettered and uneducated people. At the Sermon on the Mount, he explained that thoughts could have an evil nature or that they could be powerfully negative with strong negative consequences.

"However, I say to you that everyone who continues wrathful with his brother will be accountable to the court of justice; and whoever addresses his brother with an unspeakable word of contempt will be accountable to the Supreme Court . . . liable to the fiery Gehenna" (Matthew 5:22).

Let's strongly consider here the point regarding thoughts, mainly the ones of a negative nature, for the person who decides to harbor negative thinking will have to deal with serious consequences. Do the laws of physics give light to the possible outcomes of such negative thoughts? Considering that a hateful thought carries a frequency with a magnetic pull, then the strong emotion of hate is really amplifying the nature of that thought. The laws of physics permeating such thoughts will continue to make the intensity of the energy being broadcasted to its larger and more obvious manifestations. Those thoughts will become words of hate, those words of hate will enforce the thoughts themselves, creating bigger negative thoughts and more negative words. This will continue to influence the person sowing the nature of that energy vibrating powerfully, ultimately influencing them to act negatively. This, in turn, will create powerful negative habits, which will create in us a person of a negative character. Thus, our destiny, or personal collective vibrational pattern, will perpetuate every aspect of our lives and surroundings.

To emphasize the truth about these statements, we previously discussed how in Japan there were some scientific experiments that were done with water, proving that thoughts are things that affect physical matter. They proved in the same manner that we must realize that our body and mind, everything that makes us, are vibrating frequencies of energy into the universe, permeating all space and time and thus, through the law of attraction, creating our lives and what we experience at every instant of Planck time. It is the law. We must reap what we have sown regardless of the nature of who we are, what we are, and who we have become.

The great news is that the opposite is absolutely true by law. Our positive thoughts, as we enforce them, will create what we do desire. Our positive words will become positive actions that will translate into healthy habits of success. In turn, our character will be so powerful that we have no choice but to create our own desired destiny. Our automatic set point of vibration will bring us and create in our present reality the exact blueprint of that vibrational field. So if we want to feel good every day, to be in the career that we dream about, to do things we have thought of as impossible until now, we must know they are already in existence and that they are a reality in the energetic field of infinite possibilities. All we have to do is change the channel of our broadcast transmitter and receiver: our brain. Change what we picture, say, do, and, most importantly, what we think and how we think.

As we exercise this ability, we will program our molecular structure so that just like water will take the shaped of any vessel that we pour it into, we can essentially become what we want the most.

Practical Application

By now, we have firmly established that the laws of physics permeate our entire universe, including our set vibrational point. We may readily see what our vibration of energy is creating by making the diligent effort of observing our immediate reality. All the inputs and outputs of energy that we process are being translated into the various interactions with people, circumstances, and events that we experience. We must really start the process to examine carefully with our powers of discernment and awareness with this knowledge, what it is that is currently being mirrored back to us, as well as what has been given to us throughout our lives as a form of feedback due to our vibrational set point. This will also help us to discern what it is that will continue to be given to us as our future days continue to unfold.

As we readily examine with full awareness what we experience, we may start to hate our present reality. But this is good because we can harness that powerful emotion and decide to observe something else. We could decide to become thankful with the prospect of creating something better. So whether it is better feelings about our everyday life, more opulence in our present reality, or a relationship that can enforce positive aspects in our life, we realize that we are now aware of the positive probabilities of creating and bringing whatever we want into our existence.

But maybe we may wonder, can we really just have, be, and do whatsoever we desire? Consider this text from the scriptures that implies the nature of what our ability is supposed to be with certainty.

"Then God said: 'Let us make man in our image, according to our likeness'" (Genesis 1:26).

According to the biblical reference, God has unfathomable power, and since we are considered to be made in his image, then, in connection with him, so do we ourselves have unfathomable power. Like minigods made in his image, we can exercise our creative ability just like God did. For by exercising our abilities to speak things into existence, then it will become our nature to harness this power. It will also be proven that it is our "moral obligation" to create exactly what we want. Just like it is our moral obligation to be clean, or love our families, or save a helpless baby from drowning, so is also our moral obligation and right to pursue our dreams and goals, whatever they may be. As long as we do not step on other people's rights, desires, goals, and dreams, we can do anything. It will be proven that, like the physical laws of the universe that exist, so must our desires come into our present reality by law. And not just because we want to, but because it is our moral obligation to do so. For if we don't, the physical laws of the universe say we must die . . .

# CHAPTER 4

## Law of the Universe: Our Moral Obligation to Obtain Our Desires

*What is success? I think it is a mixture of having a flair for the thing you are doing; knowing that it is not enough, that you have got to have hard work and a certain sense of purpose.*

—Margaret Thatcher

*The desire that guides me in all I do is the desire to harness the forces of nature to the service of mankind.*

—Nikola Tesla

I BELIEVE THESE TWO quotes illustrate the basis and foundation for true success. Knowing that we wake up excited for our day because what we do puts a fire within us. That we wake up with energy and vigor because we love what we do. Realizing that long hours of work are a pleasure because they give us energy, and serving others would certainly give us purpose. Knowing that our personal desires harness the forces of nature for the betterment of ourselves and others will expand the universe into a universal paradise. We must realize that essentially this is not philosophy, but it is physics in connection to the power of our mind. This is precisely what will be proven in this chapter.

We will examine why doubt and disbelief will kill us . . . literally, but faith and knowingness will give us biological eternity. This may sound bizarre, but let's consider some texts in the biblical reference that emphasize these governing laws of the universe. As mentioned before, we will examine these ideas in the light of quantum physics and other quotes from a world-renowned scientist who has been considered to be a genius and possibly the greatest inventor of all time. Examining these statements and ideas in the light of the four scientific principles we discussed on the previous chapter will give us the assurance that biological eternity is not as farfetched as we might think. As such, we will build a foundation with the following texts:

"Faith is the assured expectation of what is hoped for, the evident demonstration of realities that are not seen" (Hebrews 11:1).

"Indeed, everything that is not based on faith is sin" (Romans 14:23).

It is of utmost importance that it is emphasized in the reader's mind that this is not theology or religious philosophy by definition. The statements here are not a "preachy sermon" that presents human beings as all evil and destined to burn in some hell fire or anything of that sort. The word *sin*, by definition, is really a misnomer. In essence, what is described in the Bible as sin is not what most people think, but far from it. The reasons? They are irrelevant, and they do not belong in this context. They will not be discussed—it will just be a waste of time.

With all this in mind, consider the exact definitions and elaborations on the words *faith* and *sin*. The Bible is describing the power of the mind and its mechanics by definition. But to illustrate faith, consider that the person who works out his muscles will experience pain the more intense the workout. The physiology of the body is programmed to repair the muscles that tore apart during the workout, and thus create new, stronger muscle tissue. The workout will progressively make a person stronger and more tolerant to pain and future workouts. This is why a bodybuilder must intensify his workouts to become stronger and more defined, otherwise they plateau. In a similar manner, faith denotes the action in which we exercise our brain muscles. The brain does need to be exercised and needs stimulation the way we need to drink water and eat food to continue living. We either progress or regress. We are either growing or dying. There is no middle ground.

By definition, the person who exercises his power of perception based on faith, whether consciously or subconsciously, is exercising a muscle that will continue to get stronger. The person of faith creates a decision in his mind to achieve something; he plainly sets an imprint in his mind of a desired outcome, a picture, and continues to hope for it. He thinks about it as much as he can with hope, or the assured expectation of it. Hope is defined as "a feeling of expectation and desire for a certain thing to happen." Then faith must be defined as "a 'feeling of knowingness' that the expectation and desire for a certain thing to happen will absolutely happen." So by definition, this is law, not philosophy, not theology or religious belief, but a law based on the fabric of the physical universe in relation to us and how we vibrate.

So according to the four principles of science, let's reason and see what is happening at a quantum level. The person exercising faith for a desired result is sending a frequency of energy that is programming his entire persona and his reality. His consistency of broadcast, through the principle that we become or we get what we think about most of the time, begins to shift and influence his immediate reality. He cannot see it immediately; therefore, he is experiencing the law of faith: "the evident demonstration of things not seen." His knowingness and positive and strong desire for his desired result adds to the power of his neurons and is creating a powerful magnetic pull, and the person is drawing in everything that must take place so that the result is exactly what he decided must happen. In actuality, such person gets what he wants, exactly the way he pictured it from the start of the process.

Through this process, the person will see his thoughts expand positively; words will reflect person's positive expectation. Feelings motivate the person to take positive action, thus creating successful habits that help such a person persevere with his actions. The massive amount of energy that is being persistently generated at a quantum physical level is permeating the entire existence of such a person. It brings the person the circumstances, events, people, and situations that are drawing the dream closer or making him match the frequency of what was already created on the infinite realm of possibilities, the etheric field of energy. Thus from the point when the decision for the dream or desired outcome was made, that dream or goal already existed on the field of quantum particle wave duality, or the ether. This is quantum tunneling. Remember the particles that were being shot against the barrier? The particles decide to go through the wall regardless of their force and inertia because they already were on the other side of the wall. Our dreams, our desires already exist in the ether. *Ether* here is defined as the field of energy where all the particles of mass exist as waves and have wavelike qualities. They are energy waves not tied into time and space or defined by such concepts.

A more precise definition of *ether* in physics is "a very rare field and highly elastic substance formerly believed to permeate all space, including the interstices between the particles of matter and the medium whose vibrations constituted light and other electromagnetic radiation." It is emphasized that the ether and all the particles in wave form are not the same but that one is a result of the other. But it will be used as a parallel to describe where all creative decisions reside as a probability of existence. Thus, the ether and particle wave duality are closely related, although not the same. For illustrative purposes, it is encouraged for the reader to watch *The Matrix* trilogy filmed and directed by the Wachowskis. Many of these principles are clearly defined throughout the movies. It helps the movie viewer to understand through illustrations what is the ether or the matrix.

> *The same inexorable agents which prevent a mass from changing suddenly its velocity would likewise resist the force of the new knowledge until time gradually modifies human thought.*

—Nikola Tesla

This quote gives a tremendous amount of data on drawing powerful conclusions in connection to our ability to create what we desire based on a brain transmission of frequency. In this instance, we choose and decide what we want, and that decision is created in an instant in time in the field of energy or the ether. Our thoughts are consistently changing the channel and thus initiating the process of bringing it into a defined collection of energy or particles in time and space—or our present matrix reality. Tesla described it here as "agents that prevent a mass from changing suddenly." If you decide that you want $10,000,000, these agents prevent you from making it happen suddenly or instantaneously.

This is good, and we can illustrate the reason this way: Imagine a man who finds a magical tree which fruit growth is based on people's desires. When the tree is approached, it mirrors instantly what a person creates in his mind. He says to the tree, "I am rich and wealthy." Immediately he is surrounded with hundreds of millions of cash at his disposal. He then says, "I want a gorgeous wife who loves me." Immediately the most beautiful woman appears in front of him, ready to demonstrate her love for him. He then says, "I desire eternal youth." And thus he feels invigorated with energy and power, and his complexion changes to that of a twenty-five-year-old. He looks at everything and realizes that he has everything he could ever want, and he says, "Wow, this must be dream. I must have died and gone to heaven." And thus everything he asked for begins to disappear, and then he dies and goes to heaven.

The point is clear: We don't always think or say positive things. In reality, we live in a very pessimistic and negative society. Imagine if you were in a zoo and saw a big, scary lion. Sometimes we wonder what would happen to us if the lion were not caged. Certainly, we don't want our negative thoughts to manifest physically in that instant. The key is that the new knowledge or broadcast of the desired result must be exercised persistently so the energetic transmission reaches the tipping point. When that occurs, there will absolutely be no choice but for us to have what we have asked, period.

Faith has always been described as a "spiritual belief," religious stubbornness, and dogma. If the reader is confused about the validity of the comment made that faith is a physical law, consider this biblical text:

"Where then is the boasting? There is no place for it. Through what law? That of works? No indeed, but through the law of faith" (Romans 3:27).

Here in these texts, the biblical reference is again plainly demonstrated to have validity and a reliable source among ancient writings. Another statement ahead of its time, or maybe not ahead of its time. We may have just regressed a little. Probably.

## The Opposite of Faith Is Fear

This sentence relates to the word *sin*, which we will now break down even more. A person of faith pictures a desired result and knows without a doubt it will happen. The person of faith, at least exercises faith so that even if he has doubts, he persists because of the strong desire. A person who exercises fear is in the habit of thinking about and talking about what they don't want to happen. The opposite of faith is fear. People who are in fear are generally mostly negative. The passage from scripture that says that "anything that does not originate from faith is sin" is, in essence, describing the same exact thing: fear. It has been said that fear is just an acronym for "false expectations appearing real." I heard a successful life coach and successful businessman by the name of Ed Foreman talk extensively about this concept and the ramifications it creates in a person's life for entertaining such thoughts in their minds. (By the way, he was elected to Congress at two different times for two different states. He is also incredibly wealthy, according to many reliable sources.)

This also denotes the idea that every form of thought or action, every form of vibrational frequency broadcasted from your brain, is either positive or negative. There is no neutral ground, no fence which one could straddle between both realms. We are either successful in creating a reality based on what we want or successful in creating a reality based on what we don't want. This will be determined based on our thinking habits and patterns of behavior, period.

Thinking about Moses, do we now realize how important it is that we listen to people who have the physical manifestations that prove that what they are saying has basis in empirical evidence? It is important that through our power of discernment, we become observing people who have successfully transferred their dreams and goals from the field of energetic waves and particles of infinite possibility to the more defined world of energy in time and space. Or do we observe people who generally have lives which manifest their doubts and fears? And more importantly, do we take counsel from them?

It is the desire now to also establish another point that we have previously mentioned. It *is* our moral obligation to create our dreams and think about what we want; otherwise, we are creating the opposite— what we don't want. It has been shown in the field of health care that stress is the number 1 cause of illness and disease, which leads to death. People are tired and sick, exhausted because the body is in a state of constant survival. The excess adrenaline and hormones that are being pumped through the body to help each person just bear his own existence obviously saps the body of strength and vigor, thus the body becomes prone to illness and disease. Stress does eventually kill us. This has been the sad destiny of all humankind since the beginning. It is funny how the biblical reference alludes to the idea of sin in connection with death, for it does say that the wages that sin pays is death.

Also think of the placebo and nocebo effect. This is established medical and scientific fact and is considered strongly every time a new drug or treatment is created to treat illness and disease. *Placebo* is defined as "a harmless pill, medicine, or procedure prescribed more for the psychological benefit to the patient than for any physiological effect." In testing, a group of people will be told that a certain drug or treatment will be given to them to treat an illness or disease that they have. Half will be given the actual drug, and the other half will be given a placebo in the form of a sugar pill. Many times, those who take the sugar pills will be cured or made better more readily that the drug which was specifically designed to help them. By observation, it is their belief that cures them even though they took a sugar pill.

Let's now consider the nocebo effect. A definition for *nocebo* is "a detrimental effect on health produced by psychological or psychosomatic factors, such as negative expectations of treatment or prognosis." In this scenario, fear of the substance or imagined negative consequence will make the body react exactly how the person was expecting; negatively, but it does not happen as a result of the thing itself that is feared.

The point must be firmly established. It seems obvious that just because we decide to think positively all the time and follow our dreams and passions, it does not guarantee that we are going to stay alive, and never die. But here is another plausible idea. If we think positively about life in the context of the following quote by Nikola Tesla (which was previously partially quoted), by law then, it is what exactly must happen.

> *If the genius of invention were to reveal tomorrow the*
> *secret of immortality, of eternal beauty and youth, for which*
> *all humanity is aching, the same inexorable agents which*
> *prevent a mass from changing suddenly its velocity would*

*likewise resist the force of the new knowledge until time*
*gradually modifies human thought.*

Here Nikola is emphasizing that the thought itself, that of immortality, eternal beauty, and youth, is possible as long as people believe in its probability. Most people accept death as natural reality and a process of life, and as such it is our present reality. These thought processes that have established our current reality are the "inexorable agents which prevent" the particles from changing suddenly. But it is new knowledge that is persistently introduced into the whole mass that will change such reality. What knowledge will eventually and gradually modify the collective consciousness agreement of death? Consider the following scriptural reference that parallels Tesla's comment:

"For the weapons of our warfare are not fleshly, but powerful by God for overturning strongly entrenched things. For we are overturning reasonings and every lofty thing raised up against the knowledge of God [universe], and we are bringing it into captivity to make it obedient to Christ" (2 Corinthians 10:4).

The weapons of warfare is referred to "knowledge of the universe itself." The knowledge of how creation works will help us remove or "overturn strongly entrenched things." The inexorable agents that Nikola Tesla described will be modified by new knowledge, for the proper recognition of the basic laws of the universe and how they relate to our personal and collective lives will enforce a new creative shift of thought in our minds. Interestingly, Christ was an expert at using the laws of physics to create powerful changes in people's lives.

We are, without question, aching because we have not discovered the solution to death. In reality, if we think about it hard enough, the only problem, or the only powerful energetic barrier we have not solved is death. The only thing wrong with life is death. The fact that we age and die is absolutely in no way natural to human beings. We are made different. Animals just live on instinct; therefore, their potential is restricted. But we have infinite potential. The laws of physics explains that it is so. Our entire human genome and vibrational blueprint testify to these truths.

Consider what quantum physics has told us about vibration in connection to the ether or matrix of energy and the constant of particle wave duality. Since particles of energy can become anything upon broadcast, and the fact that even Tesla came to the cognition of such possibility, it means biological eternity already exists in the etheric energy field. It would only take a small amount of people relative to the billions on Earth to change the present reality if they just change their mind to a much positive one. The positive energy which is much more powerful than any present negative thought will permeate the entire field, the ether, and the energy will continue to send until the tipping point spills onto the field of energy defined by time and space. Interestingly, there is one group of people that is rapidly growing, which, in essence, is introducing this powerful energy into the field. Every day, this energy is exponentially growing, and we are at the edge of its manifestation. This will continue to be discussed throughout the book.

With a sort of eternity defining our bodies and eternal youth, our potential then will be really limitless. Consider the thought that we are made in the image of God himself. Or maybe we are sons of the universe whose nature is eternal, or infinite. In essence, we are the sons of an eternal god or an infinite universe. Therefore our nature must be infinite. It is not suggested that they are one and the same but, in connection to both ideas of God or the universe, we therefore must be eternal. Since that is the case, then that is *exactly what must happen*. Or at least, it is what was supposed to happen. What went wrong? Why is that not the case? Let's examine with careful thought what we are talking about here, for as we previously stated, it is absolutely our moral obligation to achieve and align ourselves to the laws and the nature of the physical universe.

Law of the Universe: Achieving Biological Eternity

Let's think of the progress of certain technologies. Let's think of money, for example. Money is a tool that facilitates exchange of goods and services. The evolution of money has been demonstrated plainly throughout history. Let's go back to the time of nomads. They moved from one place to another in search of shelter and food. The basics were severely pursued since there were many dangers. Lack of food meant sickness and death. Nomads would become easy prey to other animals. Thus the pressures of living made them think of solutions. How to stay in one place to conserve energy. Farming was the solution. It helped them establish their livelihoods in one place and produce food without using as much energy as they would hunting. Potential life risk was drastically reduced. The "exchange" of energy was lower, thus people lived more abundantly. The land then certainly produced better and more abundantly than the availability of eatable animals themselves. The new economic system made humans progress more exponentially than the old system did.

That is not where it stopped though. Since people had more animals, bread, vegetables, or fruits than they could eat, systems of trading were naturally developed. People had more time to learn to make clothing or create tools for construction. People had more time to learn how to build homes or farm better, manage fields and workers better. All exchanges of energy were more efficient through the exchange of products and services. People were trading eggs for flour, cows for sheep, food for clothing; people helped to build homes or plant farms or vineyards for a rate of exchange, among other benefits. As a result, this helped people establish villages, towns, cities, countries, and empires.

Life pressures, though, continue to influence peoples' minds. People desired and continue to desire today more time in their lives and the energy to enjoy the fruit of their labors. We wish to experience life better, faster, and longer. We hate to delay the gratification of our lives. It really is our driving force and nature. We want more and better of the good things life has to offer. But a question does arise. How did gold and silver and other precious metals come into play as a form of exchange or money? Certainly metals are better for construction, and we hear of overlaying things with gold and silver, but what was the real value other than the observed beauty? This is a good question, since we are considering the past.

But let's continue observing the natural evolution of money as the need for better and more convenient exchange forms continued to arise. Because of the perceived value, people started to use gold, silver, and bronze to exchange for other goods. There were some issues. Carrying and traveling with heavy bags full of money for the purpose of trading was dangerous and costly. People could get cheated, robbed, kidnapped, or killed. It was also inconvenient to do large exchanges, since you had to carry large amounts of gold or silver to acquire property, animals, or other products that may have been in demand. It was inconvenient to store, and it took up large amounts of space and was costly to guard or protect. People's greed has been known to get the better of them and have caused them to kill people or pillage cities for such things. Thus the banking system came into play.

As we see it today, the exchange form is more convenient than ever before. From a society that used mostly cash, with notes backed by gold or silver, we are now a society that uses mostly electronic notes in the form of debit cards, credit cards, and Internet transactions, etc. Electronic currencies of money are the rule today. It is noteworthy how the word *currency* and *money* are used as synonyms. It is all considered legal tender based on debt. Borrowing from the future and living now. There is much debate as to the legalities and the morality of the use of such "monies" today. Maybe it is so. Considering that high interest rates and taxes and other forms of creating money out of thin air may constitute a visible negative outcome in people's lives, mainly different forms of slavery. But here is an interesting dichotomy.

Let's imagine for a second and put ourselves in a position that may seem very stressful and full anxiety. People who experience such things have been known to take their lives and those of their loved ones with the thought that it would be better to not experience the pain. We feel for such people. Either way, let's consider that an average man with a job of $60,000 a year has a mortgage; car payments; kids' college education; his own college education, credit card, or insecure debt, with high interest rates putting pressure. He is well off in his fifties. His health is waning, his energy levels are depleted. He is tired of the rat race. This is considered the "normal" life. The "American Dream." And maybe he is happy or content with his daily routine and he is looking forward to retirement.

But then we hear that he loses his job. Advanced in years, his position is unnecessary and easily replaced by technology or younger adults who will take the job for much lower pay. The company downsized, or it went bankrupt.

Whatever the reason, he now has to draw from his savings and retirement account, racks up more credit card debt with high interest rates, and maybe sell his house or foreclose. The pressure of just providing for the basic necessities of his family is getting to him. He feels humiliated, unappreciated; he is at an all-time low. He becomes desperate because he sees no way out and decides to kill himself. Obviously this can happen to anybody.

We may feel strongly about this man's situation; we could be in a similar situation right now. But do we realize that by just adding one magic ingredient, his entire perspective changes. With this one ingredient, even if his situation was worse, it would not matter. He would still feel happy and excited about his life, probably more than ever before. How? What magical ingredient is that?

Nikola Tesla said it: "eternal youth." No more aging and death. Let's exaggerate his circumstances now. His mortgage is that of $500,000, his credit card debt is up to $400,000, his collective debt, including his kids' college education and his own student loans, is an another $500,000. He is paying massive amounts of interest, so much that all his payments are going to mostly the reduction of applied interest rate. How does he feel about all that now? I believe we can realize that it does not matter. He has life as an infinite resource. He has all the time in the world to pay his debts. Even if his income was significantly lower, it would not matter. It would not change a thing about his feelings toward these seemingly negative experiences. He would be as happy as he could ever be because he knows he can change it whenever he feels like it. His debt is meaningless in the grand scheme of things. He is in full control knowing he has infinity in his side—biological eternity.

It is death that makes us rush. It is the conscious and subconscious awareness that we are going to die that makes us want to live and experience faster than ever before. We would not fret about work, money, or debt because we have eternal life. If people had this reality, would they steal, cheat, or murder? Would they doubt that they could not have abundance, or that they could one day become millionaires or billionaires? Would we ever doubt that we would make trillions of dollars? That we could build our dream estate, our own piece of paradise on ten acres of land? Of course, we would accomplish such things and more because this one ingredient changes the entire recipe. It changes everything. The perspective of humanity would shift like a massive earthquake, and nothing would ever be the same.

Unfortunately as of right now, when most of us think of creating a business or lifestyle that makes us feel free and abundant, most people have doubt and disbelief. Why? Because we know we have to exert ourselves and use resources and sacrifice things to create them with the possibility that we will fail. The problem with that is that if we continue to fail, we fear that we are exerting ourselves in vain and we will miss out on enjoying the short lives that we have. But if we have eternal youth, biological eternity, does it matter if we fail? Does it matter how many times we fail? We know that we are bound to get what we want at some point as we persevere. Then the answer is obvious: with life as an infinite resource, we could have, be and do whatsoever we desire without any fear or doubt creeping in. It would be in our nature because infinity is our ultimate resource. No matter how big or how outrageous our dream would be, we "know" we could make it happen. We would be like gods with powerful creative abilities evolving and getting better throughout infinity.

Since it is our nature to have instant gratification, death will make a human being over step other people's happiness and possessions. People will steal, cheat, and do things that we consider as immoral. We hear of people raping one another whether figuratively or literally just to gratify themselves instantly. Death pervades every aspect of society. For it is not the desire for every aspect of wealth or opulence that it is wrong in itself, but the desire to attain such things regardless of whom we overstep to get there. Fear, or false expectations appearing real, the process of thinking about what we don't want to happen literally kills us. If we are constantly in fear of not having what we desire, we may start to envy those who do. Some may start to criticize or condemn those who do, in attempt to take it away from them. We may start to fear that there is not enough for us. Therefore our instincts of survival will kick in, and like animals we may prey on others. And by the laws of the universe, we must experience exactly what we have done wrong to others. This has been the sad history of mankind. There really is no other reason for such things existing in our lives.

This examination of faith in contrast with fear and death in contrast with life is not to make the reader feel hopeless or upset, thinking that there is no way out. There is absolute evidence that these laws of the universe are kicking in to help us get out of the rat race and allow us to jump into what is our actual nature: eternity. This concept will continue to be developed throughout this book.

## The Bright Future of Humankind: For Every Action, There Is an Equal and Opposite Reaction

Let's go back to what we were discussing about the natural evolution of energy, as perceived through the example of the progress of money or currency. As we continue to look at and experience what we don't want, an equal and opposite reaction must take place, as Isaac Newton stated. We now know that as we have fear, we tend to define what we *do* want. This is that opposite reaction. When we are experiencing that which has become out of habit, creating what we don't want, we experience negative feelings, and thus we feel bad most of the time. This is the equal reaction taking place. Thus, it happens many times, that we harness the power of that opposite reaction and focus on that creation or goal in our mind of what we truly desire, the opposite of what we are experiencing. We start to experience contrast in our mind's eye. We begin to feel and emote what it would be like and how good we would feel once we have the opposite of what we have.

Interestingly, this third law of motion continues to affect our thoughts whether we are moving in one direction or heading to the other side of the spectrum. We become aware of the complete opposite from where we currently realize is our present reality. That is why we may learn of powerful examples of people whose "rags to riches" stories inspire us. Or we learn of ultrasuccessful people who fall to the bottom and their worst nightmare becomes a reality. We are either growing or dying. But all the same, it is our choice through the powers of perception that we are able to make the decision that suits us best. So if we are at our worst that we have ever been, then we can come to realize how much worse it could become. But equally present is the thought of how it could be better. Or if we are at our best and readily see how it could get better, but then we are also aware that we could lose it all.

Our awareness of such possibilities forces us to focus. It forces us to make decisions. We cannot stagnate any more than we can defy the laws of physics and wish them away. Even if we try to stand our ground, in reality we are projecting a frequency based on fear. People defend and protect what they don't want to lose. Therefore if we choose such a position, the focus of our perception is only in losing it, and thus we get what we think about most of the time. We hear constantly in sports that the best defense is a good offense. Deciding to be on the defense is nothing more than an imaginary wall. We must always remember that according to quantum tunneling, a wall is nothing more than an illusion because the particles trying to get through already exist on the other side of the barrier. It only needs to persist and with ease these particles will get through.

This is good news, since what we perceive as insurmountable stationary obstacles are nothing but illusions. Once we decide to get through, then we are through. We already exist on the other side of the seemingly giant wall. No wonder Jesus said:

"Truly I say to you that whoever tells this mountain, 'Be lifted up and thrown into the sea,' and does not doubt in his heart but has faith that what he says will happen, he will have it happen" (Mark 11:23).

As such is the reality, let's always decide to advance. This makes me think of certain scenarios that prove this interesting idea. I remember hearing on the news the story of a man of lowly beginnings who won one of the biggest lottery winnings in the history of the country. The news reporter was interviewing the gentleman who had just won what I believe to be over seven hundred million dollars. She asked him what he would do with the money. His answer, "I have no idea!" We may have also heard of dot-com billionaires, such as the creators of the Google search engine or the creator of Facebook. Seemingly without much effort and in a relatively short time, they became financially ultrasuccessful. It seems that just like records are meant to be broken, so do people's seemingly incredible achievements will be broken again. There are more billionaires today than before. The process has gone from trying to become a millionaire to trying to become a multimillionaire. And we are starting to realize that more and more people are becoming multibillionaires. We may see in the future people achieving their first half trillion dollars. The mountains are becoming relatively easier to remove.

As we progressively begin to see the world unfold into more prosperity because of this strange phenomena, maybe at some point we will realize and see the world with most of its problems virtually solved. We also realize the power of dreams and goals once achieved—that dreams, in essence, not only benefit those who are achieving them, but benefits those who also come in contact with those individuals dreams. For example: A woman opening a restaurant may hire about fifty people, and so she creates value for them. They can make money based on her desired outcome of opening a restaurant. Thus she places food on other people's tables, creates mortgage payments or rent money for the people who work for her. Her dream creates dignity and self-respect for those who benefit from her ability to create jobs from operating a business. That's value creation. Her moral obligation to pursue her dream achieved much good in her community. Her moral obligation helps her show love for neighbor.

Maybe through her use of these principles, as she exercises awareness and faith, she may be able to open more and better restaurants. Her dream could expand to that of opening hotels with restaurants all over the world and thus creating massive value for those who need such moneymaking opportunities. Let's think about it carefully. First, the operating expenses may include the construction of the buildings. This creates jobs for those whose livelihoods depend on their building skills. Once the building is up, the maintenance of the building creates value for those who provide the services required. Maybe there is a lease that needs to be paid. The kitchen appliances and machines do need regular maintenance and may need repairs from time to time. Money must go out a hundred different places to sustain the business, and by law, the owner of such operations must reap the benefits with much larger incomes. Whatever our dreams are, we can see powerful benefits being derived from them and for others.

Can we see that a world where everyone prospers is unfolding? Where everyone is able to achieve bigger and faster, influencing others and inspiring them to do the same. People will now be able to make a quantum leap, where they are no longer living to merely sustain their existence, but are living gratification most of the time. This will propel society to progress into the awareness of eradicating illness and disease. With illness and disease virtually gone, people will enjoy prolonged and better-quality lives. With everyone living in continuous prosperity, things like war and crime would become a thing of the past. No longer possible in society, the masses would be firmly established on a deep foundation of wisdom and real knowledge, and such negative concepts will no longer fit and cease to be part of people's minds. But it can't stop there, for the next step would be to eradicate death. People now will want to live forever and will exhaust every possible source to achieve it.

JULIAN VALDERRAMA

With their awareness of unlimited potential, the thought of dying would propel to desire with all their might the continuance of their enjoyment of life. Just like Tesla suggested, if enough people can permeate the ether with the idea of immortality, eternal youth and beauty, then such concepts must become our reality. It is the law.

Just like the law of progress has perpetuated technology in our day and continues to progress exponentially, so must the law of progress perpetuate our lives and value creation exponentially. And this is not a process that would take centuries, for it was not too long ago that we had giant radios, giant televisions and computers, stereos, VHS machines, and Walkmans, but now these things are drastically different today. All those technologies wowed the populace. Now we have smartphones that have integrated all those operations in one device. Everything now fits in a tiny microchip smaller than a penny. As technology unfolds, we see that everything has become more affordable and more efficient. We can realize easily why this exponential growth is taking place. As people observe these gadgets being developed, at first, they are not affordable by the average person. This makes us want them even more. But what we create collectively with that desire is the ability to afford them. But those who can presently afford them realize that they could be better. The creators of such gadgets, in turn, know that they can do better as they discover new and better technologies and integrate them into tools that expand and improve our everyday lives. Our collective vibration improves everything exponentially. We live better and faster. And so the same evolution and progress must happen with our individual lives.

This is in harmony with the texts found in the biblical reference. We will now prove that this concept has been continuing to call out since the beginning of our time. Consider some thoughts from the past:

"But the meek will possess the earth, and they will find exquisite delight in the abundance of peace" (Psalms 37:11).

"The righteous will possess the earth, and will live forever on it" (Psalms 37:29).

"This means everlasting life, their coming to know you, the only true God, and the one whom you sent, Jesus Christ" (John 17:3).

We wish to observe that these verses denote the idea of the possibility of people gaining biological eternity, eternal youth, or the exquisite delight in the abundance of peace. We must also realize that they emphasize everlasting life on a peaceful new earthly society. The suggestion of the last text may emphasize that getting to know the mind of God through creation is, in essence, the way to achieve eternity. The verse suggests that this character, as described as the one sent forth to teach us how, will gain us biological eternity. I feel we are doing exactly just that through the various fields of study—true science, true philosophies based on laws of physics, and true examples of successful people who have had the physical manifestations from the practical application of those laws. By studying how the universe works and what its laws are, we will be able to learn and evolve infinitely. As we unfold knowledge based on our desires to continue to make every instant better in our lives, through empirical evidence we have examined that our attainment of biological eternity is more than just a probability.

Since it is our moral obligation to use the laws of the universe to improve our lives and, by connection, everyone's lives, the ultimate result based on what we discussed is nothing more but the fulfillment of the law of the universe: infinity. God's desire to share infinite eternity. This is evident through what we learned in the creation account. God had created in his power a garden called Eden. The first human couple was to replicate this foundation throughout the earth. To create a global paradise was the purpose of the supposedly first human couple. Whether we personally believe this as an allegory or illustrative story, we cannot deny that through the empirical evidence, we are examining the same outcome. We can see both in the allegory and the reality of our lives that the desire for life eternal is a common denominator and a driving force in human nature. This emphasis of eternity was established since the beginning. The account describes a second tree called the tree of life. As to the nature of the tree, it is believed that once the couple partook of its fruits, it would allow them to continue sustaining their lives for all eternity.

The one called Jesus in the Bible seems to have been sent forth to correct our thinking of life and how it works. But how can we possibly replicate the quantum miracles he performed? From feeding thousands with only a few fish and pieces of bread, to eliminating illness and disease in an instant. What about the seemingly easy ability to bring the dead back to life? Certainly we have been able to do some good through technology and the progress of science, but not that extent. Have we consider that our observation of what is possible and achievable helps us to believe that we can do the same? Like a millionaire considering the idea of being a billionaire, a billionaire considering the idea of becoming a multibillionaire. What others have done, we can also do. Considering what Jesus did as it relates to reality and the laws of quantum physics, must imprint in our minds that we can exercise our power of transmission of energy and frequency to affect our reality for the betterment of ourselves and mankind. If we come to that realization, are we not in fact fulfilling Nikola Tesla's vision? Our creative process will open the solution to immortality and eternal youth and beauty. This new knowledge must permeate the ether, and it must come back to us by law. And if you really think about it, it is already happening.

Consider what Jesus said about those who take seriously the things he did and thus put effort to replicate:

"Most truly I say to you, whoever exercises faith in me will also do works that I do; and he will do works greater than these" (John 14:12).

Let's examine this suggestion in the light of the laws of physics. If we readily accept the outlandish things that he did as real, then we have no choice but to broadcast a collective frequency of energy that will create them as probabilities in the ether, the field of particle wave duality. But even if you consider them as a myth, they must still be created. What you focus on expands, whether or not you believe it as real. Albert Einstein said that the most powerful force in our hand has something to do with our imagination. So as we consider things to be myth or reality, the laws of physics will expand and make them a reality eventually.

We should consider that we must take baby steps and progressively move toward the final threshold—biological eternity. Its evolution, as we have discussed, will continue to unfold exponentially, for that which is vibrating must attract more of it. Through the law of magnetic attraction, the field must reach its tipping point and thus spill into the realm of particles defined in time and space. It must become our present reality. It is the law.

Can we see now why it is our *moral obligation* to think positively, to speak positively, to act positively, to have positive habits, and to develop a positive character? Because ultimately, it truly creates our destinies. Whether we choose fear, with death as the payment, or faith, with biological eternity as our reward. It is the law, and it must take place one way or another. Achieving what we want does mean life and death by definition. It is not religious biased; it is not religious dogma or stubbornness. It is not philosophy. It is the law of the universe as observed by our empirical science and quantum physics. It is as pervasive as the law of gravity. We must choose to create positively or negatively. We must choose either faith or fear. Either life or death.

And so ultimately, the collective energy of the masses must either perpetuate the current state of affairs, or will we dare to dream as big as Nikola Tesla did when he called for the removal of the current "inexorable agents" that prevent the mass from changing to that of eternal beauty and biological immortality?

### The Matrix of the Universe

> *Only the existence of the field of force can account for the motions of the bodies as observed, and its assumption dispenses with space curvature. All literature on this subject is futile and destined to oblivion. So are all attempts to explain the workings of the universe without recognizing the existence of the ether and the indispensable function it plays in the phenomena.*
>
> *My second discovery was of a physical truth of the greatest importance. As I have searched the entire scientific records in more than a half dozen languages for a long time without finding the least anticipation, I consider myself the original discoverer of this truth, which can be expressed by the statement: There is no energy in matter other than that received from the environment.*
>
> —Nikola Tesla

> *What has been is what will be, and what has been done will be done again. There is nothing new under the sun.*

*Is there anything of which one may say, "Look at this—
it is new"? It already existed from long ago. It already
existed before our time. . . . Whatever happens has already
happened, and what is to come has already been.*

—Ecclesiastes 1:9-10, 3:15

As of right now, the reader may be either just entertained or just plain annoyed by the amount of information that is being compared in connection to the outcomes that have been suggested as probabilities of life. They sound ridiculous, impossible, science fiction, etc. We may hear constantly opposing views about what we supposedly "know" as facts and truths. There is no right or wrong as to how we feel in regard to knowledge and the input of knowledge. It is what it is. Just like due process in the court systems of the world must be unbiased and never one sided, in the same manner, we must consider objectively all information that may completely oppose what we consider to know to be the truth. It's fine to have beliefs, as long as we are ready to let them go in the light of new and factual empirical evidence. We may find that our foundational principles that we live out and perpetually conceive will either easily collapse in the light of new knowledge or it may reinforce them. Either way, both outcomes are good. Justice calls for it, and we must be better for it.

Going back to the conclusion of the last chapter, a reference was made to a famous scene from the first movie of *The Matrix* trilogy. The Wachowskis have given us incredible parallels of the workings of the universe in one powerful illustration—the movies. If the reader has not watched the trilogy, you are certainly encouraged to at least watch the first one. If you have watched it, it doesn't matter whether you liked it or not; just like you may consider the story of Moses to be fictitious and just an illustration, then consider this trilogy under the same guise: an illustration. It will certainly help you grasp many of the concepts described so far on the pages of this book. Note that it will not be the only reference that will be suggested for inclusion in our library of information to help us grasp such concepts.

## The Ether and the Matrix of Reality

You may consider that using a science-fiction movie as a knowledge source may be going too far. Consider that the suggestion to rewatch the series was given to me by a very well-known *New York Times* best-selling author as a great reference material to learn and imprint such concepts in our mind. Did I mention that he has made billions of dollars throughout his career? I would say that, in a sense, he has what we want, and he deems the movie worthy of our time and examination. Since such is the case, I personally would take that suggestion as a command.

In *The Matrix*, the main character, Neo, finds himself going through some weird circumstances and events, and he begins to feel confused about what is happening to him. He finally meets the one he has been searching for all along to get answers: Morpheus. He explains to him "the matrix," or ether, as such:

> *The Matrix is everywhere. It is all around us. Even now, in this very room. You can see it when you look out your window or when you turn on your television. You can feel it when you go to work, when you go to church, when you pay your taxes. It is the world that has been pulled over your eyes to blind you from the truth. . . . That you are slave, Neo. Like everyone else, you were born into bondage, born into a prison that you cannot smell or taste or touch. A prison for your mind.*

Here are some simple but very accurate descriptions of what we have been talking about. The energetic field of particle wave duality, although not the same as the ether, it will be referred to in connection with the realm of energetic waves not defined in time and space. What we must understand is how it relates to us in relation with our collective vibration of frequency and the power of our minds. It is the ether, as referred to by Nikola Tesla, a connection with a field of pure energy that permeates all matter, or the field of force. This is the matrix or ether; it has a powerful influence, and it is radically pervasive like the air we breathe or the water we drink. It is like the law of gravity—it is always there even though we do not think about it, but its effects are instantly discernible.

Another factor that runs parallel to Morpheus's explanation is that we are slaves to the matrix. The context in which he describes Neo's slavery in the movie is obviously negative. We must realize that just a superficial scan of this information may completely force people to deny that the knowledge we have discussed to this point, it may seem we have but little evidence when compared or contrasted with the mirror realities of most people. For if we have such unfathomable ability and power why are our lives full drudgery and struggle? But consider that, in reality, they seem to prove that we have been hopelessly enslaved. We may wonder: if we are so powerful that we could move mountains with just our thought, how come our lives are full of misery and pain? Our lives are defined by drudgery and monotony. Our lives are defined by the ability to supersede one pain with another. It is an obvious decline toward its sad outcome: death. People seem to just be existing from one event to the next, just finding the next quick fix to distract them from the current pain. People are slaves to their most basic necessities, just barely being able to pay for their mortgages, taxes, insurance, and credit card payments, among other bills, while they try to find some comfort in the company of those who live under the same matrix reality.

Spiritual leader Paul commented, "For the creation was subjected to futility, not by its own will, but through the one who subjected it, on the basis of hope that the creation itself will also be set free from enslavement to corruption and have the glorious freedom of the children of God" (Romans 8:20). We see here strong evidence of those who have been called avatars, or powerful people who have influenced drastically the world—in this case, Paul and Nikola Tesla having similar thoughts, just different frames of mind.

The point that needs to be emphasized regarding the ether or the matrix is that it cannot be either good or bad. This may contradict the previous idea that we are nothing but slaves to it. But consider the idea of how the movie emphasized a program called "the construct." The movie defines it as a software program where individuals are connected to. Their minds are, in essence, hacked into, as if they were computers, and then they would receive a download of pictures, which translated to their awareness as being placed inside the computer program. The scene is famous for Morpheus plainly showing Neo what the literal matrix was and how it connected to people's minds. "What is real? How do you define real? If you are talking about what you can feel, what you can smell, what you can taste and see, then 'real' is simply electrical signals interpreted by your brain." He explains this to Neo while they are in what seems to be a "blank" three-dimensional space. Nothing surrounds them until all of sudden, out of nowhere, two red chairs and a TV popped up in their midst. This is later emphasized in a different scene. After defiantly breaking the laws that govern that universe during a sparring session, Morpheus calls for the "Jump Program." Suddenly, Tank, the computer program operator who is in control of what they were hacked into, downloads in an instant an entirely different scenario. The environment changes; they are now in completely different clothing and are standing on top of a building.

This, although exaggerated (or is it really?), is not far from the truth. It cannot be emphasized how beneficial it would be to watch or rewatch these movies and other recommended selections that will help us to come to powerful cognition.

When individually or collectively we are creating or formulating a new thought or the same thought, we establish that at a quantum level; a frequency is simultaneously being broadcasted and permeating all time and space. Its consistency of transmission will determine how quickly it will manifest into our present and immediate reality. This applies to us individually or collectively at every level of connection. As individuals, we transmit a collective frequency based on our entire lives. As families, we transmit collective frequencies. As communities, we transmit collective frequencies. As states or counties, we collectively transmit frequencies. As countries and continents, we transmit collective frequencies. Finally as whole, the planet transmits a collection of frequencies that by law of magnetic attraction must come back and effect and show up in our present reality.

Here are the questions: Since we are vibrating 24/7, what kind of feedback are we getting in return and why? Who is, or what is, bringing it back into our experience? Consider this: In the movie *The Matrix*, the ether first and foremost is a blank space of infinity and there is an operator "waiting for our command" to fill that blank space based on our transmission. The operator does not question your commands or your requests. He is always taking input based on your frequencies. So what are we asking for? What is our individual and collective vibration commanding the operator to present in our reality? The choice is really up to us.

Let's go back to the idea that the ether or matrix of infinite energy is based on exactly that—infinity. Then let's consider what King Solomon of ancient Israel said:

"What has been is what will be, and what has been done will be done again. There is nothing new under the sun. Is there anything of which one may say, 'Look at this—it is new'? It already existed from long ago. It already existed before our time. . . . Whatever happens has already happened, and what is to come has already been" (Ecclesiastes 1:9-10, 3:15).

Since our thoughts and ideas are created in the ether before its manifestation is reflected in our matrix of reality, then, in essence, it already existed. It has been done an infinite amount times. It already happened. Quantum tunneling proves that this is the case. Just like the particles were already on the other side, therefore, your transmission of frequency was already in existence in its blank space of infinite energy. It just has to spill over once it reaches the tipping point.

These concepts may already have been described in the previous chapters, but it is reemphasized here from a different point of view for posterity. What posterity? That we are being influenced by the transmission of others 24/7, both collectively and individually. The more people involved, the more powerful the influence on our thoughts and collective vibration. The implication and consequences cannot be overstated. This is of utmost relevance to our creative abilities. Why? Because as we quoted earlier, no one is more hopelessly enslaved than those who falsely believe they are free. This is in reference to the energetic concept and the physical laws that Tesla emphasized, which prevent immortality, eternal youth, and beauty. That biological eternity and eternal youth and beauty already exist in the ether, and it is panting or calling out to us as individuals and groups. And it must happen. This also suggests that it already exists in our present matrix of reality, that its manifestations have existed and will continue to exist for all eternity. The challenge is that they exist somewhere else and not here obviously. We must align ourselves to that present reality so that we get that reality. We must match and mirror the nature of infinity; we must become infinite or nothing. We must live in faith or in fear.

The more we exercise our abilities to think, speak, and act in harmony with that desire and reality, the consequence then must be that of a collective transmission broadcasted by those who accept the program. The energy will continue to be picked up by other brains, and thus influence the brain transmission of others. The output will influence and push forward much like the snowball effect, in that instead of continuing to perpetuate thoughts of fear and doubt, we will continue to perpetuate and influence the masses to think of that reality, one of faith and prosperity. We have previously talked about how our thoughts will affect the structure of water and completely change its molecular structure. Our brain transmission, along with our collective transmission, is permeating our reality and mirroring back to us the nature of those thoughts. Consider another experiment that is described in a book called *The 100 Monkey Syndrome.*

In this book, it is described that a group of scientists were studying a species of monkeys in a group of islands. There was no way to get from one island to another other than by boat. So they picked one island, and on that island, one scientist decided to take a sweet potato, wash it in the river, and then eat it. A monkey observed the scientist do this repeatedly for a time, and the monkey decided to do the same. The monkey grabbed a sweet potato, washed it, and then ate it, mirroring exactly what the scientist did. After some time, all the monkeys on the island started to copy these actions. The scientists then decided to go to the other islands and saw that all the other monkeys there were doing the exact same thing. They were all replicating the process that the first scientist had started. The dilemma is that the scientist did this on one island only. There was also no way for the monkey to just become an Olympic swimmer, make its way to the other islands and teach this process to the other monkeys. They called this the "hundredth monkey phenomenon." They deduced that the collective consciousness of the family on the one island that first observed the one scientist wash and eat the sweet potato permeated the ether and affected the consciousness of those other monkeys on the other islands and "whispered" to them to do the same thing. Brains do transmit and receive energy frequency, and vibration does affect physical matter. The information had reached the tipping point, and it started to permeate the minds of those monkeys relatively close to the first island.

It is the same idea with humans, our family, and our home. We must take these concepts into serious consideration and completely change the paradigm of a negative, and toxic, corrupt society into that which goal is to positively achieve individual and collective goals, dreams, and desires. Or at least, could we just considered it just like that monkey thought about for a while, whether it should replicate what it was observing this human doing with the potato? Can we just consider it, pretend what it would be like if that were the case? What would we do, have, or be if life eternal was the only reality?

We would build our dream home. We would drive our dream car. We would master every musical instrument possible. We would master every language. We would master every craft and art. We would become master engineers, or architects, or rocket scientists. Would we discover time travel? Would we able to travel at the speed of light or much faster that? Would we discover the ability to transmit things, including ourselves, anywhere else in the universe in an instant? Would we make the Earth into a global paradise of happy, fulfilled people? Would we discover other planets and create or replicate paradise in such places far away from home? With infinity and with our imaginations as the main foundational forces, our commanding and creative power will shift our realities. What could we have, be, or do then? What society will we be able to have? I believe we will be able to feel the reality of the words in this verses:

"And he will wipe out every tear from their eyes, and death will be no more, neither will mourning, nor outcry nor pain be anymore. The former things have passed away" (Revelation 21:4).

"For evil men will be done away with . . . Just a little while longer, and the wicked will be no more. You will look at where they were, and they will not be there. But the meek will possess the earth, and they will find exquisite delight in the abundance of peace . . . The righteous will possess the earth, and they will live forever upon it" (Psalms 37:9-11, 29).

"Happy are the mild tempered, since they will inherit the earth" (Matthew 5:5).

Can we see the big picture?

## Tying It All Together

We have examined laws of physics as they have been discovered and how they relate to our lives as a group and as individuals. We also observed how they are connected to all matter in the universe, including our own essence. We have also learned the implications and ramifications of applying such laws in our lives through the power of our brain frequency transmissions. We have learned of our creative ability and how it is based on either faith or fear. In a powerful conclusion, we notice that our personal awareness and realization of these facts and their practical application can either create death for us or eventually, biological eternity.

This is expressed by Nikola Tesla: It is the discovery of immortality, eternal youth, and beauty that humanity desperately needs. Parallel to Tesla's comment, spiritual leader Paul expressed the same sentiment: "For we know that all creation keeps on groaning together and being in pain together until now" (Romans 8:22). As such is the case, it must be our moral obligation to get there individually and collectively as a race. We must create a global paradise. It is the will of God and the universe. It is our law. I would go as far as to say that there is no choice concerning the following biblical reference from King Solomon: "He has made everything beautiful in its time. He has even put eternity in their heart; yet mankind will never find out the work that the true God has made from start to finish" (Ecclesiastes 3:11).

This concept creates questions. What can we do from this point forward? What is the best course of action that we can take to expedite the process and get what we want? What can we think, say, and do to influence our ultimate success as individuals and as a group? What habits can we form so as to progressively develop a strong character? How can we grow as individuals and live these concepts 24/7 so that we may create faster and better? Consider this next logical step. Since all of this will continue to be developed in the next chapters, please continue reading regardless of whether you have now agreed 100 percent with everything or not. Our inability to deny the least of the physical laws of the universe gives us the moral obligation to do so. At least consider it as a small suggestion; the choice is up to you—life or stagnation? You may find that you will come to the realization that the matrix of knowledge and creation is at your mental fingertips.

# CHAPTER 5

## "We Must Become Like a Tree Planted by Streams of Water"

*Watch your thoughts, for they become your words. Watch your words, for they become your actions. Watch your actions, for they become your habits. Watch your habits, for they create your character, and watch your character, for it becomes your destiny. What we think, we become.*

—Margaret Thatcher

*We become what we think most of the time.*

—Earl Nightingale

"THE FIELD OF Epigenetics is the study of changes in organisms caused by modification of gene expression rather than alteration of the genetic code itself." When we consider epigenetics, we find that outside influences and internal influences from our thoughts, words, actions, and habits—which create our character,—are constantly changing our human genome. Our entire library of genes gets rewritten by our inputs and outputs, as well as by that of others. Our environment has a powerful influence on our entire makeup. It really does strongly influence the way we think, speak, act, or behave, and there is no way around it. Since such is the case, it must be our mission, like a general who commands his troops on to battle, to command and influence powerfully all forms of inputs and outputs from our immediate reality. We must learn to reshape our matrix reality as we see fit.

We must do our best to take control and wage war against anything that may influence our thoughts, words, and actions negatively. We must guard our habits with our lives and with every breath we take and form our character in order to attain our best conceivable outcome. In essence, we must become "like a tree planted by streams of water" (Psalms 1:3). What does that really mean?

A tree that is purposely planted by a source of fresh, clean water is bound deeply to take root and become a fruitful and abundant tree. It becomes tall and strong. Certain animals will find lodging under the foliage of such trees. They become a stronghold for others. On the other side of the coin, if that river were to become contaminated and polluted, the outcome of that tree would be the exact opposite, and it would eventually die.

"Be on the watch of the false teachers who come to you in sheep's covering, but inside they are ravenous wolves. By their fruits, you will recognize them. Never do people gather grapes from thorns or figs from thistles, do they? Likewise,every good tree produces fine fruit, but every rotten tree produces worthless fruit. A good tree cannot bear worthless fruit, nor can a rotten tree produce fine fruit. Every tree not producing fine fruit is cut down and thrown into the fire. Really, then, by their fruits you will recognize those men" (Matthew 7:15-20).

It is noteworthy to examine that Jesus gave some of the most powerful illustrations to prove complex points. He did speak to a general population who did not even know how to write or read and generally uneducated. He also spoke to crowds with children, who, regardless of background, would be able to easily grasp such illustrations. These visual aids imbedded powerful lessons in people's minds, and the points were made effectively. For this reason, instead of creating new illustrations here, we shall refer to the biblical reference for simplicity.

This drives us back to the lessons from Moses' cognitive example: that we must learn and take information from only those who have been known to come from well-watered places, clean waters, and trees whose fruitage of success is evident. Their energetic imprint will easily influence us, and the outcomes may either be disastrous or incredibly beneficial. Let's consider the importance of our taking this council with utmost care:

"Therefore, everyone who hears these sayings of mine and does them will be like a discreet man who built his house on the rock. And the rain poured down and floods came and the winds blew and lashed against that house, but it did not cave in, for it had been founded on the rock. Furthermore, everyone hearing these sayings of mine and not doing them will be like a foolish man who built his house on the sand. And floods came and the winds blew and struck against that house, and it caved in, and its collapse was great" (Matthew 7:24-27).

Here, the point is also made clear that if we decide to not take action and learn these principles of success, then it would be as foolish as building a house on the sand. We need to strongly consider and discern that it truly is our moral obligation to understand the best possible way to get from point A to point B, whatever it is that we wish to experience. To emphasize this extremely important point, it is encouraged to the reader to reread at this time chapter 1 and how it relates to success. We may say, "But I already read it. Why should I read it again?"

*If anyone thinks he knows something, he does not yet know it as he should know it.*

—Paul (1 Corinthians 8:2)

We have all been there before; we love to watch a certain movie or listen to a certain song repeatedly. Many times, we find scenes or ideas that we seem to have previously missed. It is almost like a brand-new movie or song. It happens when we read the same books periodically. It is the same when we repeatedly do things. We do them better, and we become more attuned to the actions. Athletes are known to practice basic moves to master and remaster their selected sport. Swimmers will swim the same laps in the same pool to refine their movements in order to swim faster and more elegantly. Skateboarders will try and retry the same flips and maneuvers so that when the time comes for the competitions, they can show their skills and perform better. Basketball players will practice free throw shots repeatedly to increase their chances of winning when time comes for the real games and improve their scoring. The point is clear: repetition is the quintessence of all success and learning. If any one person desires to excel in their chosen field or career, repetition is what will determine their success. Neglecting this will create negative thoughts, which will lead us to developing a negative character, for harboring the attitude that we "know it all" is the also the quintessence of failure. This will absolutely make us fail at our personal endeavors. Or maybe we will just achieve minimal positive results.

It has been examined scientifically what happens when we develop and establish habits of study and training. Our brains will drastically change through a process called neuroplasticity. It is related to the field of epigenetics, which we will not get in here into great detail. Wikipedia explains that "it is an umbrella term that encompasses both synaptic plasticity and nonsynaptic plasticity. It refers to changes in neural pathways and synapses due to changes in behavior, environment, neural processes, thinking, and emotions, as well as changes resulting from bodily injury." The basic teaching in the field of epigenetics is that every time you have a thought, say words, take action, and develop habits, you will ingrain those thoughts into your brain in the form of neural pathways. These neural pathways will cause you to repeat such behavior, and thus continue to perpetuate the nature and vibrational imprint of those neural pathways.

This could be detrimental or beneficial based on the essence of our personal habits. These neural pathways broadcast electrical signals that are picked up by our hypothalamus. This is a part of our brain about the size of an almond. It takes those electrical signals and turns them into its own chemical, based on the nature of that electric transmission from those specific neural pathways. Like a chemical power plant, it releases those electrical pulses as neurohormones, based on the blueprint of that original electrical signal, into the bloodstream and feeds all cells accordingly. This process then rewrites the genetic code with the blueprint of the chemical feedback from the hypothalamus, for this feedback is the essence of the electrical signals originally sent by those precise neural pathways. The cells replicate and produce openings called receptors, which become more susceptible to the same chemical and thus feed much easier.

This is why people who generally tend to be more negative will become more and more negative, and thus always feel bad. The opposite is true and enforced. Positive people will generate more powerful positive thoughts, secreting positive chemicals, and thus make the body feel good. The person essentially does also feel much better. This is absolutely emphasized when we observe how the placebo and the nocebo effect have an immediate effect on the biology of the person.

"All the days of the afflicted one are bad, but the one with a cheerful heart has a continual feast" (Proverbs 15:15).

It does not take a scientist to reason that a good attitude and positive thinking is beneficial. But then again, maybe it does. We can establish clearly in our mind information and research from thousands of papers that talk about this . Our efforts in doing so will show us clearly the urgency that we have to take with our thoughts. We must take full responsibility for all our mental inputs and outputs. Please let's strongly consider rereading this book, as well as other references that will be provided to help us clearly establish and imprint in our mind these convictions.

The Basics of Input and Output

To take control and become like that tree planted by streams of water, we must realize and become consciously aware of what we are taking in. We must consider being in a deep sense of alertness as we go through our day. It is broken down into these areas. First, what we see: our eyes. Second, what we hear: our ears. Third, what we think: our brains. Fourth, what we say and eat: our words and food. Fifth, our environment and immediate contact with other energetic beings: humans and their personal reality.

What we take in collectively through all forms of input and output will absolutely influence our thoughts, words, actions, and collective behavior. Science proves it. When we watch, say, an R-rated movie that is full of negative behavior, gory images of violence and foul language, it will absolutely create neural pathways that will serve to the detriment of our overall success. That goes for music, TV shows, books, magazines, video games, computer images, etc. We can do whatever we want and decide to do whatsoever we desire, and as such, we must be ready to accept responsibility for what will happen in our lives.

It is extremely important that we discern what the immediate reality of our friends and family is, in order to determine what it is that they are getting in the form of feedback. First, we must realize the truth before we establish judgment on the physical manifestations of people's realities. The truth is, we must know that it is a mirror of their collective vibration, but also a reflection of our own matrix reality. Thus we realize that we see our collective vibration also influencing others' immediate experience, which then mirrors what we are back to us. That is why they are our friends and family. We are all on the same field of vibrational creation, and thus we create together. As such, we must make every effort to improve ourselves and establish new neural pathways that will raise us up and unplug us from that field of negative output if it reflects what we do not desire. Limited contact is encouraged with those who may enforce our negative reality. This is not to encourage or confuse us into thinking that we should look down on those who may have less than desirable circumstances. This is not suggested at all, since we must always be aware and remember that our every experience, including the experience of those around us and their collective reality, is in fact a mirror reflection of *our* collective thoughts and vibrational frequency. We are talking about our neural pathways and our DNA vibration, which includes what we have inherited through our bloodline.

We can illustrate it this way: Imagine that we have a field of produce, a farm where we have planted all sorts of seeds that we inherited from our parents and from the rest of our bloodline. Those seeds have germinated, taken root, and flourished and have produced fruit according to each kind and season. They produce exactly what they are supposed to produce. Thus we realize that we must always reap what we have sown. We eat and share the fruitage of our collective harvest. At this point, we must ask: Do we like what we are taking in? Do we like what we have produced? If we do, then we can keep on planting those seeds and thus reinforce the cycle. But if we do not like what we are taking in, then we must consider stopping sowing seeds of such nature.

As we examine our present reality, do we see and eat what we want? Do we experience happiness, joy, and bliss? Or are we constantly experiencing depression, anger, and misery? Whatever it is, we must be honest with ourselves. People tend to point fingers to external influences as the cause of their misery but readily take credit for their positive accomplishments. If our lives have been defined by mostly the negative aspect, do we fail to realize that it was us who planted those seeds of misery? Do we fail to take full responsibility and stop blaming others for what is happening in our personal lives? We are the creators of our own environments, and according to scientific data, it is an exact match to our thoughts and brain wiring. The good news is that we can change it and expand.

Many people at this point find it hard to realize that they would be the cause of the negative people, circumstances and events that continue to hem them in. Whether things took place in the past or they are presently being experienced, it really is a hard pill to swallow to know it is our fault. I know I did. But we must know that this is a powerful conviction that truly empowers us as individuals and as a society. We must begin to refine our thoughts and actions, and as such, we begin to turn the wheels toward the other side of the spectrum. Maybe the momentum has been at full speed toward the negative side; it will take tremendous amount of energy to bring it back and then make the shift toward the opposite direction, the positive side. It may be like a big hill which we climbed while carrying heavy burdens, but then we easily dropped them once we reach the peak. Everything is downhill then.

If a person is two hundred pounds overweight, then such person is in dire need of drastic and rapid changes in their life. If they wish to consider being successful in getting to the point where they are at a healthy weight, such person must take decisive positive action. A person that is only twenty pounds overweight and wants to achieve the physique of a top athlete would certainly get there faster than the two-hundred-pound person once both decide to get to such point. The person with the extra twenty pounds will not have to go through such extreme changes or take such drastic actions. Both will obviously have the need to work hard to reach their destination. Their reality is that they are at much different starting points.

But is there a system that we can plug into to rapidly change our collective vibration to that of a positive one? As we observe our present circumstances and matrix reality of particles defined by time and space, maybe we realize figuratively that we are, in essence, two hundred pounds overweight and in need of dire help to change. The momentum might be against us. It is unfortunately what our personal observation of the world's scene and what it is currently showing us, for we must realize that it is only a reflection of our own vibrational blueprint. Like the sun that collectively puts out frequencies based on its atomic structure, then in the same manner, the vibration of our own personal atomic structure is collectively putting out one frequency. We must change it because we realize the collective feedback we are getting is predominantly negative. This is true when we examine the final outcome of every human being. Why do we die? Because we create such an outcome for ourselves—this is the law of the universe. Otherwise, our nature would be infinite. And with infinity as a resource, we would always be living in a state of ecstasy and bliss. It is our moral obligation to take 100 percent responsibility for every outcome in our lives. We must start spinning in the opposite direction. How? There is a powerful system that can and will help us get there without exception. Powerful evidence will continue to be provided through the book to show of its powerful credibility. But like always, the choice is up to us to plug in.

This system will help us to continue modifying our thoughts to change the speed of the mass of inexorable agents that are preventing our state from being changed suddenly. It is also prevalent in the lives of incredibly successful individuals.

A System That Builds Us Firmly Toward Higher Realms of Reality

This system has been used throughout millennia by the most powerful world powers that have been known to exist. Like a powerful stream of water, this must be the result for us:

"He will be like a tree planted by streams of water, a tree that produces fruit in its season, the foliage of which does not wither. And everything he does will succeed" (Psalms 1:3).

Consider the benefits and the ultimate outcome of such a system:

(For objectivity, it will not be quoted verbatim but paraphrased to create posterity, since, in reality, these quotes are all based on laws of physics.)

Derived from Deuteronomy 28:

And if you without fail listen by being careful to act in harmony with these laws of physics (commandments) that you are learning about today, then the universe (God) will put you high above all other peoples of the earth. All these benefits will come upon you and overshadow (overtake) you because you keep listening and learning about the laws of the universe in relation to you and applying them positively.

1) Privileged and fortunate will you be in your home, and privileged and fortunate will you be in your discipline or choice of career or business.
2) Privileged, fortunate, and lucky will be your children, and your profits, and the profits of your children's choice of career or business.
3) Privileged and fortunate will you be when you are working on your choice of endeavor.
4) Privileged and fortunate will you be wherever you go and whatever you do.
5) The universe will cause problems and calamities that come up to be instantly resolved by you and before you. They will come from one place but be resolved instantly many different ways.
6) The universe will make a physical law of the universe, like the law of gravity, an agreement between you and the universe to make abundant and fortunate your bank accounts your investment accounts (your personal wealth), and every commitment and project or decision that you set out to do will be fortunate and privileged (blessed).
7) The universe will establish you as a revered people because you continue to apply and study the laws of the physical universe and live positively by them. And all the people surrounding you will know that the universe has appointed you as a well-known and respected person, and people will respect and honor you by giving you proper recognition.
8) The universe will make you overflow with much prosperity and abundance through your choice of discipline, career, or business.
9) The universe will open up to you its banks of infinite (energy) prosperity and make you fortunate and privileged in everything

that you do. It will be so much that you would be able to establish your own banking system based on your own wealth and others will borrow from you.

10) The universe will make you the leader and not the follower, always coming out on top and never on the bottom as long as you keep applying the physical laws of the universe in a positive manner.

It must be emphasized that this has been paraphrased for posterity and objectivity. The benefits described were given in a time and space where people's lives were much more different from our time. The intention of these benefits, as examined throughout the book of Deuteronomy, come from its laws therein as they were given to an ancient people for their own benefit. When examined carefully, it will be noticed that they are truly based on laws of physics, as described in the light of quantum physics and other principles. By law, these commandments would bring tremendous benefits to those who live by them in a positive way. If the reader wishes to learn more about this, please do so by reading Deuteronomy 28:1-14.

Note that it is not suggested that the universe is the same as Jehovah or God by definition. But it is the intent of the author to zero in on a preestablished system that has been unequivocally integrated into the fabric of the universe for the benefit of all those living in that system. The religious dogmatic approach of who is God will not be approached or discussed in this book. Just consider it as different frame of mind based on empirical evidence in the light of science and proven philosophies. With this in mind, let's consider and continue to discuss this significant singular system that will ultimately bring these incredible benefits. We are encouraged strongly that we plug in immediately and consistently for our own personal gain and those of others who may be important to us.

Books, Audio, Meetings, Relationships, and Recognition

A system that consists of reading books, listening to audiobooks, attending group meetings with like-minded people, building relationships with those who also understand these principles, and the giving and receiving recognition perpetuates and pervades in successful companies and businesses throughout the world. It is also prevalent in the lives of incredibly successful individuals. This system has been established and is used today by some of the most profitable and powerful foundations, whether in relationships, business, government, social, or religion. We are strongly urged to investigate on our own the veracity of this system and how it has affected ultrasuccessful people throughout history.

Group Meetings and Relationships: Power of the Master Mind

This systematic approach to education is based on knowing that people are a business' most valued and best asset; therefore, the profitability of our minds is truly our most precious asset. We all have read or heard the saying, "If you think education is expensive, try ignorance." So let's consider riding this "enterprise" perpetually to persevere toward a true education. In essence, you will find that it is the most powerful educational tool to transform people's minds. Having said that, let's also consider the power of collective harmony and group dynamics integrated into this "system" of personal education.

There are countless organizations and businesses that acquire massive amounts of incomes for themselves, and for the people who collectively work together for those companies. Without people and their collective power, little can be accomplished in comparison.

"Look! They are one people with one language, and this is what they have started to do. Now there is nothing that they may have in mind that will be impossible for them" (Genesis 11:6).

Here, the biblical reference describes the unfathomable power of group dynamics and how people collectively working to create one goal has tremendous benefits. So much so, that it is considered impossible to fail. We must win once engaged.

There are tremendous benefits and power when people come together and form what Napoleon Hill learned from Andrew Carnegie, the power of a "master mind." Napoleon Hill expressed that it only took Andrew Carnegie a total of twenty people to create his entire wealth. May we emphasize that it has been estimated that he had almost three hundred billion in assets? Some have estimated more. Consider that he accomplished most of it during a time when there was no Internet, TV, cell phones, and all the devices that make our lives better. Consider the amount of money that such a vast accomplishment entails. If we were to own such wealth in cash, and if we decided to spend $100,000 every day, it would take us about 8,219 years to spend it all!

The collective decision of a group of people guided by one common goal will perpetuate the matrix or ether and help establish that reality much more quickly than one or just a few people getting together.

> *And someone may overpower one alone, but two together can take a stand against him. And a threefold cord cannot quickly be torn apart.*

—Ecclesiastes 4:12

Paul had to remind the first-century Christians to "consider one another so as to incite to love and fine works, not forsaking our meeting together, as some have the custom, but encouraging one another . . ." (Hebrews 10:24-25). We realize how much progress we make when we gather with like-minded people to do things that we have in common, and thus enhancing our every experience. People will flock to arenas to watch their favorite sports, singers, movies, events, or conferences. People with common interests will sit with one another to discuss for hours, days, and weeks continually and get each other's viewpoints and frames of mind. I personally love to listen, read, and learn about concepts based on physics, philosophy, and spirituality. I have been on a personal quest since childhood to put together a harmonious integration by finding common denominators within and in connection of these subjects. I sat with and learned from people with the same ideas, have spent exorbitant amounts of money, time, and energy studying and integrating this information. To what end? That of finding practical knowledge and wisdom, whose paramount value is not only for myself, but also for others. We also develop easier, more loving, and closer bonds with those who support us in a common interest, like force of particles becoming stronger because they are in constant communication with one another (principle 4).

On the other side of the coin, we must remember, though, that "as iron sharpens iron, so one man sharpens his friend" (Proverbs 27:17), so can disharmony of thought cause tremendous damage. We must be aware of those who may not be like-minded as well as those who oppose this knowledge. They could be like rust on metal, just slowly wearing away the profitable efforts of those who desire to come together in support of each other.

We are not referring to the common disagreements of different points of view and healthy debating. This exchange of information within a healthy intention from both parties will ultimately benefit both. We previously discussed the importance of validating and integrating our common knowledge and beliefs. It will support and enforce what we know more strongly, or it will make us revalidate what we know, in the light of new evidence, so we may adjust.

We refer to parasites that feed off the value and production of others. They will eat away our goals, dreams, and hopes to validate their own existence, always envious of what others have, producing and creating illusions of dishonesty and dishonest gain. Just like righteous Job of the biblical reference, most of his so-called friends falsely concluded that because of his misery and sickness, he was being punished for serious wrongdoing.

"John came neither eating nor drinking, but people say, 'He has a demon.' The Son of man did come eating and drinking, but people say, 'Look! A man who is a glutton and is given to drinking wine, a friend of tax collectors and sinners. All the same, wisdom is proved righteous by its works" (Matthew 11:18-19).

Just like the Pharisees created lies and attributed Jesus's work to the ruler of the demons, so will people demonize our efforts to do what is right and our pursuit of our dreams and goals.

In the same manner, this information, has been repressed and hidden from those who would need it most. Kevin Trudeau emphasized that it is because they do not want competition. In the same way a parasite will bring on more parasites, so does those who decide to be judgmental of our endeavors and dreams as if we had nothing but bad motives.

This system of personal education will propel us to incredible heights of success, and it is being suppressed by the current worldly systematic approach to education. Before we discuss the other facets of this system, we will and must build a foundation, or it won't work. There are certain principles that must be established firmly into our mind in order for us to reach certain true success.

What is being denoted here is despite that any cognition and understanding that the reader may have come to until this point, there is 95 percent chance that it won't work in your current set point of collective vibrational output unless something takes place first. Jesus illustrated it like this:

"Nobody sews a patch of unshrunk cloth on an old outer garment. If he does, the new piece pulls away from the old, and the tear becomes worse. Also, no one puts new wine into old wineskins. If he does, the wine will burst the skins, and the wine is lost as well as the skins. But new wine is put into new wineskins" (Mark 2:21-22).

It is what Tesla described about the nature of mass, in this case, preestablished neural pathways: "the same inexorable agents which prevent a mass from changing suddenly its velocity would likewise resist the force of the new knowledge until time gradually modifies human thought."

We cannot build a brand-new structure on top of an existing structure. The old property must be demolished, and then a new structure may be built. In essence, we must burn or demolish that old property. We must replace completely our thinking patterns like emergency surgery, thus cutting away a dead, cancerous organ. How?

Sharpening Your Ax: Do We "Know" or Just "Know About"?

*If an iron tool is dull and one does not sharpen its edge, he will need to exert much effort. But wisdom helps to achieve success.*

—Ecclesiastes 10:10

*My son, if you accept my sayings and treasure up my commandments, by making your ear attentive to wisdom and inclining your heart to discernment; moreover, if you call out for understanding and raise your voice for discernment; if you keep seeking for it as for silver, and you keep searching for it as hidden treasures . . . you will find the knowledge of God.*

—Proverbs 2:1-5

It is known fundamentally, that we must be teachable when it comes to learning and understanding what it takes to succeed. But in reality, very few people truly understand how far this concept can go.

We can illustrate this idea by acknowledging the fact that when scientists study the cosmos, the farther they go and look into outer space or the universe, the more they emphasize and realize how much we don't know. Also, we are beginning to understand that the further we look into the microcosmos and the fabric of the universe, we realize how much we just do not know. It is a strange paradox, but we see that knowledge just begets more knowledge. We learn one link, and it seems that three other concepts are shown to us based on that first connection. Then we look at those three interconnections and we realize that nine more questions come up. Knowledge continues to exponentially expand, seemingly to infinity. And just like learning units of knowledge, we see that within those units there are an infinite amount of smaller parts within one piece of information. For example, when we take the number 1, there is also 0.01, 0.001, 0.0001, 0.00001, and so forth, within that unit. In essence, we continue to learn infinitely in all directions.

To illustrate further, consider watching the episode of *Stan Lee's Superhumans* featuring Shi Yan Ming and his one-inch punch. Shi Yan Ming is a Shaolin monk who has a school for Shaolin martial arts. Raised in the original Shaolin temple, he was trained from childhood. He defected from China and is now teaching somewhere in New York City. In this episode, his strength was tested based on Bruce Lee's famous one-inch punch. It was claimed that Shi's power has reached a much higher level than that of Bruce Lee's. A test group set up a crash dummy and hooked it up to computers to measure the force of impact, just like it is done in crash tests for vehicle safety. The conclusion was mind-blowing. The little Chinese man, at five feet three inches, could generate more force against the dummy with his one-inch punch than a 30 mph car collision. This punch would certainly kill a person in a single blow.

It is understood that there is such a thing as a single punch. But according to the results, it is discernible that he had to harness and receive some very specific and repetitive training to be able to achieve such force in a punch that was an inch away. Interestingly, he has been quoted as saying: "I am not afraid of the ten thousand strikes you know you have practiced once. I am deadly afraid of the one strike you know you have practiced ten thousand times." (Your Wish is Your Command, by Kevin Trudeau) The reasoning is logical and powerful in itself. It is the ability to integrate neural pathways and learning a few simple convictions and mastering them to a level of efficiency that supersedes the simple overview and quick scan of learning or doing something just once.

Kevin Trudeau and infomercial king, explained this extensively in an audio series entitled *Your Wish Is Your Command*. In a rare coincidence, he explains that he himself took Shi Yan Ming into his house as a guest and was personally trained by the monk himself. This is where he learned the quote about practicing a single move ten thousand times. Kevin Trudeau explains that it is the basics that we must master by going over them repeatedly. That each time we listen to an audio material, read a book, or listen to a lecturer, since we are a different person each time we do those things, we will take in the information much differently. We will take in new discoveries, cognition, and realizations that will help us integrate even further the knowledge that we are building. Like spiritual leader Paul emphasized:

"If anyone thinks he knows something, he does not yet know it as he should know it" (1 Corinthians 8:2).

The Kingdom Interlinear Translation of Greek Scriptures states the same verse this way:

"If anyone is thinking to have known anything, not as yet he knew accordingly as it is binding to know."

It is true we must continue to bind our neural pathways based on this knowledge so that we come to the point of not just "knowing about," but truly "knowing," allowing us to live these principles and produce discernible evidence or create physical manifestations in the real, physical world that prove that we "know." It is just like this monk whose punch was measured to be stronger than a 30 mph car crash. He certainly *knows* how to throw a punch.

Solomon truly had the right idea. We must pursue mastering knowledge the same way we would pursue a hidden treasure. We readily realize that if we found a treasure map like Indiana Jones, we would not spare any effort on finding such treasure. Jesus, in connection to the Kingdom gave a very appropriate illustration, saying:

"The Kingdom of the heavens is like a traveling merchant seeking fine pearls. Upon finding one pearl of high value, he went away and promptly sold all the things he had and bought it" (Matthew 13:45).

Do we realize of the intricacies and high value of this training and knowledge based on real-life principles, supported and grounded in the light of quantum physics and empirical evidence? Are we humble enough to realize that we do not know anything and that we need help? Are we too proud to receive counsel emphasized by powerful evidence? Since we do not deny the existence of technology because we readily see it, then how come it is so easy to envy and criticize those who have better success than we do? Isn't their technology as evident and tangible as it is with a cell phone or computer? Since we do not understand how these things work, then why should we take upon ourselves to destroy people's reputations just because we don't understand their success? Would it not be much better to learn and apply the common denominators of success that they themselves have learned to achieve what we want?

This is the exact reason the biblical reference explains why Jesus was executed unjustly. He had technologies at his beck and call and performed observable miraculous actions, and for that, the rulers of that world hated him. Persecuted him. Made fun of him. Ultimately murdered him. It is because they thought they knew it all and had the ultimate call on the ultimate truth and philosophy and could not accept the reality of their ignorance. It was too shameful that they knew nothing, and their attitude showed that it was true. This kind of hateful persecution has happened consistently throughout history to those who pioneered movements of knowledge that we are now seeing having a positive impact on our everyday life. It is as Albert Einstein said: "Great spirits have always encountered violent opposition from mediocre minds."

The Teachability Index: Quoting Kevin Trudeau

This conviction will have profound effect in our lives once we realize how we can turn it into a powerful one-inch punch. If you have not done so already, I would encourage you to get your own copy of this CD series by this renowned author. In this series of audio, he talks about how he himself defected from a private group of elite people called "the Brotherhood." In this private, exclusive club, he was mentored and taught all of these principles of success. This book you are now reading was strongly influenced by his teachings. Thus, to review these common denominators of success, they must be compared with the foundational principles of empirical evidence in the fields of quantum theory, but mainly with the Bible.

In my opinion, other than the biblical reference, this next concept has not been better explained and simplified more efficiently as Kevin Trudeau does in the audio series *Your Wish Is Your Command*. It truly does give me personal validation of the veracity and validity of the Bible and its most basic teachings for personal success. Mr. Trudeau has demonstrated plainly in his life how efficient and powerful these principles are. They are timeless and used by all the most successful people in the world.

## The Power of Being Teachable

*First we are taught that we must be teachable and coachable. The qualification to enter into these secret societies and learn all the levels of apprenticeship, is whether you are teachable and coachable. Not how much we know, how smart we are, but do we "know" how dumb we are, and how much we don't know.*

—Kevin Trudeau

In *Your Wish Is Your Command*, Kevin Trudeau explains that you must have a high teachability index. It is based on two variables: willingness to learn and willingness to accept change. It is explained that our willingness to learn can be measured from a scale from 1 to 10, 1 being a low willingness to learn, and 10 being a high willingness to learn. The same can be applied to the second concept and our willingness to accept change. If we consider that if we have a 10 in our willingness to learn but we have a hard time applying them and accepting change—which would mean 0 willingness to accept change—we would have a 10 × 0 teachability index, or a zero teachability index. But if we can get our variables to be 10 × 10, we would be the "perfect student," with a teachability index of 100.

We can examine that the biblical reference has explained these thoughts in very simple illustrations. Mirroring the importance of having a high willingness to learn, we have discussed the sacrifices that the merchant did to obtain a pearl of high value. He sold everything he had just to acquire what he wanted. Are we willing to sacrifice our time, money, and resources in the same manner in order to learn these concepts? Are we willing to search as for hidden treasure or money? Our time and money truly are some of our most priced and valued possessions. Can we give things up to acquire such knowledge and understanding so that we may learn from those who have the capacity to teach us? Do we readily accept the evident demonstration of what they have and their success as physical manifestations of the reality of their personal knowledge? As Paul emphasized, do we realize that we have not come to "know" and integrate knowledge as we should: "bindingly," irrevocably.

Our willingness to accept change is determined also by the same things but mainly by our decisions to observe and live by such teachings. Kevin Trudeau emphasized that we must be willing to give up things we love doing and thus freeing up time, energy, and money to acquire and learn these basic teachings of success. We are known to be creatures of habits. These habits that we have already established originate from our most prevalent thoughts. We have patterns of behavior where every day, we will occupy our time in things that are either building us up or tearing us apart. "If we want things in our life to change, we must change things in our life." We cannot do same things over week after week, month after month, year after year, and expect we'll achieve something different and better than what we currently have. People spend massive amounts of time, energy, and resources on entertainment and other things we may not be willing to give up easily.

How much time do we spend watching TV? How much time do we spend on the Internet looking up trivial things? How much time do we spend drinking, or eating, or clubbing? None of these things are wrong in themselves, but are they helping us get to where we desire to go? Are we willing to think, speak, act, form habits, and develop the character traits that we must have in order to replicate the success that we desire? As we examine our lives carefully, can we truly give the proper answer? And let's not just ask once but continue to ask ourselves indefinitely as we progress toward our dreams; what is our teachability index? Why?

"Everyone who comes to me and hears my words and does them, I will show you whom he is like: He is like a man who in building a house dug and went down deep and laid a foundation on the rock. Consequently, when a flood came, the river dashed against that house but was not strong enough to shake it, for it was well-built. On the other hand, whoever hears and does nothing is like a man who built a house on the ground without a foundation. The river dashed against it, and immediately it collapsed, and the ruin of that house was great" (Luke 6:47-48).

"For if anyone is a hearer of the word and not a doer, this one is like a man looking at his own face in a mirror. For he looks at himself, and he goes away and immediately forgets what sort of person he is. But the one who peers into the perfect law that belongs to freedom and continues in it has become, not a forgetful hearer, but a doer of the work; and he will be happy in what he does" (James 1:23-25).

Is it not interesting that when we compare these texts to people's success discoveries, in essence, they are telling us the same things? James said that as we learn, essentially we are looking at a mirror. Reasoning through the foundation of scientific principles previously discussed, our vibrational frequencies will continue to pick up lessons and illustrations that will mirror our need based on that moment. It also emphasizes that we will be happy when we are doers and not forgetful hearers because we are observing the perfect law of freedom.

"You were taught to put away the old personality that conforms to your former course of conduct and that is being corrupted according to its deceptive desires. And you should continue to be made new in your dominant mental attitude, and should put on the new personality . . ." (Ephesians 4:22-24).

"And clothe yourselves with the new personality, which through accurate knowledge it is being made new . . . clothe yourselves with the tender affections of compassion, kindness, humility, mildness, and patience" (Colossians 3:10, 12).

In conclusion, really, there is no way around it. We are either progressing or regressing. We either are in a state of perpetual learning or stuck in a rut because we believe we know it all. If we desire to achieve the success promised under these laws of physics as stated in the book of Deuteronomy, we must become coachable and bring our teachability index to 100.

Hopefully it is properly and clearly defined in our mind by now, with all this information and how it relates to our personal attitude, that we must maintain indefinitely and continually a teachable attitude. This will help us to grasp and take root in a firm foundation so that we may become like a tree planted by streams of water—so that everything we do may have success.

It must be a strong emphasis that we must firmly establish knowledge based on the physical laws of the universe, for we must make it a part of our entire human genome. These are the hidden treasures that we must search for as we would a literal chest full of gold, for it really is for our ultimate benefit. In essence, it would mean our literal lives.

The Power of Books and Audio

*The book of the Law should not depart from your mouth, and you must read it in an undertone, day and night, in order to observe carefully all that is written in it; for then your way will be successful and then you will act wisely.*

—Joshua 1:8

*Everyone must be quick to listen, slow to speak . . . But the one who peers into the perfect law that belongs to freedom and continues in it has become, not a forgetful hearer, but doer of the work; and he will be happy in what he does.*

—James 1:19, 25

*He must write for himself in a book a copy of this Law . . .*

—Deuteronomy 17:18

These three biblical references highlight the course of action that should be strongly considered when referred to reading books and when listening to audio material. What books and audio material? A list of these materials has been provided in the reference section of this book, which will help establish a focus. As readers, we should read and listen repeatedly so as to master and imprint completely such concepts into our minds. This will include some audiovisuals that will powerfully influence our minds so we may absorb much easier these lessons based on laws of the universe.

"That is why it is necessary for us to pay more than the usual attention to the things we have heard, so that we never drift away" (Hebrews 2:1).

We must get to the point where we are studying and reexamining books and audio with regularity. As we emphasize such laws and principles, we must observe them carefully so we may become successful in our actions and in every facet of our lives. This is also to strongly imprint the information in our brain, creating a network of neural pathways that enforce these principles and laws of the universe. We should also consider doing what the previous kings of Israel and other rulers did, specifically writing and rewriting concepts, thoughts, words of wisdom, lessons, ideas, notions, texts, and descriptions of what can create success for ourselves. If we desire to create our own "kingdom," should we not do exactly as those who were known to have literal kingdoms?

Is it being suggested that we transcribe word by word books and audio? Certainly it would be of tremendous benefit, but we should not be discouraged if we feel we cannot take on such a task. Let's use our powers of discernment and agreement to know what we can or cannot do. But let's strive to do the best we can. Our dreams and goals, and ultimately our lives and the lives of people we love, demand it.

Let's now consider and observe what is happening to us and all around us, as we take step by step of reading and rereading, writing and rewriting concepts and the written word in books. According to epigenetics, the quantum energy and environment in which we bath on when we read books will permeate our entire genome. The collective vibration of such books will influence our entire being. The collective neural pathways that continue to be established and rewritten will affect and influence positively our entire biology. We learned that our hypothalamus will create chemicals that will nourish our entire biological cellular structure based on the nature of those neurons. We will become what we read and write; in essence, in a very literal way, we will become what we think about.

Consider what we will be able to vibrate and broadcast 24/7 as we progressively study and review these laws and principles of the universe. As we transform our entire energetic structure, we must continue to become more powerfully aware of how the laws of the universe relate to our lives and the lives of others. By law, we must become wiser, understanding, discerning, learned, etc. We will also influence the entire etheric field of energy, which by law of attraction and magnetic force, it will influence back strongly other people's brain reception in our environment, and ultimately affect their DNA once the populace is influenced by the information to think and act more positively. The populace can and will pick up on those transmissions, helping our entire society integrate progressively these understandings.

We must become better for it and because of it, whether individually or collectively. Positive energy must encompass every facet of our lives, internally and externally. Whatever negative energy that exists will be gradually diminished and maybe become nonexistent, canceled, and neutralized or at least drastically reduced. These benefits will become universal law, as they were described in Deuteronomy 28:1-14, mainly the intention behind them.

Maybe we feel doubtful and see all these hopes or prospects as farfetched, but the laws of physics emphasize what Albert Einstein said: "We cannot solve our problems with the same thinking we used when we created them." The laws of physics tells us that it is our thinking that originates and creates the problems we see today. Therefore it takes extraordinary thinking and creativity to transform our reality into a different and much more positive one. If we continue to think like we have always thought, we will continue to get what we have always gotten. If we want things in our lives to change, we must change things in our lives.

It was once outlandish and crazy to think that the Earth was round. It was once insane and ridiculous to think that it was the Earth that was revolving around the sun. It was once outrageous to think that our universe was in actuality bigger than just the Milky Way. It was once blasphemy to think that the universe is billions of years old and not just a few thousand. It was once ridiculous to think that one day we could fly or go to the moon.

Do we dare then to think and realize that the transformation of our world into one of "exquisite delight, and abundance of peace," where wealth and freedom and infinity as a personal resource, is just plain lunacy? Or at least can we consider that we can achieve worldwide peace and prosperity even though we may never figure out how to achieve life eternal? If we doubt, then, like those who persecuted the people who have transformed our world and made it a better place, we will become obsolete and irrelevant. Why? Because the laws of physics prove that we must become what we think about most of the time.

The general population continues to think, speak, and act in manners where they believe that doom and death is the only certain reality. Our imaginations thus have worked in horrendous ways; we have come to learn how to destroy each other and commit suicide more efficiently and creatively. From the use of weapons of mass destruction to the ability to destroy this world many times over, recent times have clearly shown us what we have all been collectively created through our most prevalent thoughts. Governmental sources know this to be the truth and are making plans to eradicate the collective energetic pattern that death is preferable to life. They know that if they allow for such a pattern to continue, then we can only hope for the destruction of the vast majority of the human race.

Only those who align their lives to universal policy can hope to survive such cataclysmic event.

We are at the threshold of a decision. Will we use our abilities and capabilities, our power of imagination to improve or destroy? Faith or fear? Life or death? This thought validates strongly what Einstein said about the power of our imagination, for it is more important than knowledge.

> *Logic will take you from point A to point B. Imagination will take you everywhere.*

—Albert Einstein

> *A new scientific truth does not triumph by convincing its opponents and making them see the light, but rather because its opponents eventually die, and a new generation grows up that is familiar with it.*

—Max Planck

Certainly it is not being suggested here that life eternal is an established scientific truth, but merely a hypothesis. But even the scientific concept of quantum tunneling and the ramifications of the field of energy that permeates all time and space suggest of its infinite probability. The hypothesis must be tested extensively. We have established background research based on empirical evidence. We have constructed a hypothesis, and now we must experiment individually and collectively. When time comes, we must analyze the data and draw conclusions. But is there scientific data that may suggest of our potentiality, like what Tesla and Jesus said in reference to biological eternity, eternal youth, and beauty? This will be discussed in a later chapter.

The Power of Recognition

> *Rejoice with those who rejoice; weep with those who weep.*

—Romans 12:15

"Love is not jealous. . . . [It] believes all things, hopes all things." (1 Corinthians 1:4,7) In simple terms, we must strongly consider and be self-aware of how we feel about other people's successes or failures. Recognition is a form of love and ties in the entire systematic approach of this learning system. Like a step-by-step formula for success, this foundation has to, by law, eventually create and explode our abilities to improve our every facet of life. Being happy with sincerity for others' success, without judgment or criticism, is extremely important to our personal success.

Let's consider the science. A person's success is no more than that person's ability to finally get what they have been thinking about most of the time. A person's desire for that outcome through his faith won the battle against his personal doubts and disbeliefs. Our fears are constantly bombarding us with negative thoughts. For example, we may hear in our minds thoughts such as the following: I can't do it, it won't work. What is the point? What if I fail? What will other people think or say? I don't have the education, I don't have the expertise, I don't have experience. I am too ugly, too short, too incompetent, not smart enough, not intelligent enough. There is too much competition. They will think I am joke. Other people are better than me.

But we can also have positive thoughts such as the following: Of course I can do it. This is certainly a possibility. Others have done so, why would I not be able to do it as well? I must do it, I will do it. I am smart enough, intelligent enough. I have enough education. Who cares about the competition? I am certainly as good. I have confidence, I have patience, I have self-control, I have faith. I am strong, I am resilient, I am hopeful. My dreams are real, and I can do whatever I want. I am thankful, grateful, and appreciative. Everything always works out for me, I always land on my feet. I love challenges, I love opportunities. Failure is not an option; success is the only option. I am positive. I love my life, and I love others. I know what am doing is right. I know what I have to offer others will benefit them. I will make them eat their words. I will come out on top.

People's success is a result of their arsenal of neural pathways that support their dreams. Accomplishing nothing is also a result of their neural pathways which support fears. Henry Ford is quoted as saying, "If you think you can or can't, you are right." It is your thinking that makes it so. Do we see other people's success for what it is: a powerful triumph over the forces of evil? People love watching movies or reading books where the forces of good always seem to be suppressed by the forces of evil, but in the end, good always comes out on top. The *Star Wars* series is a strong example of the excitement and personal gratification it brings us to see such things occur.

A strange paradox does occur in real life, though. It seems that the general attitude of the populace is to be critical and judgmental of other people's success. We must do an honest examination of our feelings in connection to other people's success. Do we feel happy for them? Do we feel excited for them? Do we feel love for them? Do we realize we are better for it because it helps us to believe that our goals and dreams can become reality? Do we realize that it was a fight they endured, but all along, who were we rooting for to win? If we have jealousy, does that mean we subconsciously desire for others to fail? Does it make us feel bad because we believe they are better than we are?

Whatever prevalent frequency gets activated will be sent to them, but ultimately, it only comes back to us to hunt us down. We must reap what we sow. But on the other hand, if we realize that we have appreciation and positive strong recognition for other's successes, then our most prevalent positive thoughts of happiness for them will also be picked up by these people but also ultimately create and enforce our success. We are happy and genuinely excited for their success; therefore others will become genuinely happy and excited for our success. Our success, thus, must be created in our present reality.

Another factor is that with results being tangible, we can now examine these examples of success to see how they created what they wanted in their life. We can empirically and objectively observe how they thought, how they spoke, how they acted, and how they responded to adversity. We can also examine what habits they developed and what character traits they possess. Acknowledging their success for what it is—empirical evidence, forms of physical manifestations that prove their validity—will help us to replicate their proven hypothesis and experiment successfully. Thus we must get the same desired results.

Proper positive recognition will enforce the complex processes to achieve what we want in life and turn them, by law, into simple, easy-to-replicate processes in the form of strong neural connections. This process hardwired into our being will rewrite our genetic code, simply programming it for success now and the future. Like baby steps, we will struggle from rolling, to crawling, to easy, natural walking. Our success will become a reality by law, and whatever we set out to do must happen positively without a doubt.

Recognition energetically will permeate the duality of particles, and its vibration must continue to spill over into our matrix of reality and permeate all time and space. It will and must make us better as whole. The mass must gradually change and be modified by the prevalent thoughts of those who acquire and develop a complex neural connection of positive thoughts. These will vibrate 24/7 and will send frequencies back and forth, reinforcing what is being presented to the universe. In this case, a collective vibrational frequency, a prevalent attitude of happiness and expectation of other people's success. A world of love and happy recognition must become the reality.

It must become our moral obligation to develop our powers of perception and train ourselves to acknowledge positively other people's quantifiable successes.

Putting It All Together

This is the most effective foundational system that has been put together that is proven to create individual and group success. At least, this is the case so far. Whether we decide to create successful, supporting, loving relationships; whether we want to build a life of freedom and wealth; whether we want to just feel happy, content, or excited for our lives; this educational system will construct a powerful foundation to create what we desire. But it is up to us to engage and have our teachability index kick in like military training. It is a battle of the mind. We must exercise to win against the negative feedback that we are constantly being projected, thus be at cause and in power over the influences we create around us. So whether it comes from our own preestablished DNA patterns and thinking, or from our immediate environment, or from the frequencies we pick up from others in the field, we now know what we can do to win.

The Bible, ahead of its time, aptly warned us saying; to be aware "of the system of things of this world, according to the ruler of the authority of the air, the spirit that is now at work in the sons of disobedience" (Ephesians 2:2). We must be self -aware of our thoughts and emotions, for it is the ether, with all the collective patterns of thoughts, that will influence us the most. It will continue to download into our mind the most prevalent thoughts that are in harmony with our mental habits. This is significant for when we fail to comply to the laws of physics and act in harmony with these principles that govern us, our lives must become chaotic.

Scientists are able to precisely calculate the travel path of rockets in space because they have been able to clearly define these laws and obey them. The slightest error in calculations have proven disastrous. In a similar manner, we could go off and continue to do our own thing, just act according to what we feel is right, and thus continue to create what we have always created. If we love what we have, then let's continue creating that. The observation and decision is up to us.

It is strongly suggested that like a tree purposely planted by a river of clean, abundant water, so we must immerse ourselves and root into all five aspects of this system. Reading books, listening to audio materials, and watching audiovisuals on a regular basis, will help us develop strong neural connections. Attending group meetings, whether for learning or just to have loving, fun fellowship with like-minded people, will enhance exponentially our learning experience and how fast we achieve that which we desire. And finally, let's change our mind so as to train our powers of perception to lovingly recognize, with genuine interest and excitement, the celebration of people's triumph over the forces of evil, as readily as we watch the movies with such stories. "In brotherly love have tender affection for one another. In showing honor to one another, take the lead" (Romans 12:10).

Let's celebrate and dedicate positive particle flow by applauding and cheering for those who have acquired success. Then, and only then, we will have no choice but to be successful.

# CHAPTER 6

## The Power of Giving: Exercising Our Mental Faculties with the Power of Faith

*There is more happiness in giving, than there is in receiving. . . . Practice giving, and people will give to you. They will pour into your laps a fine measure, pressed down, and shaken together, and overflowing. For with the measure that you are measuring out, they will measure out to you in return.*

—Acts 20:35, Luke 6:38

I WOULD SAY THAT this is probably the most important chapter in the entire book, and rereading and studying and taking notes is paramount. We have expanded throughout the previous chapters *why* we are able to accomplish anything we desire. We are brilliantly designed to accomplish in reality anything we could conceive in our imagination. Our abilities exponentially grow and become more firmly established as we learn to follow specific instructions and work with principles that are founded on the laws of the universe. The scientific field of physics has truly made tremendous breakthroughs in helping us clearly define these laws and how they relate to our personal lives. As previously mentioned, it continues to help us see that truly, we are "designed for accomplishment, engineered for success," as Zig Ziglar said.

With our faith being properly exercised and nourished, we can now expound upon the laws of physics and integrate them into specific patterns of activity. For what? Until now, we have talked about why we can be successful, clarifying that it is by understanding basic principles and laws of life that will determine our success. It is understanding that our success is based on our patterns of behavior and being alert to what outcomes we may have received due to our transmission. But what we have not gone over is the specific foundational action plans that we could decide to take to get from point A to point B.

It is now with this instruction that, after we have developed the habits of studying and personal development, we will now be able to create powerful universal commands based on integrated actions for the creation of our best possible outcome of our positive dreams and goals.

### Self-Awareness and the Present Moment: The Power of Contentment and Discontentment

People define success and wealth in many different ways. What we want to establish here is that true success is our personal desire for our entire happiness pie to be filled. People who may have great material or financial wealth may struggle in keeping their relationships under the same agenda. People who may have built strong, happy relationships with their families may be in constant struggle and stress as they live paycheck to paycheck. On the other hand, people who may have a great career and find fulfillment in what they do may be experiencing health problems that eat away their happiness pie. The challenge we then face is that many times, our unhappiness in one area spills over onto other areas where we may have easily built success. We hear constantly that marital problems and arguments come from financial situations that may have been persevering on their peace of mind. Or it could be that a career could be very time consuming and leaves too little time spend with their loved ones. Being kept away from loved ones for prolonged periods of times can be very distressing.

It is a balancing act of energy. Unfortunately we may believe that we can only have one or the other. Maybe we believe that we can only focus on one thing at a time. Maybe we can only shift our focus on two, perhaps money and family while sacrificing career fulfillment or good health. Someone may focus on their health and career, but sacrifice time with family. It is almost like discontentment is constantly defining our lives with everything we do.

Discontentment is not being suggested here as a bad thing. This is because our thoughts ultimately decide how we decide to look at such specific feelings. The same can be said about the connotations of the word *contentment*. For example, a person who is content could experience both negative and positive consequences. We may have seen people who may be morbidly obese and still feel happy with who they are and who they may become. A big and famous comedian who calls himself "Fluffy" said that he would rather just be happy eating whatever he desired, than worry about working out and exercise in misery. "I rather die full and content than sore and hungry" was his joke. The prevalence of his lax attitude about his health may have consequences. It is his decision. It could also be that a person loves their job and makes just enough to sustain their life. But their lack of ambition may eventually affect their peace of mind, for outside influences such as inflation and the rising cost of living may catch them at a disadvantage. The natural laws of the universe will foment people to move from their comfort zones, which they may not be ready to accept or adapt to.

But on the other hand, if we are too content we may never be motivated to resolve a situation that may be adversely affecting our lives. A person who cannot afford the things they want, but keep charging on credit cards, could eventually experience financial ruin and wreak havoc on people who are close to them. Unnecessary burdens may be multiplying on top of each other. A person who just eats fast food will eventually pay the price with their health and well-being in the long run. A measure of discontentment would ultimately do them some good.

On the other side of the coin of discontentment, people may readily achieve success. It is obvious that discontentment can actually make somebody get up from where they are and try to improve the situation that is bothering them. A financially poor person may become so fed up with their living situation that they become a powerful rags-to-riches story. The battered spouse who is constantly abused either physically or verbally might become so fed up with the situation, they will eventually leave or find better circumstances. Maybe they'll take control and improve their present challenges. The obese person who finds shame in their condition may come to grips and start an exercise routine or health program that completely turns them around, and thus shape themselves into a fit and healthy being. The discontentment of a family head with his career and how it takes so much time away from loved ones may finally make him decide to jump into a better opportunity or simplify their lives to basic essentials for the sake of family closeness.

On the other hand of discontentment: we always hear of the multimillionaires who are constantly trying to get their fix by making more money. The spouse who may have a perfectly fine relationship with their partner but can't seem to get enough attention from others of the opposite sex. The person who is constantly looking to feed their alcohol or drug addiction is maybe consistently trying to mask their discontentment. It will always be there once they've had their fix. A healthy amount of contentment will certainly help them shift focus. Self-awareness is the key, and knowing ourselves is paramount.

Maybe the reader is right now experiencing a combination of contentment and discontentment on certain areas of life. Specifically, we might be learning this information because we have been wondering what could be the best way to achieve and improve such aspects. Maybe you have been praying for an answer. Maybe you are on a mission to learn what it takes to change your personal situation. Obviously this is not far from the truth when it comes to everyone. We all want something, and we want it now, or at least as soon as humanly possible.

Now going off on a tangent from the main subject, let's consider the shift of contentment and discontentment if we had biological eternity. The person experiencing discontentment in one area of life will have all the time in the world to change it. For example, a family head experiencing too much time away from family because of work will never feel too bad about it because they know they can change it anytime they want. The family who may be experiencing such absence from that person will know that they have an eternity to be together. The billionaire will not feel the need to make more money just for the sake of having more money. The spouse will not have to worry about personal attention from their spouse because they know they have all the time in the world to be together. A person can have any career they want at any time they desire, for they may change their mind regardless of profits or time spent. With all the time in the world, youth and beauty will be a given. People will have all the time and resources they could ever need to create their personal ideal situation. This continues to prove that Tesla's call for eternity and youth is, in essence, the real foundation of life. These laws of physics, considering how they are interconnected to the fantastic benefits of biological immortality, are strong observations of how life is supposed to be. Why is it not, then? We'll continue to discuss this in a later chapter.

## Contentment and the Power of Feeling Good

The title of this chapter refers to the key to acquiring everything we desire. We must understand that the laws of physics demand that we give first so we may receive that which we want most. "Where there is no wood, the fire goes out" (Proverbs 26:20). We must but only give the frequency of what we want. Everything in the universe is energy. Therefore we are to offer the vibration or match the frequency of what we want. It is all based on the laws of physics that govern the matrix of particles of energy.

Let's carefully examine these thoughts. We generally desire things because we want more contentment, and we want to feel good. These feelings of desire are stronger the more we experience what we do not like. Our low income makes us feel bad, therefore we want a lot more money. Our crappy car that breaks down all the time makes us feel bad, therefore we desire a nicer, newer vehicle. People who makes us feel bad makes us desire people who will make us feel good. We want heat and food because we feel cold and hungry. In essence, we want energy because we lack energy.

So if we think about what we want, in reality we must match and give consistently the frequency that we desire to experience. First, we realize that we must feel content and feel good in this instant and offer that frequency in order to continue to receive it. Since we want things to feel content and feel good, then we must first be content and feel good now. Contentment and feeling good about our present circumstances sets the foundation for us to receive that which we are asking. But how can we possibly send out a frequency of what we want when our set point might be mostly negative?

This certainly is a good question and a strange paradox. We have established that we want things because we are experiencing what we do not want. Also we want things because we have experienced them and we want more of them. Because we have felt good, we want more of that which made us feel good. Therefore when we experience lack of that which makes us feel good, it makes us feel bad. But how can we match the frequency of what we want when it is in a much higher vibrational field? Since we are currently vibrating lower, which means we lack that which makes us feel better than we feel now? And how can we match the vibration of what we want when our collective vibration is set to matching that which we do not want? This is true because when we are broadcasting negative thoughts and feelings, it is because we are looking at something we do not desire; with this, more of those things will continue to come into our experience and match our frequency. We start to feel worse, and our negative thinking and feelings are being enforced because of its attractive magnetic pull.

First, we must know that there is no right or wrong, and that both have advantages and disadvantages. But preferably, we desire for our current vibration to be that of contentment and happiness regardless of circumstances. Newton's third law of motion, as previously described, states "that for every action, there is an equal and opposite reaction." This will help us understand why this the case. Along with Newton's law, which is enforced by the law of magnetic attraction, we must know and realize that we always have a choice. Another way of saying that we always have a choice is this: We must know and realize that our brain has the ability to create and transmit any frequency we desire based on our command.

Once we decide and transmit a positive frequency based on what we want, we must move on progressively to the positive direction of feeling good. Let's say we raise ourselves from feeling contentment to feeling joy; that will continue to be matched by its reaction. People will react to our joy, and therefore make us more joyful. It will continue to propel us upward to our most positive emotions. But we have found that the opposite is true: someone may say negatively and sarcastically, "What are you so happy about? Wipe that stupid smile off your face," or "Get off that cloud and come back to reality." Certainly if we allow it, such comments will bring us down. This law will consistently force us to make a decision. We will either choose to focus on the positive or the negative. The more prevalent our set point of vibration is, then the more prevalent the pull will be in regard to our decision to be able to sustain that feeling.

If we feel angry, then by the law of attraction, we will continue to create situations and circumstances that will fuel that feeling. We may decide to calm down and move ourselves away from the trigger that is causing our anger to flare and go for a walk. Or we may decide to fuel the fire by holding on to what made us angry. Self-awareness dictates that we know what fire we are presently fueling. Our energy could be depressed, anxious, or sad, or it could be content, happy, optimistic, or passionate. Whatever it is, our present vibrational frequency will continue to permeate our reality, and the universe will mirror back that which we are giving. The caveat is that we will always receive an opposing frequency to help us appreciate contrast. It is paramount that we realize and have self-awareness of the opposing reactions in our present reality so we can focus on the positive and change our vibrational output.

Since it is our desire to always feel as good as we can, then when we are feeling bad, our subconscious mind and body's defense mechanisms will always give us solutions to improve the situation. Maybe we need to relieve stress through exercise, playing a game, watching a funny movie, etc. But during the times when we feel really good, those who feel bad will send us negative feedback. Know that this is good in reality because it helps us to appreciate contrast. We will know that since we do not want to feel again like those who are feeling bad; thus we can make the conscious decision to continue enforcing the current vibrational point defined by our present good feeling.

People will continue to feel good by enforcing and focusing consistently on that good feeling. So whether we decide to engage conscious positive thoughts, words, and actions to enforce our current good feeling, it is still our conscious decision to do so. Actions such as working out, running, walking, laughing, or smiling on a regular basis will also help us to powerfully perpetuate our decision to feel good. It is our personal decision to create the shift from negative to positive, or vice versa. We must emphasize the point that we are either growing or dying. Progressing or regressing. We must consciously give the frequency for that which we desire.

## ALWAYS BE REJOICING, GIVE THANKS FOR EVERYTHING

*Always be rejoicing. Pray constantly. Give thanks for everything. . . . Do not put out the fire of the spirit.*

—1 Thessalonians 5:16-19

JULIAN VALDERRAMA

The biblical reference indicates aptly that our focus needs to be in our happiness. We must take steps to positively expand the current positive points that are being presented to us.

We do not want to be in morbid fear of our negative thoughts and feelings; instead we should be empowered by them by giving thanks for them. We should appreciate and feel thankful for these low feelings, for in reality what they do is give us contrast. They will launch us into giving us the proper pattern of action so we may feel good more often more consistently. It helps us to develop neural pathways that will help us form habits that will make it easier to move through our negative emotions toward more positive ones.

As we develop the conscious awareness of our negative thoughts, words, and emotions, we can exercise the same awareness to shift our focus to that which we want. As time passes us by, we will have developed a multitude of positive habits in knowing that every time we are confronted with a negative vibration, we will take positive action and develop the habit to think about that which is of a positive nature. This will continue to shift our set point of vibration to a progressively higher frequency; thus our positive pattern will continue to be enforced.

But why is feeling as good as we can so important in relation to what we want? And why are feelings of contentment and discontentment powerful tools to help us create? Also, how can we become more self-aware of these feelings?

## We Must Be at Cause and in Control

Simply, if we accept the fact that our present reality are indicators of our current set collective broadcast of frequency, as specified by the laws of physics, then we must know we are at cause of our current situation, whether positive or negative. We created and generated vibrations in the past and continue to do so based on our thoughts, words and actions. Our present reality is but a reflection of that which we have broadcasted with our brain and our DNA. Our brain transmits powerfully based on our most prevalent thoughts, words and actions. Our DNA was preprogrammed based on the collective vibration of our parents passed down the bloodline. Our DNA is also continually being reprogrammed, as we have continued to experience and observe what our DNA has been offering 24/7 based on our DNA set point of vibration. This means that most likely, up to this point, we have only been reacting to our unconscious creations. It is like a stranded boat just being tossed around by the waves and the winds of the sea, wherever they decide to take us.

Our DNA vibration is also enforced and reprogrammed based on our habits of thinking, words, and actions. Our habits and our character traits are truly our destiny, as the former prime minister of England aptly put it. The point of destiny in this sense is that it is the set point of prevalent energy programmed into our DNA based on our bloodline. It is not implied that some deity has determined every facet and experience of our life or that there are strange forces at work, making our life predestined regardless of our choice and personal power. What we desire to really be aware of is that our DNA vibrates 24/7 based on the positive and negative programming of our bloodline. The great news is that we can consistently make it better and upgrade it as we desire to experience what we do want and not what we do not want.

As we persistently become more aware of our patterns of behavior with our present lives, then we will continue to positively make choices that will eventually change our DNA programming and our habits of thinking. To do the opposite is to continue practicing mysticism and superstition. People who are superstitious or mystics generally look to outside things, people, and influences as the cause for their misery and negative feelings. They always will blame everyone else except for *themselves*, the true cause of what is happening in their lives. We hear of sayings like "If you point a finger at someone, there are three fingers pointing right back at you." As the bible reference aptly puts it:

"Stop judging that you may not be judged; for with the judgment you are judging, you will be judged, and with the measure that you are measuring out, they will measure out to you. Why, then, do you look at the straw in your brother's eye but do not notice the rafter in your own eye? Or how can you say to your brother, 'Allow me to remove the straw from your eye,' when look! a rafter is in your own eye? Hypocrite! First remove the rafter from your own eye, and then you will see clearly how to remove the straw from your brother's eye" (Matthew 7:1-5).

It is noted that this refers to our negative thoughts toward those who are closer to us. But in reality, the emphasis here is on "stop judging." Stop blaming outside influences, stop pointing the finger at other things, and stop judging things because the reality is that our vibration is only coming back to us. It is all mirror images of our thoughts and everything that these broadcasted thoughts generate and create. It is all in our experience because we are the cause of those things that are either negatively or positively affecting our lives. The irony is when we create good things that make us feel good, we take full credit, but we will never take full credit for our own shortcomings and the negative feedback we receive from our present awareness.

The prevalence and constant exercise of this single concept of thinking will always make us feel empowered. Thus when we realize that negative events in our life are there because of the magnetic pull of our collective broadcast, then it will also be empowering to confess and accept full responsibility for everything that is happening in our lives. We must strongly consider that we are at fault and we are the only ones to blame, period.

"Therefore you are inexcusable, O man, whoever you are, if you judge; for when you judge another, you condemn yourself, because you who judge practice the same things" (Romans 2:1).

"When under trial, let no one say: 'I am being tried by God.' For with evil things God cannot be tried, nor does he himself try anyone. But each one is tried by being drawn out and enticed by his own desire" (James 1:14).

We reap what we sow, positive or negative. This is when, like properly trained Navy SEALs, this training must kick in on the battlefield. We must take these concepts and powers of discernment and take control. We must stop blaming outside influences for what is happening in our lives and take full responsibility for them. It will shift us to saying "Forget everything, I am in control and let me create and focus on exactly what I do want." This is the real power of feeling good now. It is knowing that regardless of our circumstances, we can always make them better. So we may bring this question back: Why is it so important to feel good? Because when we feel bad, it is only because we created it and we are focused on our negative thoughts. We are focused simply on what we do not want. We are in fear of what we don't want; essentially we are exercising faith in creating what we don't want.

Considering that our habits may just be a product of DNA inheritance and reinforcement from our thoughts will help us become fully aware of who we really are. It will also help us to know where we stand in connection to where we want to go. Are we figuratively two hundred pounds overweight? Are we ahead of the game, or are we losing? We must know plain and simple. Thus, do we feel good, or do we feel bad most of the time?

With this in mind, we must accept the truth of negative events. They exist because they will help us focus. They happen because they warn us of the frequency we are giving off, for we must turn to self-awareness and realize that we must change what we are thinking. Negative events happen because, in essence, they launch us out of, or into, either discontentment or contentment. It makes us better and will make us grow if we decide to take hold of them and have them serve us. Just like a servant ready to do our bidding, do we command it to become that which we want?

Negative outcomes will make us feel better if we choose it to be. It is not the seemingly negative consequences that are good but the feeling that they give us. Why? Because then we can focus those feelings and thoughts in the opposite direction and then decide what we truly want to experience. Then really, there is no reason to ever feel bad just for the sake of feeling bad. It is an opportunity to broadcast a frequency powerfully and to create more precisely and positively. No need to fret or worry. Everything is always fine. When we realize this, it then makes sense why we can give thanks for everything. We can be thankful for those negative events because they can help us get exactly what we want and need. Such negative feelings will propel us to take action; we could become so angry about a situation that it will move us to make massive action to shift into a different direction. Whether our set feelings are sadness, depression, despair, boredom, hatred, rage, or frustration, among others, we will know that we want to feel enthusiasm, eagerness, joy, and other forms of happiness.

Another reason negative events may occur in our life is because we are actually broadcasting the most powerful and positive frequency we can possibly offer. We are giving out exactly what we want for the purpose of receiving that which we want. We may be in complete alignment and focusing precisely on our hearts' desires, but because of this strange paradox, weird phenomena, or confusing oxymoron, we must experience what we don't want. *Why?* We will discuss this in a later chapter.

## BEING AT CAUSE OVER NEGATIVE FEELINGS OR EVENTS

Now that we have established the importance of self-awareness in connection to our conscious decisions, feeling good becomes paramount. Our good feelings then become a perfect foundation to create what we want, but not the only way to be able to create and obtain what we desire. Feeling as good as we possibly can is absolutely the optimal way of doing things and thus create the best results. But also, some effort in broadcasting what we want regardless of how we feel will absolutely create some results. Fifty percent of something is better than 100 percent of nothing. Consider the following scriptural illustrations:

"Then he went on to tell them an illustration about the need for them to always pray and not give up, saying: 'In a certain city there was a judge who had no fear of God and no respect for man. There was also a widow in that city who kept going to him and saying, 'See that I get justice from my legal opponent.' Well, for a while he was unwilling, but afterward he said to himself, 'Although I do not fear God or respect any man, because this widow keeps making me trouble, I will see that she gets justice so that she will not keep wearing me out with her demand.' Then the Lord said: "Hear what the judge, although unrighteous, said! Certainly, then, will not God cause justice to be done for his chosen ones who cry out to him day and night, while he is patient toward them?" (Luke 18:1-7).

Also this other account has a similar connotation:

"While she prayed for a long time before Jehovah, Eli was watching her mouth. Hannah was speaking in her heart, only her lips were trembling, but her voice was not heard. So Eli thought she was drunk. Eli said to her: "How long will you stay drunk? Stop drinking your wine." At this Hannah answered: "No, my lord! I am a woman under great stress; I have not drunk wine or anything alcoholic, but I am pouring out my soul before Jehovah. Do not take your servant for a worthless woman, for I have been speaking until now out of my great anguish and distress."

Then Eli answered: "Go in peace, and may the God of Israel grant your petition that you have asked of him." To this she said: "Let your servant find favor in your eyes." And the woman went on her way and ate, and her face was no longer downcast" (1 Samuel 1:12-18).

Although it was emphasized that feeling good now, regardless of the situation we may currently experience, is the most ideal place to broadcast a decision or desire, we should not conclude that we should wait to feel really good to decide to transmit such a decision or desire.

In the first illustration spoken by the teacher, it was emphasized that we can persistently ask or broadcast a transmission, especially if we have negative feelings. The agony and discontentment of the widow asking the judge for justice must have been of epic proportions. We can discern this to be true since her strong discontentment and distressing situation was moving her powerfully to persist on her request. Her ability to persist was so precise, that even though the judge was aloof and cold to her misery, he still considered yielding to her just because "she was wearing me out with her demand." Obviously the widow was not in a place of feeling good, but her intense negative emotion obliterated all possible resistance that may have prevented her from getting what she desired. Her focus was precisely on what she wanted because she was experiencing intensely what she did not want. Thus the lesson is that we must persist boldly in our request and broadcast frequencies based on our desires without giving up regardless of how we feel. Also, we must broadcast and focus on what we want, especially when we are feeling the worst.

In the second illustration, we see a woman who is also in great distress and sorrow. Her life was made difficult by an adversary, her husband's second wife. We can see that in her time, polygamy was widely accepted and practiced. In a time where a family's economic status was supported by the increasing of numbers within the family arrangement, this woman was experiencing barrenness. Women were expected to give birth to many children and thus preserve the family name and land. The high numbers in a family also helped to cultivate the land they possessed. Hannah had not been able to give birth and was considered barren, or unable to produce progeny for her husband. Thus the second wife comes into the scene and is able to give him several children. Hannah's situation was made more distressing because the rival wife kept taunting her and belittling Hannah for not having children.

JULIAN VALDERRAMA

Her situation is now irrelevant to us, but we do want to give light to Hannah's specific course of action in regard to her transmission of brain frequency: her desire. The account tells us that she was in so much emotional pain, that while she was making a request to God, she seemed to others as drunk. Key words in the verse emphasizes that her transmission was of long duration. Her trembling lips and visibly anxious emotional state describes to us that she had powerful emotional energy being transmitted in connection with her desire. It was obvious she was not happy or anywhere near feeling remotely good, but that did not prevent her from focusing on what she truly wanted. She shifted her emotions toward exactly what she wanted.

Two more points we can take to heart is the description of the nature of her prayer or transmission of frequency. It was mentioned to us that she poured her soul, and that afterward, she was no longer concerned with her affliction. It would be good to ask ourselves whether our desire may have such intensity in our hearts that we feel like we could give anything for it. This collective vibration based on her personal request was also left alone, as if once asked and ordered, she knew she would receive what she wanted. Have we realized that we can possibly leave our desires into the hands of someone or something much more capable of accomplishing than that of ourselves? This question will continue to be developed in a later chapter.

One thing is for sure though: we must not be discouraged if we feel we have a long trip ahead of us;. What we mean by this is maybe we realize our collective vibration mirrors to us that we are really behind and in need of tremendous work. Maybe we notice that we feel bad most of the time, with just slight superficial fixes that only mask pain temporarily. Maybe we observe that our surroundings are less than desirable and we consistently find ourselves wishing for somebody to come to the rescue. But what we must know for sure, regardless of our present circumstances, is that success has been many times been defined as "what we learn on the road to what we want and not the destination itself." It is not what we have, but the person we must become that will truly give us the best feelings of happiness. Therefore, we should never delay our decision to define our dreams and goals and to begin to transmit powerfully that which we desire most.

But what action can we best take to get what we want? Are there specific steps we can take to make things happen?

## THE POWER OF PERSEVERANCE AND ASKING FOR WHAT WE WANT

*Nothing in the world can take the place of persistence. Talent will not do it; nothing is more common in unsuccessful men than talent. Genius will not; unrewarded genius is almost a proverb. Education will not; the world is full of educated failures. Persistence and determination alone are omnipotent.*

—Calvin Coolidge

*Pray constantly.*

—1 Thessalonians 5:17

Whether we believe in prayer or not, it is irrelevant. As we have examined the laws of physics in relation to the power of our mind, we have deduced that, in essence, prayer is nothing more than putting out a conscious transmission being broadcasted from our brains. When people pray to their deities or gods, in reality the transmission of frequency is transmitted, and therefore the laws of physics kick in to bring that vibration back. The difference is knowing that we can create whatever frequency we want, and being aware that there may be resistance holding us back and preventing us from receiving what we want. What will eliminate or reduce resistance? The previous subheadings about contentment, discontentment, feeling good, and self-awareness will greatly reduce our resistance and diminish the chances of us not receiving what we want. Although these are all great foundational bases for receiving what we want, there is one thing that is powerful enough to give us what we want regardless of our happiness, self-awareness and contentment.

The biblical reference has highlighted through some simple illustrations the power of persistence and perseverance. The combination of effort with the power of our conscious transmission will create powerful results in our lives. Our power and ability to "give" on a consistent basis will determine the speed and the efficacy of our being able to receive that which we are asking. It is of utmost importance that persistence becomes prevalent and ingrained into our makeup through our neural pathways and DNA vibration. As emphasized by the quote, "persistence and determination alone are omnipotent."

Let's consider some illustrations from the biblical reference that will help us learn and grasp the power and meaning of persistence and determination:

"Suppose one of you has a friend and you go to him at midnight and say to him, 'Friend, lend me three loaves, because one of my friends has just come to me on a journey and I have nothing to offer him.' But that one replies from inside: 'Stop bothering me. The door is already locked, and my young children are with me in bed. I cannot get up and give you anything.' I tell you, even if he will not get up and give him anything because of being his friend, certainly because of his bold persistence he will get up and give him whatever he needs" (Luke 11:5-9).

"In a certain city there was a judge who had no fear of God and no respect for man. There was also a widow in that city who kept going to him and saying, 'See that I get justice from my legal opponent.' Well, for a while he was unwilling, but afterward he said to himself, 'Although I do not fear God or respect any man, because this widow keeps making me trouble, I will see that she gets justice so that she will not keep wearing me out with her demand'" (Luke 18:1-7).

The illustrations are simple and drive the point home. The power of persistence and determination will get us what we want regardless of people, circumstances, or situations that we may have in our lives. The success of those who received what they wanted was determined by their ability to not give up. Never giving up is the paramount object when it comes to transmitting a frequency of vibration, as we are broadcasting and asking for that which we desire. The corrupt judge who couldn't care less about this widow's problems gave in just because he did not want to be worn out from hearing her cry. He got sick and tired of her presence; therefore, he had no choice but to give in to what she wanted.

So whether we decide to pray to our choice of deity, god, or universe, it is irrelevant. We can ask in prayer, and use thoughts, words and speech;

in harmony with our intention in the form of a conversation, as readily as asking a friend or in the form of a demand like the widow to the judge. But in reality, one of the best ways to ask for what we desire is commanding it to happen.

"Have faith in God. Truly I say to you that whoever tells this mountain, 'Be lifted up and thrown into the sea,' and does not doubt in his heart but has faith that what he says will happen, he will have it happen. That is why I tell you, all the things you pray and ask for, have faith that you have received them, and you will have them" (Mark 11:22-24).

It must be emphasized here now in our mind, how unequivocally this key scripture teaches that we have the power to command whatever we want to happen with our spoken word. The illustration puts the one asking in the position of master or boss. Like an employer telling his worker to do a certain task, the employee does HIS bidding without question. The illustration also emphasizes that *anybody* can command with their words for their desires to come true. We can literally speak things into existence. The laws of physics according to quantum tunneling allows for these processes to occur. It is the law that if we have the assured expectation of what we have commanded to happen or asked for, we should consider that it is just like we have already received them.

Many religious people may have confusion about this understanding. The illustration encourages faith in God. But then Jesus goes on a tangent, emphasizing that we can command the literal mountain to move from land into the sea. Are we commanding God, as if God were our servant? It almost seems to suggest that. I feel more inclined to think that since the biblical reference has described mankind in general as being created in the image of God, in essence, we can create and speak things into existence in a similar manner that God said, "Let there be light." Some people may think that it is ridiculous to believe that we are like gods. But the biblical reference leaves no doubt to this thought. Consider the clear authority that this passage specifically described our potential for creation:

"'For instance, which is easier, to say, "Your sins are forgiven," or to say, "Get up and walk?" However, in order for you to know that the

Son of man has authority on earth to forgive sins—' then he said to the paralytic: 'Get up, pick up your stretcher, and go to your home.' And he got up and went to his home. When the crowds saw this, they were struck with fear, and they glorified God, who gave such authority to men" (Matthew 9:5-8)

In harmony with the authority of commanding a mountain to transfer from one place to another, here, the biblical reference clearly states that what Jesus was able to do with such ease, so can mankind. We can command anything we desire to happen for just like Jesus commanded the paralyzed man to get up and walk to his house. The same way that the paralyzed man had no choice but to do so, also must our desires expressed in the form of commanding words occur. The current state of affairs had to completely change on the paralyzed man, therefore he was able to go home healed. The biblical reference, in its pages, clearly highlights that we have such authority. Quantum physics portrays that it is a reality. People who create amazing success know and understand that they have such power; therefore they create whatever they desire. Obviously in this instant in time, we may not command things to happen as easily and discernible as this account portrays Jesus as being able to do, but the potential does exist.

"Most truly I say to you that whoever exercises faith in me will also do the works that I do; and he will do works greater than these" (John 14:12).

It is our moral obligation to exercise our innate abilities to the point that our faith will allow us to achieve things and command things to happen as big and drastic as what Jesus did with seeming ease. The great news is that our faith must only be as big as the size of a mustard grain.

"Truly I say to you, if you have faith the size of a mustard grain, you will say to this mountain, 'Move from here to there,' and it will move, and nothing will be impossible for you" (Matthew 17:20).

But how can we exercise our faith to such degree? We must take baby steps and start creating little by little. Perseverance and determination is demonstrated in the following illustration:

"Keep on asking, and it will be given you; keep on seeking, and you will find; keep on knocking, and it will be opened to you; for everyone asking receives, and everyone seeking finds, and to everyone knocking, it will be opened. Indeed, which one of you, if his son asks for bread, will hand him a stone? Or if he will asks for a fish, he will not hand him a serpent, will he? Therefore, if you, although being wicked, know how to give good gifts to your children, how much more so will your Father who is in the heavens give good things to those asking him!" (Matthew 7:7-11).

It is aptly described here that our ability to receive a desired result comes from not giving up in asking, seeking, and knocking. We must also readily know that we will receive from the "given" transmission through the laws of the universe, that which matches our broadcast of frequency. We must know that doing so is like asking the best possible parent in the world, in this case, the laws of physics working diligently for us, thus we will receive that piece of bread or fish. What we want is already created in the ether, and it is as easy to manifest into our reality as a parent giving his son that piece of bread or fish. Does it not make sense that when we command something to happen, since it is law for us to receive, then our feeling must be as if we already received it?

We are truly masters of our universe, and according to the biblical reference, it was God who gave us such authority over the physical universe. It is like a genie that is at our disposal, ready to do our bidding, like a servant who is eagerly working for us because it wants to please us. The Bible essentially has always taught us that we do indeed have our own personal genie ready to grant us our every wish. The laws of physics prove this to be true. Biblical text illustrates this simply too.

"Now the apostles said to the Lord: 'Give us more faith.' Then the Lord said: 'If you had faith the size of a mustard grain, you would say to the black mulberry tree, "Be uprooted and planted in the sea!" and it would obey you. Which one of you who has a slave plowing or shepherding would say to him when he comes in from the field, "Come here at once and dine at the table?" Rather, will he not say to him, "Get something ready for me to have my evening meal, and put on an apron and serve me until I finish eating and drinking, and afterward you can eat and drink?" He will not feel gratitude to the slave because he did what was assigned, will he?'" (Luke 17:5-9).

Here it is emphasized that our faith is strongly connected to our ability to realize that we can command what we desire to happen. The universe will comply as readily as we feel like a master commanding his slave to do his bidding. We should not be in expectation of it as if someone greater than us were doing us a favor, and thus we feel indebted or unworthy. If we feel like slaves fearfully asking for what we want, we will not receive because we are already in fear or are conscious of what we do not desire. Many times we fear those who have greater power or authority than ourselves. We look up to those who are our bosses or leaders. Instead we must have the attitude of not even feeling gratitude for what we assigned the universe to do for us. In the same manner, if God himself commands his servants to do something and does not feel gratitude for it, then we realize we are the universe's gods, and therefore we do not feel indebtedness or gratitude for doing what it was commanded to do. This must be our mental state and predominant attitude toward our transmissions of desire to the universe if we are to receive what we want.

Give Us More Faith!

Another key ingredient is realizing that we may not have the faith that we need to create that which we want the most. The biblical reference emphasizes that we must ask for such faith as a desired result *first* before we try to ask for that which requires at least a measure of faith the size of a mustard grain. We must develop such faith by broadcasting the intention that is exactly what we desire. We can ask for the freedom to ask or command for that which we want. In essence, if we desire to progress in this process, it is our moral obligation to command that we must be given such faith, and thus it must be developed within us.

## THE OTHER SIDE OF THE COIN OF FAITH: WORKS

*Indeed, just as the body without spirit is dead, so also faith without works is dead.*

—(James 2:26

Faith has been previously defined as "the assured expectation of what is hoped for," the evident demonstration of realities although not beheld. It is the feeling of knowingness that we will have the desired outcome, event or thing. Our hope expects it until what we want is in our present reality. The question then arises, can I just lie on my bed and command things to happen? Don't I have to do something? Can I just have hope and faith that it will take place without any action on my part?

One joke illustrates it like this: A lady was praying to God, saying, "God please make me win the lottery." A second time, the lady prayed, "God, please allow me to win the lottery, for I have lost my job." After some time, the lady prayed again. "God please make me win the lottery, for my kids are hungry and I don't a have job yet." A little more time passed as well, and she kept praying, "God, please, I am asking you with despair, my husband left me, my kids are hungry, and I have no job, so please allow me to win the lottery." Then the heavens opened up and God said, 'Lady! Would you please buy the lottery ticket already!"

Another joke goes like this: A priest owned a church in town, for he was God-fearing. A warning for coming storms and possible flooding was issued. People were told to leave town because the danger was imminent. The priest was told to leave his church, but he responded, "I don't have to leave, for God will take care of me." The rains came and started to flood the town. The priest was told to leave town again, but the priest responded with the same thing: "I don't have to leave, for God will take care of me." The floods started to rise, and then a boat came to the priest. "We are here to rescue you," they said. The priest responded in the same manner. "I don't have to leave, for God will save me. Then the floods kept rising. The priest was on the roof, and then another boat came—"We are here to rescue you." The priest insisted, "I don't have to leave, for God will save me." Then after a while the flood kept rising even more, and a chopper came by and said, "We are here to rescue you." The priest again replied, "I don't have to leave, for God will rescue me." The floods then rose to the point of drowning the priest, and he died and then went to heaven. Mad, the priest asked God, "What happened? I had faith that you would rescue me and you let me die." God responded, "Dummy, I sent you two warnings, two boats, and a chopper."

The point is simple: faith without works is dead. We must act in harmony with our transmissions of frequencies to have real power. We must give our energy, time, and effort if we are to create or receive that which we have asked. Our faith is enforced through our actions to make things happen. For example, if we desire to be in shape and picture a result, then we must realize that doing things that are in disharmony with this goal will not help us create what we want. We cannot get a hardcore six-pack or defined chest sitting on our couches watching TV or playing video games while eating junk food all day long. As we begin to exercise and change what we eat to that which will help us get in shape, we will begin to receive people, circumstances, and events that will continue to enforce our desire and motivation to continue exercising. This will perpetuate the energy in our field or matrix and will continue to do so, ultimately helping us create the body we desire.

## DIFFERENCE BETWEEN KNOWING THE PATH AND WALKING THE PATH

In the movie *The Matrix*, the character Neo was confused about the feedback he got from the Oracle, who was a guide that would help him achieve ultimate power. Morpheus explained to him that Neo only heard exactly what he needed to hear, and that was all. Morpheus added, "Neo, sooner or later, you're going to realize, just as I did, that there's a difference between knowing the path and walking the path." But what does this really mean in reference to our goals and dreams?

Simply put, if we desire a better job or more income, we may begin to broadcast what we want: a better job or more income. The universe will begin to present us with people, circumstances, and events that will help us get closer to what we want. But we must know first that we should not wait on such responses from the universal field to take action, for we can demonstrate our faith by taking the initiative. We can begin to search for a new job or improve our skills and expedite the process, at which point the universe will continue to guide us in the right direction for our desired outcome or result.

One thing that is paramount is that we must realize the truth of the matter: that works, skills, or actions, are *not* really the key. We must take this as a warning because then we will create resistance. This is the warning:

"So, then, it depends not on a person's desire or on his effort, but on God [the universe], who has mercy. . . . For what reason? Because they pursued it, not by faith, but as by works. . . . but God [the universe] kept making it grow, so that neither is the one who plants anything nor is the one who waters, but God [the universe] who makes it grow" (Romans 9:16, 32; 1 Corinthians 3:6-7).

This is a strange dichotomy and paradox. Consider the steps: We make the decision that we want something and we want to create it. We first transmit using our brain the dream or goal in the form of a desire. The broadcast of frequency will continue to permeate our matrix, adding more energy to it as we continue to think, talk, and act on that dream. Our positive feelings of expectation amp the power of our transmission or vibration of our thoughts, words, and actions. We create habits that generate more energy based on those thoughts, words, and actions, which continue to perpetuate the transmission from our brain even more powerfully. The energy gets to the tipping point where the scales come to the other side of the matrix—the field of particles of energy defined by time and space. The result? The universe, through its most foundational laws, creates people, circumstances, situations, events, and things to make it happen in our life. We get exactly what we want by law.

The paradox is this: it is not our works, actions, skills, or plans that create and make what we want happen. It is the accumulation of energy from all the thoughts, words, and actions that continue to broadcast the already-created dream from the matrix of wave particles to our observable universe, the matrix of particles of energy defined by time and space. It is the energy generated and broadcasted from our brain, the total accumulation of all our thoughts. The words are thoughts. The actions are based on thoughts originated by the original desire.

As the biblical references point out, it is up to God or the universe to create it in your field. We are the ones watering and fertilizing the seeds of our dreams, but it is the universe or God that brings them into our existence. We want to emphasize here that we are not suggesting that the universe is the same as God. This parallel just describes that it is laws of the universe that engage and work for us and with us to create what we want. It is all for posterity and objectivity.

This highly suggests that our entire makeup is not separate from our universe but unequivocally connected to us, connected to who we are and what we are. Essentially we may be the singularity of our own universe. The warning then is this:

"Do not be misled my beloved brothers. Every good gift and every perfect present is from above, coming down from the Father of the celestial lights, who does not vary or change like the shifting shadows" (James 1:16).

The warning is that when we are focused on our actions or how to achieve things, we will not get what we want or we will not create it. It is our faith, perseverance, and persistence and our ability to continue giving that frequency of energy so that we may receive that which we have established as the desired result.

For example, let's say we decide we want a brand-new car. We find out the car is worth $80,000. We notice that it is out of our income range, and there is absolutely no way we can buy it or finance it. The first thing that comes to mind is, "How in the world am I going to buy it?" Since we do not see in our present reality how to buy it, then we give up on the idea of getting it. The broadcast was weak and instead it creates fear and doubt. The focus is now on the absence of the car as opposed to having it. Therefore, it will always not be there because that is the current state of mental focus. Then the nature of the words become that of "There is no way how," "I can't do it," "I am not good enough," "I will never make that much money," etc. The universe will then mirror that agreement, and we will not see a how to accomplish getting the car. That agreement will spill over and affect other desires related to money, health, relationships, and even spiritual matters, among other things. Habits of thought will invite an equivalent or similar form of thought that will affect our decision making.

Instead, what we must realize is that the *how* to achieve it, really, is not up to us. What is up to us is our ability to sustain and persevere in holding a state of transmission while acting in harmony with what we desire. We may start researching how other people get the car. We may also find out that people who get such seemingly expensive items have businesses of their own, and therefore we may decide to look to establish our own business. We may start doing research on different kinds of businesses we could possibly engage in. We may start to take classes to improve our skills or start taking certain courses to learn specific businesses or jobs that provide such income that will allow us to receive that which we want. This is what it means to act in harmony.

Remember, we now know that it is the universe that will ultimately help us create it in our present reality. While we are engaged in this process of acting in harmony with what we want, then we may find that through some strange circumstance, we get exactly what we want. We will find that it will happen not through the way, or *how*, we chose to get what we desire. The universal laws will push us in a certain direction tangential to what we are currently engaging in. Maybe everything falls apart and another way or *how* presents itself, and that may be the way to get there. What we must know that it is paramount that we exercise our ability to sustain that transmission long enough to achieve our dream or goal. This is the creation process, and it must be firmly established in our mind if we are to progress and move from our present reality.

The present reality that we may have created thus far may be so out of place and so far from what we desire, that it may essentially make us feel like failures and that we are hopeless. But what we must understand is that it is the accumulation of the energy that is vibrating into the ether or matrix of wave frequencies that will create the result. The dream or goal has already been created there, but to bring it into our existence, we must continue to give energy until that big ball of energy reaches the tipping point. Then the universe, with all its laws, creates our goal in our reality. These are the mechanics, but in essence, it is our decision to acquire something we want that starts the whole process. As long as we hold on to that decision, regardless of circumstances, we will create it through our transmission, as the laws of the universe begin to operate from the conception of that decision.

## THE SUCCESSFUL FAILURE

*You unreasonable person! What you sow is not made alive unless first it dies. And as for what you sow, you sow, not the body that will develop, but just a bare grain, whether of wheat or of some other kind of seed; but God [universe] gives it a body just as it has pleased him, and gives to each of the seeds its own body.*

—1 Corinthians 15:36-38

JULIAN VALDERRAMA

*Nobody sews a patch of unshrunk cloth on an old outer garment. If he does, the new piece pulls away from the old, and the tear becomes worse. Also, no one puts new wine into old wineskins. If he does, the wine will burst the skins, and the wine is lost as well as the skins. But new wine is put into new wineskins.*

—Mark 2:21-22

We may feel confused because many times we will set up a goal or desire and work really hard without seeing any results. This will absolutely happen. Another scenario that will consistently happen is that when we choose to pursue a goal or desire, the *how* will completely collapse and end up not working out. Maybe the business fails, or we see very minimal results. This is when a shift in our consciousness must take place: We must know that failure is just a sign that we are getting closer to what we want. Thomas Edison was quoted as saying that he did not fail ten thousand times when creating the incandescent lightbulb. He said, "I successfully found ten thousand ways it would not work." This is very positive and the reality of the laws of physics. How and why?

Before the eighteenth century, the concept of science was created through the scientific method. Empirical evidence became paramount to establish facts and replicable results. It has unleashed an enormous amount of information that continues to make technology progress exponentially. The laws of physics are more clearly defined and explained in ways that are easily described by mathematics. It is now being shown that through integration of physics and numbers, the entire cosmos can continually be described by mathematical formulas. These formulas are then translated into physical laws of the universe. Interestingly, it was the laws of physics that were first established as a theory and then proven through complex mathematical formulas. The law always precedes the formulas that describe them.

This means that mathematics is intertwined and integrated into the fabric of space. Simply put, without the concept of time and space as an "observable notion," then we would not be able to measure time or space. One could not exist without the other. The dimensions of the rooms in our homes and buildings all have been first established through careful foundations of workable mathematical concepts and laws of physics, for they all must be applied precisely without error for builders to be able to establish replicas of what is designed on paper. Everything, in essence, is constructed through preestablished basic foundational principles, or laws of physics defined by mathematical concepts observable by our minds. But what does time and space have anything to do with the concepts of failure and success?

It has everything to do with it. Realizing that we must accept the preestablished physical laws of the universe allows us to replicate a simple predetermined quota of movements or actions to create the result. Failure, by definition, is described by the infinite nature of the universe as it relates to time and space. The ramifications of infinity aptly explain or highly suggest that we must fail an infinite amount of times before we succeed. The opposite is also true, for infinity says that we must succeed an infinite amount of times before we fail. This is a strange paradox, for how can we ever succeed if we are to fail an infinite amount of times and vice versa?

This has been referred as infinite regress. It means that principles must be founded on another principle. It may be illustrated like the weird optical illusion of mirrors reflecting each other, ever onward into infinity. Principle 1 requires the support of principle 2; the truth of principle 2 requires the support of principle 3 and so forth, ad infinitum. Zeno's paradox is defined in the story of the tortoise and Achilles. A turtle gets a head start of one hundred feet against Achilles, and as such, Achilles can start running once the turtle hits the one-hundred -feet mark. Logically, the runner catches up to him rather easily and will win the race. But in essence, according to the laws of physics and how they relate to time and space, that is impossible. Why?

Because the laws of physics describe that the runner must always reach an infinite of halfway points before he catches up to the turtle. The runner must reach the fifty-feet mark, but before that, he must reach the twenty-five-feet mark. Before that, he must reach the 12.5-feet mark, and before that, he must reach the 6.25-feet mark, and so on and so forth. This process, through the laws of math, requires the runner to go through a paradoxical and infinite amount of points before he reaches the turtle. Thus, he can never catch up to the turtle. This has blown away the minds of philosophers, scientists, and mathematicians. It is a radical idea.

At this point, the reader may be totally perplexed by the implication described here therein. This is in line with the thought by King Solomon of ancient Israel:

"He has made everything beautiful in its time. He has even put eternity in their heart; yet mankind will never find out the work that the true God has made from start to finish" (Ecclesiastes 3:11).

We may realize logically that the runner never catching up to the turtle is ludicrous, and therefore, he will always catch up to him regardless of what the laws of math say in connection to the fabric of time and space. Of course this is true because that is what we *know* must happen. Have we considered that it is the strong, powerful faith, the assured expectation of what is hoped for, the knowingness, that Achilles has what it takes win the race? It is his faith that makes him go past the turtle. It is this knowingness vibration from his mind that allows his particles of infinite possibility that permeate the runner, which program him and allows him to reach the goal and pass the turtle. The runner, from the start, has already passed the turtle in his mind without a shadow of doubt. He has already predetermined that he has beaten the turtle and there is nothing the turtle can do about it. The turtle has no choice but to lose.

So according to the laws of physics, the runner has already lost an infinite amount of times to the turtle, and thus has gone through an infinite amount of points trying to reach it. Therefore it is Achilles's strong "faith" that allows him to "win." It is a strange radical paradox, but faith is a mathematical concept preestablished in the laws of the universe essentially tied into quantum particle physics in connection to the realm of time and space. Our consciousness "knows" we can outrun the turtle; therefore our faith makes it happen, and that is exactly what we must observe. We get what we want.

In the same manner, our faith must catch up to our desires. Our decision that we already have what we want makes it happen. It is our doubt and disbelief that create failure and make us give up. But it is our persistence and patience that determines, through our faith, whether we will receive what we want or not. Success is truly just a decision away.

Albert Einstein said that we cannot solve the current problems with our preestablished thoughts and habits that have created them. Tesla said that the energy mass that prevents us from achieving what we may desire will not change until the new thoughts of knowledge gradually changes the status quo. We cannot currently achieve what we may desire because our mass must change to match that which we want. We get what we want because we must *become* what we think about most of the time. Failure through Isaac's third law of motion forces us to focus on whether or not we will be able to achieve what we want. It reinforces our decision to create what we want based on our current situation. It will either convince us that it is impossible and make us quit, or it will help us more clearly focus and desire more strongly. This is that which must continue to take place until we create what we want by means of our strong focus on thought transmission. We cannot sew a new patch onto an old garment, as suggested by Jesus. We must completely transform and become new to get the new. How?

## LIFE AS WE THINK WE KNOW IT IS IMPOSSIBLE; THEREFORE WE MUST FOCUS

The essence of persistence and perseverance is *focus*. Consider what a lower life-form is programmed to do by instinct. Plants, in this instance, have been described as being able to efficiently process light—photons or particles of light—to create their own food source and nourishment. They are a factory that recreates light into infinitely denser energies. According to classical physics, this is really impossible. Why? Because the particles that compose plants are dense and defined in time and space.

We can illustrate it like this: Imagine parallel steel beams placed a quarter inch from each other. Imagine that we have a wall of billions of these beams placed in front of us from side to side in one line, from left to right. Then we observe that there are also billions of these beams placed in front of this wall and past the wall. Therefore we observe that this structure is billions of steel beams wide and deep. Consider that each successive steel-beam wall is placed randomly in front of the space that separates it from the first wall, and down the line, you find that the pattern continues with each wall. Like a dense crowd of people with no discernible arrangement or alignment, we would have to maneuver our way in carefully without touching anyone to move through the crowd.

Imagine that in the middle of this dense crowd of random steel beams placed a quarter inch from each other, there is a billion dollars for the taking.

The challenge, we are told, is that we must go through the dense structure blindfolded. As we stand in defeat in front of the problem, we find that it is impossible for us to reach the center and get our reward. In the same manner, the photons of light are even less likely to reach the center as we are reaching the center of this massive structure. This is because the plant makes up trillions upon trillions of atoms of thickness in length and width, height or depth. The radical paradox is that plants are able to efficiently draw and make those particles of light reach its center to create its own food. They grow and prosper. How?

The laws of physics at a quantum level allow this to take place with perfect efficiency based on the "decision" and "focus" of the consciousness of the plant. Simply put, the focus of the plant is to produce food by means of the photosynthesizing core. The focus and decision of the plants makes the photons that collide with itself to become wave particles. This is called quantum superposition (principles 1, 2, and 4). In essence, it takes the photons defined by time and space and turns them into wave particles. Imagine us being multiplied by the trillions of possible routes we could take in this massive structure of beams standing in front of us. Then imagine taking each possible route simultaneously until the shortest, quickest route is found. Remember that photons of light cannot consciously decide to swerve between beams, but blindly it continues to collapse against the particles that make up the plants. In the same manner, hitting every possible beam must be accounted into the multiplication because we must blindly travel through the maze. Finally, from all the possible routes one could take, the successful person does reach the center and grabs the prize.

The plant collapses all the trillions of possible routes the particle could take that did not reach the center and therefore observes the only one that does reach the center, and it becomes the only possibility. In reality, it becomes the only choice because the plant's focus and decision makes it happen. In an instant, the trillions of possible superpositions defined and allowed by the duality of particles must take place. All decisions and routes must take place simultaneously and calculated until the only favorable choice takes place. The information or choice travels back in time and becomes the single and only possible observation in time and space.

The double-slit experiment allows for information to travel back in time and create a different outcome. This was observed when scientists decided to observe the wave particles hitting the second wall at the last instant. What they observed was mind-blowing and confusing. What they saw was no longer an interference pattern, but a defined pattern. Almost as if the particles went back in time and decided to go through both slits, just as particles with solid properties do.

This may be very hard to comprehend fully, but it is described herein to establish that failure only happens because we decide to observe failure. We, as human beings, are more powerful than any plant. We can focus our mind to the outcome of our success, and that dream or goal must become the only choice. This does not mean that we will experience an insurmountable amount of routes on our way to success, but that we will experience the only route to our desired result. Successful people seem to be quoted saying similar experiences on their way to success. Consider a few:

*If there is no struggle, there is no progress.*

—Frederick Douglass

*If you want to be happy, set a goal that commands your thoughts, liberates your energy, and inspires your hopes.*

—Andrew Carnegie

*As long as the mind can envision the fact that you can do something, you can do it—as long as you really believe 100 percent.*

—Arnold Schwarzenegger

*In the middle of every difficulty lies opportunity.*

—Albert Einstein

JULIAN VALDERRAMA

*Everything you can imagine is real.*

—Pablo Picasso

*Don't worry about failure; you only have to be right once.*

—Drew Houston

*If you are going through hell, keep going.*

—Winston Churchill

You can find similar quotes describing the same ideas about failure and perseverance throughout many sources, and thus the point is firmly established. Sometimes, we must experience what we don't want to clearly define and pursue what we truly want. We must exercise our mental faculties to use the power of o u r imagination to picture the result as the only option. Our photosynthesizing process of the wave particles in the infinite energetic field of our matrix will spill over until it is the only choice in our present reality. Our focus, perseverance, and determination is unfathomable and omnipotent. Nothing can change that law, for if we desire to achieve what we want, this process must be engaged, period. So focus!

The Best Energy We Can Give to Achieve Financial Wealth

*"Bring the entire tithe into the storehouse, so that there may be food in my house, and test me out, please, in this regard," Jehovah of armies says, "to see whether I will not open to you the floodgates of the heavens and pour out on you a blessing until there is nothing lacking."*

—Malachi 3:10

*Honor Jehovah with your valuable things, with the first fruits of all your produce; then your storehouses will be completely filled, and your vats will overflow with new wine.*

—Proverbs 3:9-10

Clearly we must exercise our faculties of giving. Here it is emphasized throughout the biblical reference that, as a result of our efforts to give, we will receive an exchange of abundance. People become poor out of their own volition and their habitual mentality in the focus of lack. People are poor and broke because they are mentally focused on beliefs that there is not enough. We may ask: How can we give if we don't have enough for ourselves? This is an illusion and a decision that will continue to perpetuate our reality, and thus we will never have enough.

This commentary is absolutely not just regarding money, but every conceivable aspect of success, happiness, and abundance. For example, an individual who feels lack of love from a mate or suffer from loneliness may envy other individuals who have managed to create such riches and abundance. The antisocial and easily offended individual who feels lonely for lack of friendship and real friends may criticize and condemn those who may be more popular because of their more outgoing and caring personalities, for as a result, friendlier individuals will draw to themselves people who love their company. Thus the same principle applies to those who feel financial stress or pressures, for their lack of resources is the result of their own doing. It is all based on their conscious awareness of energetic prosperity and their corresponding physical manifestations.

It has been known that the biggest philanthropists have been known to be incredibly financially successful. People may say that it is because they are financially rich that they have a surplus to give. Although this may be true in some cases, the truth, according to the laws of physics is that they continue to receive more because they have been giving more since the beginning. They give first before they spend on themselves. And by law, they reap what they sow—they become more successful and attain bigger and more abundant riches. The saying that the rich get richer and the poor get poorer is true based on the laws of physics. The law of magnetic attraction has to match what you have given out. The seeds that you continue to plant and fertilize become trees that produce abundant fruit. Thus we must be self-aware of the nature of those trees. Have we planted seeds of lack or abundance?

Let's consider a story in the biblical reference that will empower us. It is found in 1 Kings 17:1-16. The reader is strongly encouraged to read the account, for it teaches a powerful lesson.

To establish background information, Jehovah, the God of the Hebrews had appointed a man by the name of Elijah to become his spokesman for the nation of Israel. During that time, there was great economic turmoil because the nation had forgotten to pursue and obey the law that was originally established for their own good and prosperity. They were paying the price for failing to follow some very simple principles founded on the laws of the universe. To care for his messenger, he sends him to a widow in a land called Zarephath. Once Elijah reaches the place, he meets a widow with an only son. According to the record, the widow has nothing. There is drought in the land; she is a widow with no source of income, she has a son, and all she has left is a small jar with a little oil and a handful of flour to bake some bread. Her situation is so dire and desperate that she believes she and her son will die after this one meal.

It is an interesting paradox because God had promised Elijah food, shelter, and provisions through this widow. After Elijah requested a round cake for himself, the widow expressed her grief on how she could not provide what was requested. In response, Elijah says:

"Do not be afraid. Go in and do as you said. But first make me a small round loaf of bread with what is there, and bring it out to me. Then you can make something afterward for you and your son. For this is what Jehovah the God of Israel says: 'The large jar of flour will not run out, and the small jar of oil will not run dry until the day Jehovah makes it rain on the surface of the ground'" (1 Kings 17:13-14).

What a strange request. The story points out that the means of provision would not run out as long as she *first* gave what she had. The lesson is clear: we can absolutely always give something of ourselves regardless of our circumstances, for it is highly unlikely that they are as bad as this widow's situation. She gave all she had first for the benefit of others. This is not to imply that we must give everything we have to others, but what about just 10 percent of our income, resources, time, or energy? The words of Malachi are based on the laws of the universe, for they will activate and we will continue to increase even though we are giving our resources. No matter how little we have, we can give at least 10 percent off the top first for the benefit of others. The bigger our contributions, the bigger our return of investment must be.

People will save and invest in real estate, stocks, savings accounts, or businesses with the hope of getting some returns. Many do, and many do not. But according to this principle, we will absolutely, with 100 percent certainty, get a return on our investment. If we were given a stock pick that guarantees a return of investment of a hundredfold, would we not do it? Imagine that the stock is guaranteed by the state treasury, the president and vice president of the country, the Federal Reserve, and even the Securities and Exchange Commission. You see that, under contract, all the signatures are set. All you have to do is sign the paper and make the investment. Would we not do it?

The laws of the universe will act in favor of our agreement and will bring us by law a greater return on investment. The neural pathways that we develop will continue to vibrate and create people, circumstances, and events that will continue to give us more opportunities to give more. Therefore we must have a lot more to give. To whom should we give our resources? It is up to us to decide what we wish to do. There are charitable organizations that have great causes. Our family members may need our help. Whatever we decide, we can really give our resources away for any cause or to anybody, and by law, it must make us wealthier. We become what we think about, and therefore we broadcast the nature of those thoughts and actions. There is more happiness in giving than receiving because we get more and can continue to expand our reality by giving more of ourselves. Let's make sure we understand why this is true by continuing to expand on these concepts, for by reviewing them repeatedly, we will live these laws and see powerful results in our lives.

This all proves that there is absolutely more happiness in giving than receiving. Then by all means, let us all resolve to persevere in our ability to give away as much as we can give so that we may continue to receive even more abundantly than what we have given. It is the law, under contract.

## Tying It All Together

May we suggest that this chapter be reread not once, but many times. The entire chapter focuses on helping us become more aware to

JULIAN VALDERRAMA

the vibration we are offering. It is the nature of what we are giving out that will determine our success. Knowing that contentment and striving our focus to feel as good as we possibly can will set us up to create better and faster. As we give thanks for every experience, whether good or bad, we will continue to perpetuate our neural pathways and focus on being able to stay at cause and in control of our lives and the things we create. Our perseverance and persistence to send out a transmission of frequency to its point of manifestation in our physical lives is also the key to create whatever we want. It is paramount that we understand that is how we create.

Realizing that our actions and skills are not really important but our ability to sustain a transmission of frequency is the most relevant cognition will help us supersede negative thinking and stop worrying about failures or minor setbacks. Being aware that there is a difference between knowing the path and walking the path to our goals will help sustain our focused vibration. This will remind us that our goals and dreams are not defined by the amount of failures we may experience along the way. Knowing that failures are just powerful energy to help us more precisely and more strongly define our dreams and focus on them will give us fantastic opportunities to renew the power of our output. Our transmissions of frequency for our dreams will be amped, and we will create more efficiently.

Giving resources and money will propel our dreams because as we freely water others, we will be freely watering ourselves. It will become law that as we focus on helping others to improve their lives by our giving 10 percent of our income, or whatever amount we choose, that in itself will propel us to achieve and create our dreams much faster and better, proportionate to what we have given. Giving is the key to our happiness and the realization of our dreams. Practicing our ability to give is what will create more abundance in our lives more than anything else we can possibly do. As we exercise our faith and ability to focus, we will continue to permeate the ether with our desire, and we will find the floodgates of the heavens opening to us so much prosperity that we will not know what to do with it. It is the law.

# CHAPTER 7

# The Unfathomable Power of A Master Mind

*Look! they are one people with one language, and this is*
*what they have started to do. Now there is nothing that they*
*may have in mind to do that will be impossible for them.*

—Genesis 11:6

THIS CONCEPT IS powerful. We may want to consider that it is the most powerful system that we can plug into. In a previous chapter, it was stated that Andrew Carnegie mentored Napoleon Hill to codify success. Napoleon Hill learned the master mind teaching from Andrew Carnegie, the richest man in the world at the turn of the century. This conviction is also found through the scriptures, mainly through the example of Jesus. He successfully replicated his knowledge through his best friends and ultimately had them do the same. This replication process perpetuated until it transformed the thinking of that known world. This is not to emphasize on a set of spiritual beliefs over others, but it is to emphasize that this basic concept of "action" as a foundation will permeate and perpetuate success, whatever we choose that to be.

If we desire to get in the best shape possible, we can gather a group of people that will support us in that endeavor. If we desire to develop a certain skill, we can get together with like-minded people with the same goal. If we desire to engage in a business, this support system will propel us to incredible heights of success.

The "master mind" is a group of people that support each other in their endeavors. They all have one common goal, and that is to support each other's dreams or goals, whatever they are. For example, let's imagine that a group of seven friends form a master mind, and they make a solemn promise to each other that they will get together on regular basis to discuss each other's dreams and goals. Let's suppose that each individual states their dreams in the following way:

Person 1: Become fit and healthy.
Person 2: Find a spouse/soul mate.
Person 3: Pursue a career in business.
Person 4: Improve relationship with spouse.
Person 5: Increase monthly income by $2,000.
Person 6: Increase monthly income by $3,000.
Person 7: Start a coffee shop.

Each individual in the master mind will state to each other their goals and desires, and everyone else will agree to support and help each other by transmitting positive recognition for each other's dreams. It could happen that a master mind may choose a single common purpose. Maybe they choose to put a portion of their incomes together to start up a company based on product X or service Y. As such, under one common goal, they will be more likely to accomplish what they want faster than if they were to try to do it individually.

The following eight-step pattern for success is a proven method that can help us form a powerful master mind that we can engage with, for whatever purpose and goal we may desire to achieve. Whether the master mind is set up to support each individual's goal or the collective decision to accomplish a common goal. This pattern for success can be applied to one's personal endeavors, regardless of a person having a master mind or not; thus it could be used to start a business or project of achievement.

## THE EIGHT-STEP PATTERN FOR SUCCESS

This system is used by some of the most financially successful individuals, as well as companies. This system perpetuates success faster than anything else. A billionaire described this system as a proven method and not a theory. It is a fact that it helps people become financially successful or independent.

Although money may not be our goal or dream, it is important that we realize that real, physical cash and the things it can buy are quantifiable. We can see it, touch it, smell it, and feel it with our senses. They are real, physical manifestations in the real, physical world that we live. These people have been able to broadcast the frequency of their desired result and have it permeate their matrix of reality to the point where they are able to see the results of their prolonged broadcast. They have successfully focused so much energy into the field of wave frequencies to the point of it spilling over into the particle field of energy. It takes the dreams already in existence in the ether of infinite possibilities to the realm of energy defined by observation, time, and space. Refer to chapters 2 and 3 for emphasis of these physical laws of the universe.

This system is also essentially described in detail in the biblical reference. We may want to strongly consider using this systematic approach to success to create what we want, since it is referred by the triad of knowledge: science, spirituality, and philosophy. The foundation of this system lies in our ability to make the decision that we will become successful. This decision is defined by its first step:

## STEP 1: CLEARLY DEFINE YOUR DREAM AND GET A BURNING DESIRE FOR ITS ACHIEVEMENT

> *Write down the vision, and inscribe it clearly on tablets, so that the one reading aloud from it may do so easily. For the vision is yet for its appointed time, and it is rushing toward its end, and it will not lie. Even if it should delay, keep in expectation of it! For it will without fail come true. It will not be late!*

> —Habakkuk 2:2-3

This is the first step and the most important one. If we fail to do this correctly, the rest of the system will not work. This is of foremost importance, and it is paramount in this system that we do this single step appropriately. On a white sheet of paper with a pen with blue ink write down the following, in order:

– Write "Dreams, Goals, and Desires" as the title of the paper.

- Write down all the things that you would have, be, or do if money were not an object.

It is important in this step that we do not prejudge goals and dreams. We must use our imagination and really dream. Consider what Tesla was able to accomplish. He has had the most influence on all the technology that currently exists today. Also, as we have read, he imagined and dreamed of a society and a world of people who live eternally in youth and beauty. He saw it as the aching need of humanity. If that was his dream and thus his drive to create so much as a result, then in reality, it is our imagination that we must exercise to broadcast the proper frequencies. It is our moral obligation to do the same as Tesla did; we must dream big.

Obviously our dreams could be of a spiritual nature. We may desire happiness, contentment, joy, peace of mind, or more love. Maybe we desire better qualities in ourselves, such as kindness, goodness, patience, or more self-control. We could desire more faith in life and in our thoughts. These would be outstanding goals and dreams, and we can certainly create a magnificent lifestyle based on these principles. It would certainly create an abundance of happy feelings in our lives and may probably be the best way to go about making sure we feel good most of the time. "Happy are those conscious of their spiritual need" (Matthew 5:3). Thus we can write these things as goals and desires if that is what we truly want on our list.

Maybe we desire a mate or partner in our life. We may desire relationships of one sort or another. We may have desires for people in our lives that share our common interests, hobbies, business, or intellectual pursuits. It is fantastic to know also that we may desire more opulence and wealth in our lives. The exercise of fear in any area of our lives will influence and spill over to all other areas or our lives that gives us happiness or contentment. If we desire bigger homes or mansions, luxury cars, sport cars, yachts, trips, furniture, clothing, more money, or anything that is of a material nature, that is absolutely fine and commendable.

Many people may have limiting beliefs or misinterpretations from sources that seem to give credence to such beliefs. This creates fear and chaos in people's lives. For example, many sources quote money or material things as the root of all evil and credit such principles to the biblical reference or other spiritual references. Rest assured that when we carefully examine such thoughts when referencing spiritual leaders, most of the time, they are being misconstrued or misinterpreted. The Bible does not teach that money is the root of all evil, but instead it specifically says in 1 Timothy 6:9-10: "But those determined to be rich fall into temptation and a snare and many senseless and harmful desires that plunge men into destruction and ruin. For the love of money is *a* root of all sorts of injurious things" (emphasis mine). Another verse also emphasizes the contrary. "I pray that in all things you continue to prosper and enjoy good health" (3 John 1:2).

It is clear here that it is not money itself that is wrong but that love of money can trap people into harboring wrong desires, and thus money can become a root of all sorts of injurious things. It is a general statement that we must examine with careful discernment. People will steal or sell things that are harmful to others. For example, a drug dealer will kill and corrupt others in order to profit from others' addictions. His desire for money is stronger and far more powerful than any love he may have for the good of others. And it is others' peace of mind and goodness that are sacrificed for the greed of a drug dealer. That is why most of them end up in jail or dead. People will create schemes to dispossess people of their property and valuables. Wars have been started in order to take away others' possessions and natural resources. People will gamble hard-earned money or sell possessions to continue gambling with the hope of quick riches, and in the process, they lose it all. People will prostitute themselves or their children for the sake of money. People will kidnap others and ask for ransom money in exchange. The list goes on and on.

Clearly it is not money in itself but the love of money over the love of people that is evil and a root of all sorts of injurious things. If we desire for money through honest and hard work or by creating a service or product that truly brings benefits to others, then it would be loving to do so. It is our moral obligation to provide such goods for others to benefit. We must never sacrifice other people's happiness and well-being for the sake of our own dreams, goals, and desires. If we do so, we are just acting out of fear and disregard for the value of life. We will never attain happiness by taking it away from others because by law we must reap what we have sown, and thus our happiness and well-being will be taken away from us.

JULIAN VALDERRAMA

It is paramount that we realize that unlimited wealth is our inheritance, for when we examine carefully how we are made, we understand that eternity is our nature. We previously established and suggested that with unlimited time and youth as a resource, then we can create whatever we desire without any fear or doubt.

## Dream Book and Dream Board

This step is paramount to continue establishing strong neural pathways of our dreams so you can get a burning desire. Creating a dream board and a dream book will help you focus and experience the things you desire in your mind as if you already had them. Previously, we discussed how the focused decision of plants powerfully affects particles of light so they become what they need. In the same manner, we must get or become what we think about most of the time.

Take the list you wrote of your dreams and desires and cut out pictures and place them on a big board on the wall. We can go online and find anything and everything we may desire. Pictures of cars, houses, furniture, home improvements, trips, yachts, etc. People smiling and enjoying time together can mean that you desire contentment or happiness. If it is freedom you desire, then think of things you would do if you had more free time and money. There is no limit as to what we can acquire and experience. We can have, be, and do whatsoever we desire.

Do the same thing with your dream book. Grab a three-ring binder, put pages in, and paste pictures. Nowadays people are looking at things on computers or cell phones. These things may be helpful, but we must remember that just like physical words will affect the molecular structure of water, physical pictures with words expressing our dreams can help us make them a reality. The vibrational frequencies of these pictures will permeate our neural pathways and our DNA. We will begin to transmit what we want 24/7 to the point of its physical manifestation. This is why it is so important that we have hard copies of pictures because of their specific transmission.

When we are observing images through computer screens, the pictures are not there in our reality. These images on a computer do not have the vibrational imprint as real pictures do. Real hard-copy images have energy, and they permeate the energy of our living space when we put them on a dream board or dream book. As we carry our dream book everywhere, its collective vibration will permeate our collective vibration. This detail will help us create faster.

It is also important that, if we can, we physically go out and touch and see our dreams and goals. Go look at the house. Go sit in the car. Put the clothing on. Experience the new living room. Drive by rich neighborhoods. Watch shows about people who have accomplished big dreams. This helps us become inspired by the fact that they have successfully created what they want in their lives. Other people's success stories must and will have a tremendous positive influence, for we can replicate and apply the same processes to our respective goals. We will also find that their focus of attention was entirely on one specific dream, with a corresponding burning desire for its achievement.

Napoleon Hill, in his books, had emphasized that we must focus on one thing at a time. We may start the process by building on the smaller dreams that we have now put in our dream book or dream board and progressively work on our bigger goals as they unfold in our present awareness.

## What to Expect

*Look! A sower went out to sow. As he was sowing, some seeds fell alongside the road, and the birds came and ate them up. Others fell on rocky ground where there was not much soil, and they immediately sprang up because the soil was not deep. But when the sun rose, they were scorched, and they withered because they had no root. Others fell among the thorns, and the thorns came up and choked them. Still others fell on the fine soil, and they began to yield fruit, this one 100 times more, that one 60, the other 30.*

—Matthew 13:3-8

Although this illustration was specifically pinpointed to the effects of Jesus's message about the kingdom of God, its connotations are closely relevant to our dreams and desires. Consider that we are constantly sowing seeds of desires in our minds. Whether it is for more money, a house, health, or fitness, these are specific neural-pathway imprints that will become fertile with proper care and nourishment. We will reap

JULIAN VALDERRAMA

fruitage and results based on those seeds of desires. There are warnings, though, that could prevent us from reaching the point of reaping fruit.

The first one is referred to seed being eaten up by birds of the field. This is a dire warning that we must take to heart; if we decide to put our dreams and goals where others can easily see them, we risk losing those seeds by having others steal our dreams or goals. How or why? Because most people are negative and have envy. People generally do not like others to become more successful than themselves. People will criticize and condemn others' goals, dreams, and accomplishments that themselves may not have. They will attribute them to wrong motives, selfishness, and greed. Or maybe they will testify to "facts" or "opinions" of other people's experiences and suggest that our endeavors will not work out.

For example, we may want to start a coffee shop. If we decide, out of excitement, to start telling others of our dream of having a successful coffee shop, they may start spewing negativity to us. They may say, "It won't work," "There's too much competition," "You are not educated enough," "I know of so and so, and they failed," etc. We must keep our dreams to ourselves and work on them almost like if it were our secret mission. Exposure to the enemy risks the success of the operation.

The second part of the illustration explains that our seed may fall in rocky ground without deep soil. It sprang up but the sun scorched it. The key here is that the root cannot go deep, and thus the plant that sprang up was exposed to the sun. We must build a deep foundation in ourselves if we wish to become successful in our endeavors. That is why the system of reading books, listening to audio, and attending meetings with like-minded people who support us is paramount. Building ourselves up as people and building our belief in ourselves is essential in having deep roots whenever we make the decision to achieve a desired outcome. As such, we will have every advantage to make it happen.

The sun's scorching heat also could represent our own negative thinking that may eat away at our dreams and goals. We already discussed that others' negative input will have a dire impact on our desires if we easily expose our dreams to them. But in reality, even if we decide to keep our goals to ourselves, the time will come when we have to face our own negative input as well as others. This will become evident as we progressively make our dreams come true. Our lack of pillars of belief in ourselves and in our ability to do it can burn up our plans. Also, as we experience challenges, we may get discouraged from persevering to reach our goals or dreams. We may get near the finish line and decide to just give up right before crossing it and attaining the prize.

It is paramount that we realize that continuing our personal development will enrich the fertile soil where our seeds will be allowed to grow and prosper. Let's be resolved to not let anyone steal our dreams, including ourselves. It is our moral obligation to do whatever it takes to acquire what we want.

The third part of the illustration explains to us that there are thorns that may surround our seed and prevent it from growing. The scriptural reference refers to thorns as anxieties of the world or distractions. The world is full of weapons of mass distraction. Our media, entertainment, hobbies, and other seemingly necessary things will rob us of the time and energy that may be needed to be focused on our dreams to accomplish them. Like previously discussed, the entire focus of all plants is to reach photosynthesis; in the same manner, we should strip from ourselves time stealers so we may have laser focus on our desires. We must remember that it is our ability to persevere and persist that will allow us, using our brains, to transmit a beam of frequency so powerful, it has no choice but to manifest in our present reality. It is the law, and it demands it.

## STEP 2: MAKE SOME COMMITMENTS

*The kingdom of the heavens is like a treasure, hidden in the field, that a man found and hid; and because of his joy, he goes and sells everything he has and buys that field. Again the Kingdom of the heavens is like a traveling merchant seeking fine pearls. Upon finding one pearl of high value, he went away and promptly sold all the things he had and bought it.*

—Matthew 13:44-46

Making commitments is another important key to acquiring that which we want. Our ability to make a solemn promise to achieve our dreams is required if we are to see its physical manifestations in our reality. The illustration states plainly that we must, in essence, be willing to give up and sacrifice whatever it takes to achieve our dreams. It is the law, and it demands for it. The person hid his treasure and then sold everything so he could buy the field where his treasure was. He sacrificed everything and was glad to do it. He knew it was necessary. The other showed the same industriousness, and thus the merchant, finally finding the fine pearl, promptly sold all the things he had to buy it.

Many people are aware of an interview that Larry King had with Bill Gates. In this interview he emphasized on 3 key ingredients:

1. *Being at the right place at the right time.* This means that as we establish a goal or dream, we will get people and circumstances that will help us get what we want. Like the illustration, we will finally find our fine pearl of high value, translated into an opportunity or a certain means to achieve what we want. We will see that we will be given every advantage to achieve what we desire by the universe. The physical universe will mirror to us exactly what we need. But just being at the right place at the right time is not enough.

2. *Depth of vision.* Bill Gates had depth of vision when it came to the potential of personal computers. We can readily see a track record of what kind of vision he had. Today he has become one of the richest people on Earth. "Where there is no vision, the people go unrestrained, but happy are those who observe the law" (Proverbs 29:18). It has been said that when people are not given a purpose, or something to do for that matter, they become depressed and frustrated. It is imperative that when we realize that once we transmit a vibration for our desires and a *how* presents itself, we must do our due diligence and research such opportunity. We may also be forced to see the potential of such opportunity so we may readily engage.

"Again the Kingdom of the heavens is like a dragnet let down into the sea and gathering fish of every kind. When it was full, they hauled it up onto the beach, and sitting down, they collected the fine ones into containers, but the unsuitable they threw away" (Matthew 13:47-48).

We may also find that we may have many opportunities falling right into our lap, and we may become confused or bewildered. At this point, like hauling many fish, we must do our due diligence and use our powers of perception based on our personal strengths and weaknesses, choose one single opportunity, and engage by focusing on that opportunity.

> *The wise man puts all his eggs in one basket and watches the basket.*

> —Andrew Carnegie

> *Your eyes should look straight ahead, yes, fix your gaze straight ahead of you. Smooth out the course of your feet, and all your ways will be sure. Do not incline to the right or the left. Turn your feet away from what is bad.*

> —Proverbs 4:25-27

These illustrative teachings are precise and to the point. We must know with certainty from the beginning that it is our perseverance and commitment to our dream through a singular means precisely what will create our success. We should also be aware of distracting opportunities that may come up along the way, so that, like thorns choking our seeds, other opportunities may not prove fatal to our already committed ways and have to start all over. We cannot jump from opportunity to opportunity thinking that one is better than the other. Our original seed will not get the proper watering and fertilizing and will not grow to produce fruitage.

3. *Massive immediate action.* It has been established already that we must be teachable and coachable. We must be willing to give up and sacrifice things if we are to achieve what we desire. "The lazy one says: 'There is a young lion in the road, a lion in the public square!' A door keeps turning on its hinges, and the lazy on his bed. The lazy one buries his hand in the banquet bowl, but he is too tired to bring it back to its mouth. The lazy one thinks he is wiser than seven people who give a sensible reply" (Proverbs 26:13-16).

What did King Solomon mean by the lazy one screaming lion in the market? This reference is understood to refer to the "lazy" person's negative thinking. His fear of trying to accomplish anything in his life overwhelms all logic and desired outcome. In his mind, through his

JULIAN VALDERRAMA

fear, a lazy person will picture in his mind every possible scenario that will make his pursuit fruitless. Therefore, the lazy person will stay in his bed, inactive, or will start a project (putting his hand in the food platter) but never finishes the task to the point and cannot bring the project to completion. And like a completely unteachable person, the lazy think themselves as wise; therefore, they feel like they know it all and will always have a negative opinion about everything and everyone.

> So if any one of you is lacking in wisdom, let him keep asking God, for he gives generously to all and without reproaching, and it will be given him. But let him keep asking in faith, not doubting at all, for the one who doubts is like a wave of the sea driven by the wind and blown about. In fact, that man should not expect to receive anything from Jehovah; he is an indecisive man, unsteady in all his ways.

—James 1:5

Here, the idea is rather simple, under the context of being committed and taking massive immediate action. The person who doubts will not have the positive vision of a positive outcome, but instead he will see negative outcomes. The doubtful person's imagination will prevent them from taking any possible action because they already decided it will not work.

The only hope we have if we have such mental disposition is to ask for wisdom, as suggested by the text. Our doubt will keep us in a state of indecision because we believe every path will lead to a "lion that will eat us alive." How could we ever finish any task or accomplish anything if we are in constant fear of failure?

This is not to put aside any acknowledgment that failure will happen. But we already discussed the true nature of failure. Most of the time, failure is inevitable, and as such, we will experience pain. But like a pregnant woman in labor, the woman will quickly forget her pain when she sees her child and the product of her pains. In the same manner, once we begin working hard and taking the necessary actions toward the fulfillment of our desired outcome, as long as we persevere regardless of failures, our energies will continue to be redirected toward its fulfillment as long as we keep our commitment.

We must remember that the energy of our decision and commitment is not attached to one specific how, but our ability to stick to our dreams while working toward them is what will manifest it into our reality. It is the energy that is being transmitted 24/7, day after day, week after week, month after month, year after year, that will continue to be at work until finally we receive what we want. The paradox is that we do need a how, or a means of receiving so we may open our hands to receive. We must make the decision to act and stick to that decision as if it is the only option. We must truly be willing to give it all we've got. It is the law, and it demands for it like the government demands taxes.

## STEP 3: BE A PRODUCT OF WHAT YOU ARE GIVING

This step has been defined as using the product or being a product of the product. Another way of saying this is being a product or a positive outcome of what we are selling. "A (positive) man brings out of his good treasure from his heart, but a (negative) person brings out of his bad treasure from his heart, for out of the heart's abundance the mouth speaks." (Luke 6:45) (wording was changed a little to convey the intention of the principle with objectivity, author is not trying to present anyone as wicked as the actual and original rendering denotes)

This teaching relates more closely to our ability to make money in a way that we absolutely love. We must get to the point of loving what we do or doing what we love. For example, if we examine the most common denominators of people who are ultrasuccessful, it is because they are doing what they absolutely love, and they also inherited the abilities necessary for such success. People are ultrasuccessful partly because they are really good at what they do. "Have you seen a man skillful at his work? He will stand before kings; he will not stand before common people" (Proverbs 22:29).

Athletes become super athletes because they love the sport they engage in. Artists love to perform in front of audiences or the camera. Chefs receive Michelin stars because they absolutely love what they do. Restaurateurs open magnificent, successful restaurants because they love to be hospitable, thus the term *hospitality business*. Scientists love to find out how things work, deconstructing them and reporting their findings. The point is being made clear to us today: It is not the money that will give us the satisfaction but finding out what our passion is and pursuing that with all our heart, strength, and desire. We must know and come to find out what our strengths and natural abilities are in order to access real wealth and prosperity.

We may at times wonder what exactly is our passion, but the reality is that the answer is always in front of us, right under our noses. Some people have found the answer by asking: What things do I absolutely cannot go without doing? There are many sources that can help us define this clearly, but there is an even greater shortcut. We can command the universe (God), what exactly is our brain wiring, our nature, to zero in on our passion, or what is the one thing we personally are really good at doing, in essence our gift to the world. .The answer will come up continually as we exercise our awareness of our thoughts, emotions, and the many people and circumstances that will mirror to us exactly the answer to what we have been asking.

To give you an example, one day I was speaking to my boss, who was the owner of a very successful high-end restaurant. I asked him if he liked what he did. My boss was well in his seventies, and with the enthusiastic, vivid Texan way, he said, "I love it, there is nothing else I would dream of doing." I asked him whether this was what he studied for. He said he was going to become a lawyer but that it did not pan out. He ended up serving tables at various restaurants and then becoming a manager. Then he finally opened the restaurant he always dreamed about.

Then there are others who are born into already successful family businesses but do not love doing business. They may have become financially successful but not necessarily love what they do.

I personally struggled to find my true niche in connection to my natural abilities. I come from a very humble background, with parents who, even to this day, struggle to make a living. I did not inherit money or wealth of any kind. I only had certain passions that were passed down to me. I did not finish college for lack of character and decision. I knew I loved reading, research, and science. Math came easy to me as well. I loved to build things and put together things like furniture. As a kid, I would spend hours and hours playing with my toy building blocks and build structures by deconstructing and reconstructing. I also came to find out that it was easy for me to get specific concepts that are hard to understand and that I was able to break them down to their very basic principles. I found that I was a good teacher, but I was not a great speaker.

I did find I was good at writing with persuasion and tactfulness. I had all these facts but did not know how to put them together in a way that would allow me to cash in on my strengths.

I asked my wife to help me transmit a frequency to find out what I could do to accomplish our desires and manifest what we wanted. Interestingly enough, up to this point, we have tried various avenues of pursuit but they all failed miserably. The main focus we had chosen, which we had been working on for almost four years came to a halt, and by circumstances beyond our control, the avenue we were pursuing was dismantled at the last minute. It had to do with a money-making opportunity, but certain government authorities, at the last second, came in and changed the whole program. I lost all interest in the program. I had invested a substantial amount of money with no real results. Something amazing did come from it. I now had powerful information that had improved the most important aspects of my life. Each facet of my life was better, thanks to something that seemed to be a failure.

My wife and I began to see a big picture of what I could do. She started to get feedback from the universe, telling us to write a book. She was watching movies and TV shows where there were successful writers being portrayed. I kept getting similar feedback. As such, I decided to write a book based on these principles of life and the fabric of the universe and how it relates to us, the biggest minority: the individual. Since childhood, I had read and reread the biblical reference with a very personal positive impact. I could see my life was better off than most people who did not follow specific principles contained there. But I also saw that there were people who applied such principles even though they did not read the biblical reference. Their life was also better, not because of a book, but because they knew, consciously or subconsciously, the principles of life that are inherent in the nature of humans as they relate to the physical universe and its laws. I found there were many philosophical theories that referred to these principles and paralleled those found in the bible.

Finally I came to study principles of success, as found through the many exclusive societies throughout the world. This instruction gave me a powerful realization: I knew that there was no way for people to achieve super wealth and success without readily applying certain principles in the universe. It was the law. I always understood that people who had what I wanted knew information I did not know. What would blow my mind away is that many people could not reconcile spiritual beliefs with philosophy and new discoveries in science. I did realize that there was enough common denominators found through these fields of study that, if expanded upon, would allow us to see a powerful way to learn our personal abilities and exploit them. I wanted to write this book mainly because it is a way for me to transmit a frequency for the desires I want. I also realize that this may not be the ultimate way for me to get that which my wife and I desire, but it feels right, and I feel good doing this. It comes with certain ease, in my opinion, to write this book.

So we encourage the reader that, by all means, please do the same and ask for an answer of what it is that you do better than anyone. It is said that sometimes, when we do things that we find easy and fun to do, we believe others can do the same things much easily or as easily as we are able to do it. The reality is, that is not the case. Our natural abilities are unique in themselves, but it is true that it is through perseverance and persistence that we must exploit such abilities. Our potential will continue to be untapped if we do not exercise our innate faculties and abilities.

This is true success and commitment: that we love what we do while doing what we love. That at the same time we are using our innate deep abilities, we are creating value for others and enriching their lives. Knowing that it is our lives that are also made prosperous and happy will give us fulfillment and appreciation for life; it will help us to continue finding joy and passion for our individuality. Being a product of what we are giving means also not selling out for the sake of profit. We cannot succeed and truly be happy if we are giving or selling something that we do not have a strong, powerful belief in. We must at least know that it is a good service to others. But to reach ultrasuccess, we must focus on something we absolutely love. That is the true commitment that we must practically apply, for by asking the universe or God—take your pick—we will find the essence of what we are designed to do. It must happen; by law you must get an answer, but the choice to pursue will be up to you.

## STEPS 4 AND 5: FIND A PROSPECT
## AND SHARE THE PROGRAM

This is an interesting definition of action: *Prospect* is defined as "the possibility or likelihood of some future event occurring." Synonyms to this word are *hope, expectation, odds,* and *probability,* among others. Another definition explains that it is a person regarded as likely to succeed or as a potential customer, client, etc. The verb form is also rather interesting. *Prospect* in verb form means "to search for mineral deposits in a place, especially by means of experimental drilling and excavation." It denotes the idea of exploring, surveying, scouting, and inspecting, among others.

> *Into whatever city or village you enter, search out who in it is deserving, and stay there until you leave. When you enter the house, greet the house hold. If the house is deserving, let the peace you wish it come upon it; but if it is not deserving, let the peace from you return upon you. Wherever anyone does not receive you or listen to your words, ongoing out of that house or that city, shake the dust off your feet.*

—Matthew 10/11-14

People believe that they must be skillful salespersons to achieve what they want. Like an orchestra of perfect symphony, selling skills will add to your abilities and are useful, but not necessary. A prospect is just that—a possibility, a potential. When offering our program through networking or other means of advertising, we must know what nature or what the laws of physics will do when we put our name or product to work.

> *The Kingdom of the heavens is like a mustard grain that a man took and planted in his field. It is in fact, the tiniest of all the seeds, but when it has grown, it is the largest of the vegetable plants and becomes a tree, so that the birds of heaven come and find lodging among its branches. The Kingdom of the heavens (our personal desire outcome) is*

JULIAN VALDERRAMA

*like leaven that a woman took and mixed with three large measures of flour until the whole mass was fermented.*

—Matthew 13/31-33

Let's examine what is being implied here by these illustrations. First, we must know that when we are talking to individuals, in reality we are searching out those who are "deserving" of our services. Since it is suggested that we may have a strong belief in the benefits of what we have to offer, then, like mining and digging for gold, we will find many people that will say no to us, our services or products. Our intention, and not the intention of selling one specific person, but that we desire to find those who want and desire what we have will helps us to continue and persevere in moving on to the next prospect. This puts things into perspective, for we will just shake the dust off our feet whenever we find those who have no interest.

Second, the interesting part is that a powerful physical law is being implemented here through this process. Our transmission of frequency will begin to permeate our matrix reality, thus every time we do a presentation of services or products, the other person's exposure to such things is also a broadcast of frequency. In essence, they are helping us to transmit our desired outcome regardless of their response. It will exponentially help us to bring it into our reality. This is why the more times we expose our product to others, regardless of their response, the faster our desires will reach the tipping point to its physical manifestation. Like leaven fermenting a whole mass, the collective transmission of all the brains will continue to permeate the ether until it reaches critical mass. This is what Nikola Tesla suggested in relation to the "inexorable agents that prevent a mass from changing suddenly its velocity." It is the thinking that will eventually change the present circumstances to the desired outcome—nothing else does it. The hundredth monkey effect will kick in, and our energy of our desired outcome will land in other people's brains, and eventually we will absolutely find those who desire what we are offering.

This is why we must be resolved to continue in our ability to persist in what we have to offer, since it is not our skills, but the collective transmission of what we desire that will create it. Knowing this by nature will help us to know that, regardless of how many failures we have or refusals that we get, such responses are irrelevant in the grand scheme of things, or the systematic and order of things according to the universe. Napoleon Hill said that we must dig through tons of dirt just to find a few ounces of gold. By all means, let's find our gold by digging deeper.

So like a tiny mustard grain that we plant, by watering and fertilizing of our seed, we share the program with as many people we can until that seed becomes a big tree where others find shade and other benefits.

## STEP 6: ANSWERING QUESTIONS AND OVERCOMING OBJECTIONS, FOLLOWING UP, AND FOLLOWING THROUGH.

*Look! A sower went out to sow. As he was sowing, some seeds fell alongside the road, and the birds came and ate them up. Others fell on rocky ground where there was not much soil, and they immediately sprang up because the soil was not deep. But when the sun rose, they were scorched, and they withered because they had no root. Others fell among the thorns, and the thorns came up and choked them. Still others fell on the fine soil, and they began to yield fruit, this one 100 times more, that one 60, the other 30."*

—Matthew 13:3-8

This text was previously discussed in connection to our seeds as dreams, but it also relates closely to what we can expect from individuals whom we may come in contact with. For example, we realize that most people may say no and show no interest, but since they send out a transmission as they contemplate what we desire, then we want to buy as much time as we can from them. Skillfully answering questions and overcoming objections to have them think about our program in a positive light will help us to plant seeds in their minds of their own dreams in connection with our desires and services. By following up and following through, we can continue to water and fertilize those seeds so that we may expand upon that vibration of frequency.

## What to Expect

The illustration of birds coming to eat up the seeds will help us realize that we will absolutely find those who have interest, or at least, consider what we offer. The reality is that sooner or later, they may change their own mind through their own cognition or from others' negative influence. Either way, it does not matter.

Others may begin to engage in our program but have no real deep interest. Their interest may just be polite, superficial. Others may come up and become excited about our program, but others' opinions will supersede their desire to be truly committed. Finally, as we persist in marketing our program, it is the law that we will continue to find those who will give us the fruitage we desire. It is our desire to find those who will replicate our efforts through business relationships. "No man will make a great leader who wants to do it all himself or get all the credit for doing it." (Andrew Carnegie) The hope of pursuing this system of following through and following up is to create a master mind where, through a common interest, we can exponentially reach ultrasuccess. It is paramount that we realize that, just like Andrew Carnegie, who had a master mind of twenty people to achieve what he did, we can also scientifically replicate such success.

## STEPS 7 AND 8: START THEM RIGHT BY PLUGGING THEM INTO THE SYSTEM

Our goal at this point of the program is, once we have replicated this process and created a master mind for our desired result, to lead by example and to plug our master mind into these systems. What systems? Consider that in the biblical reference, Jesus first chose a group of people, mainly twelve disciples, so that his efforts in spreading his teachings would be replicated. The replication would be perpetuated through the next generations. This process has been replicated and continues to be repeated and engaged by many successful companies and organizations. We are looking for those who will commit to their dreams and goals, not just have a superficial interest.

Reading books, listening to audio, attending events with like-minded individuals while participating in giving and receiving recognition are all necessary for progressive milestones of success. It is this first system that we must hand down to replicate, so once we find fine pearls who will engage in their dreams by means of our chosen field or program of services or products, they also become successful. But first, we must be reading books and listening to audio every day before our master mind does. First, we must attend educational meetings and personal development seminars to have our master mind do the same. And finally, we must first engage in giving proper recognition for their success by making every possible effort to make our master mind successful. Then truly we will become successful because what we focus on expands, and that which we nourish and strengthen must grow first and prosper before we can reap fruitage. Zig Ziglar said, "You can get everything in life you want if you just help enough people get what they want."

The second system is replicating this eight-step pattern of success by sharing this with our master mind. It is paramount that we acknowledge and give positive recognition to our master mind's goals and dreams, and by doing so, we will get what we want faster. It is important that we help them make a commitment to their goals and dreams so they may focus and achieve them. We easily root for our favorite sports teams, and therefore it is insanity if we don't cheer for those who are close to us in a harmonious master mind. It is imperative that we help our master mind group to find their innate abilities so they may find their niche and accomplish their dreams and goals. We must also find the time and energy to support our master mind in prospecting and marketing their chosen field of endeavors.

Finally, it is paramount that the master mind meetings continue to be built upon a unanimous agreement, where everyone promises to engage in this system of reading books and listening to audio, which helps the master mind be built up by information and instruction. Proper recognition of each other's dreams must be positive and applied to the successes of each individual member. What must happen is that the master mind will get together in harmony in the spirit of love and compassion for each other. A real brotherhood of love will perpetuate positively throughout the master mind, and everything they do will have success.

JULIAN VALDERRAMA

## Skipping All the Nitty-Gritty Work

The details of creating a master mind, a brotherhood where people will support us and each other's dreams and goals in the spirit of love, can seem to be daunting. Not to worry, there are many organizations in the world that have successfully found preestablished niches of people who do just what we have talked about. We may search the Internet and find specific interest groups based on our personal likes. But to create a powerful master mind based on information that is timely and truly beneficial can be daunting.

Remember, understanding whom we must listen and take counsel from is a very important task. What books will our master mind read? What audio material will our master mind listen to? What personal development programs will we attend? In this book, the reader will be pointed to what I was personally invited to plug into. A system founded by elite members of society, ultrasuccessful people who have real-time physical manifestations that prove they have mastered these techniques. I can testify that this system has nourished me and thousands of others to be trees planted by fresh and clear waters. Our lives are better for it.

This system was brought to me due to my personal transmission of energy. Through people and circumstances, I am now privileged to be mentored by incredibly successful people. I have strong belief in its leaders, and I have come to find out that they are people of strong integrity. The company is filled with positive, enthusiastic people who also come to know the integrity and power of this system. Like-minded people are drawn to each other. There is an overabundant exchange, and thus the compensation of those who engage in this system get tremendous value from its core values. The most important value and asset that we will derive once engaged is that we will develop a powerful belief in ourselves. This will be touched on in a later chapter.

# CHAPTER 8

# The Alchemy of the Universe

"Most truly I say to you, unless a grain of wheat falls
to the ground and dies, it remains just one grain; but if
it dies, it then bears much fruit. Whoever is fond of his
life destroys it, but whoever hates his life in this world
will safeguard it . . . What you sow is not made alive
unless it first dies."

—John 12:24-25, 1 Corinthians 15:36

THE WORD *ALCHEMY* originates from an interesting belief
from medieval times. It was thought to be the practice of
chemistry where matter could be transformed and given a new essence.
The main reason people would pursue this was because they wanted
to learn how to transform any metal into gold. Whether this was truly
done or not, it is mostly considered a myth. And although considered a
myth from the past, scientists have been able to apply a form of science
through chemistry by recreating gold from other metals. But why is this
chapter named after a myth, now a proven scientific process?

Let's consider that the opening scriptural reference is pointing out
to a fantastic understanding of the nature of the universe, regarding our
progressive realization of our dreams and goals. This chapter is designed
to help us become aware that once we activate a seed of creation based
on our biggest desires, milestones of experiences must happen that will
let us know exactly where we stand in connection with the progressive
realization of our dreams.

# WHAT HAPPENS AFTER MAKING A DECISION

We have talked about what is necessary to make our dreams and goals come true. We have discussed the science behind the power of our minds. We have discussed what happens when we transmit a vibration based on our desires. We have also described what happens to the universe and the etheric realm and how our dreams are accomplished by the influence of the universe. We have also talked about the attitude we must develop to be able to get what we desire. We learned how faith plays the most important role.

But here is something that is incredibly rare. I have been personally exposed to incredible amounts of information and have only seen glimpses of the concept. I have examined thousands of pages in books, thousands of hours of audio material, from teaching systems scientifically designed to personal mentorships from multimillionaires, to books written by ultrasuccessful people. This following concept is touched on briefly or discussed slightly throughout these sources. But most don't see this lesson because most people, in reality, do not want to hear it. Subconsciously, it shuts people off even though it is one of the most wonderful principles of success that will make everything we want happen faster and faster. I know for myself that it took me more than five years to really grasp this concept. It seems I was just not ready to receive its lessons. I feel it is mind blowing and exciting to know what this new ounce does to our collective vibration. But what does it do?

In essence, what is happening is that the universe plays blacksmith, chemist, and metal refiner. It takes our being and ignites a fire so intense that it infuses us with power beyond what is normal. The fire is so intense under us that it brings scummy dross out from our entire essential energy to turn us into that which we most desire. Like the mythological alchemy, this process will absolutely turn us into precious, refined, and pure gold. The irony is that it only happens when our decisions are destroyed and killed, and like a seed that falls to the ground and dies, only then will it sprout and spring with life and fruitage. We must let go of what we already may have accomplished so far, and as John D. Rockefeller aptly put it, "Don't be afraid to give up the good to go for the great."

# THE IRONY: THE UNIVERSE CONVINCES
## YOU THAT IT IS IMPOSSIBLE

We must pay close attention, and let's be aware. We now know that it is our transmission of vibration that creates what we want. There is an irony to which we must be self-aware and attentive that pervades the universe. Yes, it will bring you people, circumstances, and events that bring you closer to what you want. The question then, is this: What exactly is the nature of those people, circumstances, or events?

## The Nature of the First Set of PCES:
### "Being at the right place at the right time"

Consider that the acronym almost sounds like the word *pieces*. It stands for "people, circumstances, events, and situations." So just like pieces of a puzzle, the universe will bring you people, circumstances, events, and situations that puts together our dreams and makes them come true.

The first PCES, like a miracle, are presented into something that will speak to us so deeply as the solution, idea, or highway to the result that we are looking to get. It will also fill us with hope, motivation, and energy that drives us forward with full confidence to our desired outcome. It makes us decide to follow it to its conclusion. We will feel like luck or God is on our side, holding our hand, telling us that it is ours. What is happening, in essence, is that the laws of magnetic attraction are being made powerfully active in our seed of desire based on our decision to create what we desire. But then the irony of all ironies kicks in:

## The nature of the second set of PCES:
### "Have we been convinced that it is impossible?"

The irony, it seems (let's pay close attention), is that the universe seems to begin to betray you. Suddenly PCES beyond our control begin to destroy our hope, motivation, and energy. In essence, this second set of PCES begin to eat away our dream or goal. They start to give us fears and doubts, and they begin to convince us that what we want is impossible to achieve. At this point, we become confused, frustrated, and wonder whether we have made the right choices. This is where most people quit.

But since this phenomenal concept must happen, as it is integrated and programmed into the hardware and fabric of space, how can we ever accomplish what we want? This is the great irony.

This is that intense fire. It is the key that will absolutely make our dreams come true. We must know and be self-aware that once this seemingly negative force begins to occur, we come to the threshold where we decide to continue our pursuit, regardless of what seemingly negative situations have come up. We either decide to follow through somehow anyway or quit altogether. This is the universe playing alchemist. This is the universe trying to rid of our scummy dross, the worthless qualities and mentalities that are holding us back. Nikola Tesla called them "the inexorable agents which prevent a mass from changing suddenly its velocity" that "would likewise resist the force of the new knowledge until time gradually modifies thought."

It must be clarified and precisely stated now that what we must realize that our decision to continue or quit is not connected to the *idea*, the *how*, or the means of achievement that we may have chosen to achieve what we want. For example, we may decide we want financial freedom. As we continue to transmit the frequency of "financial freedom," we will meet with the lucky circumstances that tells us, "This is the how." It could come in the form of a business opportunity, if what we want is a measure of financial prosperity. It could be that a really great relationship begins to develop, if our focus of transmission is companionship. The irony is that this how or means of achieving the desired outcome will just fall apart many times due to reasons beyond our control. It may also cost us an incredible amount of resources and energy, thus we will meet with feelings of great disappointment and may feel like it was all a waste. What we must know once we have arrived at this point in the journey is that all the energy that we have given to this point is being reinvested into its final outcome. Like a high-interest investment account, it will continue to accrue till it matures, and thus we will cash in on its dividends. This is the decision we must reestablish.

We must notice that these unlucky circumstances and situations do not prevent us or stop us from transmitting what we desire. It only challenges our faith, perseverance, and ability to continue focusing our desire. This is why most people quit. It is because we may not realize that it is not our dreams that are being crushed, but our ability to persevere and ability to hold on to our vision. For every action, there is an equal and opposite reaction. It will either help us focus on what we want more intensely, or we may decide to focus on the lack and the absence of our desire. It will either help us transmit a collective vibration of energy so powerful that it will absolutely permeate our universe to make what we want happen, or it will completely shut us down and completely convince us that it is essentially impossible. Our decision must be reaffirmed.

The scriptural references gives some powerful illustrations of this concept. The story of Joseph, the eleventh son of Jacob, son of Isaac, son of Abraham, is such story. If the reader has not personally read it, it is certainly encouraged that you stop reading at this moment and read that account for posterity. It is found in Genesis chapters 37 through 47. The illustration will become a vivid, powerful mental lesson that will kick in to remind us to continue, once we find ourselves in need of it. The mind pictures and lessons will become powerful arsenal, for when the time comes, we can engage in energetic combat and win.

## Joseph's PCES

Joseph seemed to have been favored by God himself. God had given him approval by giving him the ability to interpret dreams. This did not go well with his brothers, since they kept making fun of him, to the point of envying him so much that they started to hate him. Their hatred toward their brother was so intense that they conspired to kill him. Although they did not follow through with their scheme, they ended up selling him into slavery.

On a side note, this account really emphasized some points about our dreams and goals. Once we make a decision, we must be careful not to describe what we want to unfavorable ears. They will hate us for it and envy our determination to pursue that which we want. This could be really detrimental to our mental stability and our ability to sustain a frequency for long durations of time without any resistance.

Another point is realizing that we may have come into a place where we feel that a lucky star is shining over us; thus, like Joseph, it will also seem like we were given really favorable PCES. Joseph was filled with hope and dreams since he was little. He was told that they were favored by God and his angels and was promised incredible wealth and power. Joseph's ability to receive dreams from God and interpret them does seem to have given him ample validation of his blessed status. The irony is that for years, he finds himself receiving PCES that begin to frustrate him and confuse him.

This in a very real way, will absolutely happen to us. We are all endowed with very specific innate abilities. The universe will match us with PCES that can exploit and train those innate abilities so that we can achieve our ultimate potential. Therefore we will receive what we ultimately want much faster. The fascinating lesson here is that we do not receive what we want until our training is completed. Once we have learned the necessary powerful lessons in our personal lives, then and only then will we qualify to receive the bigger dream. This is again the universe playing alchemist, turning us into refined gold.

The Nature of the Third Set of PCES: "A taste of success"

The nature of the third PCES will fill us with hope and happiness. They will absolutely with 100 percent certainty through the universe wet our appetite with success, triumph, and a measure of affluence. Then the compulsive force kicks in once again. A repetitive exchange in our awareness begins to be presented to us, for the events and the nature of the second set of PCES and the third set of PCES begin to program us. This takes place in our energetic blueprint. Thus, back and forth like a tennis ball, we are tossed from what seems like failure or dissatisfaction, to a measure of success and prosperity, and the process repeats itself.

Joseph ends up working and managing a political branch; the scriptural reference called it Potiphar's house. At this point in his life, things seem to be turning around.

"But Jehovah was with Joseph. As a result, he became successful and was put over the house of his master, the Egyptian. And his master saw that Jehovah was with him and that Jehovah was making everything that he did successful." (Genesis 39/2, 3)

But just when everything seems to be working out just fine, everything collapses right under his feet. Potiphar's wife becomes romantically interested in him and tempts Joseph to commit adultery. Joseph, doing the right thing and realizing it would be wrong to take advantage, fled. This backfired on him, and he was put in prison under the wife's false accusation of attempted rape.

In the same manner, it will seem that although our success is imminent and we have arrived at something that is good, the universe again tries to convince you it is impossible. Through PCES beyond our personal control, everything seems to not work out or just plainly fall apart when we think we are ahead. The irony kicks us out of our comfort zone.

The Nature of the Fourth Set of PCES: "The green light to failure"

This is the paradox of paradoxes. One of the ironies of irony. This will really test us and compel us into extreme confusion. It will absolutely happen at one point, that when we get the green light to pursue a course of action, we will be convinced by the universe that it will get us to our destination. Thus we are forced to take massive and immediate action. This is acting in harmony with our faith in connection to our desire, and we know it has to happen. We plunge into what is presented to us through fortunate circumstances, but then it happens: it blows up right in our face and we are made to fail through PCES beyond our control. (Bummer!) The unfortunate part is that it happens when we feel that success is already ours. We will feel like we have almost achieved what we want, like a runner who has exhaustedly and progressively run toward the finish line but steps on a rock and completely loses the race because of a sprained ankle.

We must accept that this is not an exception but the rule. We will absolutely be given the green light beyond a shadow of doubt; moreover, the nature of the PCES will absolutely disappoint us beyond belief. An example of this energetic concept, or alchemy, is found in the scriptural reference in Judges 20:17-35. This account is much more obscure and not as commonly known as the account of Joseph, but it still drives a powerful point home. I would certainly encourage you to read it for posterity. In this account, the nation of Israel finds itself having a civil war. One of the twelve tribes of Israel, the Benjaminites, had allowed a small city to go unpunished. Its citizens had gang-raped a traveling fellow countryman's wife. Not only did they do so, but they abused her for a whole night to the point of death.

The nation was consulted by this man, and finally the nation decided to punish the perpetrators by having them put to death, but the guilty tribe did not want to give up the men. The nation had a system of support where they were able to access God's counsel and approval whenever they felt the need to engage a campaign. This time, they were about to start a civil war and wanted to know from God whether they should begin such a course of action.

*They got the green light!* As we read the account, the nature of the fourth set of PCES kicks in. Even though they had Jehovah's approval and the green light, they lost the first battle. Confused and frustrated, they asked Jehovah once more, and lo and behold, they get the *green light again!* Ironically, they lose the battle this second time too. After the third time, the nation "wept and sat before Jehovah, and they fasted on that day until the evening and offered up burnt sacrifices and communion offerings before Jehovah."

The third request for favor was finally endowed with success. Although this may be an extreme case, this civil war does teach us a valuable lesson. It is our ability to persevere relentlessly that will enable us to conquer that which we are trying to achieve. "Keep on asking and it will be given you, keep on seeking and you will find, keep on knocking and it will be opened to you." (Interestingly, on a side note, the word *Israel* means "persevere" or " contender.")

It is when this begins to occur that we must acknowledge that we are being tested and refined. We must let our resolve intensify and use the negative emotions we will experience to focus. This will project nuclear explosions from our transmission of energy to create what we want once we decide to use such amplified power to our benefit.

### The Nature of the Fifth Set of PCES: "We Win!"

"But Jehovah continued with Joseph and kept showing loyal love to him and granting him favor in the eyes of the chief officer of the prison. So the chief officer of the prison put Joseph in charge of all the prisoners in the prison, and everything that they were doing there, he was the one having it done." (Genesis 39/21,22)

Ironically, God seemed to have allowed this seemingly unfortunate event happen to Joseph. At some point, Joseph's apparently useless ability to interpret dreams comes in handy. As he interpreted the dreams of the Pharaoh's chief cupbearer and chief baker, it seemed that a lucky coincidence has now come to his aid, for an opportunity to be set free. Joseph, in faith, asks the cupbearer to remember him once he is out and to give good word of Joseph so that he may be freed.

Again, ironically, once the cupbearer had resumed his position before Pharaoh, he forgets about Joseph and his interpretation of his dream. But finally, at the end of two full years, Pharaoh had a dream which only Joseph could interpret, which caused Joseph to be freed from prison. Joseph then gets appointed to a position only second to Pharaoh, with authority over all the kingdom. Overnight, he went from being a lowly prisoner to the second most powerful person of that nation.

But why would the universe make us go through such personal ordeals or seemingly negative situations when we ask and transmit the frequency of our desires as we are exercising our faith? Why do we go from one negative situation to a measure of peace, to only experience the same thing again? Why must we go through things like a hamster uselessly running on its wheel? Why did Joseph have to wait another *two years* after using his miraculous ability before he saw any real results? Was God being stubborn, unfair, and just plain mean, as if to say, "You will get it when I say so"?

The answers has to do with the nature of energy in the field of particle physics defined in time and space. These occurrences remove what is being referred by Tesla as the "inexorable agents which prevent a mass from changing suddenly its velocity." God, in this instance, was molding Joseph and making him go through rigorous training, refining him like metal, drawing out scummy dross by putting him into an intense fire to turn him into what he needed to become: the second most powerful ruler of that known world.

As we continue to read the account, Pharaoh's dream came true. The seven years of prosperity and the seven years of famine occurred, at which point Joseph was then, and only then, capable of fulfilling what was before his future assignment. Joseph successfully managed to fulfill his role and saved the lives of millions of inhabitants. Entire nations benefited from Joseph's experience of being able to handle somebody else's goods during his training.

*The person faithful in what is least is faithful in much,*
*and the person unrighteous in what is least is unrighteous in*
*much. Therefore, if you have not proved yourselves faithful*
*in connection with the unrighteous riches, who will entrust*
*you with what is true?*

—Luke 16:10-12

The point is clear and simple: what we currently are, or our current vibrational set point, cannot possibly receive that which collective energetic vibration is much higher. Our dreams and goals, when bigger than ourselves, will modify the inexorable agents and remove the things that are preventing us from achieving or becoming what we desire. It is imperative that we become what we must become to receive that which we desire and learn the valuable lessons along the way as they are being presented to us. In essence, we do become what we think about most of the time, but it will take some time.

We cannot hope to receive what we want tomorrow if its energetic blueprint and field is at a much higher frequency. It is only our relentless transmission that creates it. So as long as we perceive that we must persevere in holding on to its constant transmission, then and only then we will receive what we want. The spill effect from the vibrational creation from the etheric field is what is going to make it happen. If it were to happen when we think is more convenient, it would just fall apart. This is why it happens many times that people who win the lotto and acquire massive amounts of money all at once end up just as broke or worse than before after about five years. It has to do with the person we become and not the destination. It is not the money or goal in itself that transform us, but the lessons we learn along the journey that qualifies us to receive what we have been asking for all along.

## Tying the PCES together

It is of utmost importance that we realize that like a game being played, we must know what is expected from each of the players. We must realize what the rules are and how the game is played. The milestones in our route to success have now been laid out. There are not many books that have codified such principles and laws of nature. Since such is the case, it is our moral obligation to know how to play the game better so that we may improve upon it. We now know what is to be expected once we make the decision to direct our personal energies towards a campaign of achievement. We must know that the bigger our dreams, then the better we must become for it. The lessons we learn on our way to what we want will propel us to infinite heights.

If we sit back and think of people who are ultrasuccessful based on their personal physical manifestations in the real, physical world, then we can readily observe a powerful movement and shift in those people's minds. Let's think for a second about the person who has billions of dollars of assets at his disposal. What do they have? What do they do? What do they wear? Where do they live? What are their lifestyles? Some of these people have hundred-million-dollar yachts. They buy super sport cars that cost hundreds of thousands of dollars. When traveling, they reserve suites and rooms that cost anywhere from $10,000 to $40,000 a night. They spend $400,000 dollars a year in traveling expenses, not including the price of their private jet ($40,000,000). How much does it cost to dock and maintain a yacht? Are they buying $5,000 shirts, suits, and ties? Do they live in thirty-million-dollar homes?

Have we ever really sat down and thought about what these people dream about? They are already there where many people would love to be, but what else do they dream about? What are their goals once they have reached such heights? These questions are not about material things or about buying what our perception considers to be expensive, but this is about our ability to sustain a vibration for a prolonged period of time to its manifestation. It is a powerful scientific observation of empirical evidence to us when we are able to observe these people's efficacy in materializing what they desire. It is wise to remember that our current vibrational set point may be far from such things. And as such, the inexorable agents that need to change through these various firewalls may indicate that a rigorous amount of energy must be exerted to its final completion. The person who is two hundred pounds overweight must refine their entire character and habits of behavior and essentially remove inexorable agents that have created their undesirable situation if their dream is a healthy and strong body. The person who is a criminal and is in dire need of reform must also refine their energetic blueprints if they are to become exemplary citizens. Regardless of the goal or dream, much energy must be exerted.

The story of Joseph illustrates this point well. He had to go over a number of firewalls to finally get to the point where he qualified to receive such a position of responsibility and stewardship. This is not to say that every goal or dream is just going to be some arduous process where our sanity will be tested to its limits. It is considering the gap between vibrational blueprints that require the manifestations of our desires. It is the difference of personality from the person we are to the person we want to become. A person who is two hundred pounds overweight cannot hope to accomplish to become Mister Universe in the next couple months. It will certainly take more considerable effort than the person who is just fifty pounds overweight. The person who is born in the projects and grows amid crime and injustice can certainly become a lawyer or a successful politician, the same way a person who is born in a privileged family can. The starting points of these examples are two different spectrums, but one will have to exert much more energy than the other in comparison. Either way, both can eventually get there.

It is an exciting journey to know that we can become whatsoever we desire. To have, be, or do whatsoever we desire is an absolute certainty. But is there a way to know for sure that what we may choose to acquire is truly the best for us? We have all heard of the miserable lawyer who wanted to open a restaurant. His real dream was never accomplished. Or the young man who was groomed to acquire a huge business enterprise, just to forfeit all to become a Formula 1 racer. The doctor whose parents pushed her to become so, when in reality her true passion was to become an actress. The successful business owner who inherited wealth, but his dream really was to explore the world through the field of archeology. We get the point.

## HOW TO UNFOLD YOUR OWN PERSONAL LEGEND

*O the depth of God's riches and wisdom and knowledge!*
*How unsearchable his judgments are and beyond tracing*
*out his ways are!*

—Romans 11:33

*Call out to me and I will answer you and readily tell you great incomprehensible things that you have not known.*

—Jeremiah 33:3

At this point, it is the desire of the author to advise the reader of the possibility of letting go consciously to what they think is the best goal or dream and what isn't, let me explain why. Maybe at this point, you are already integrating this knowledge and looking to apply it in your personal life. I know I did, and I still do. We have arrived at a point where I feel there is power beyond what we have talked about. At this point, I will be going off on a tangent and express my personal opinion on limited information, and thus acknowledge I could be 100 percent wrong. But maybe not.

As we have been discussing carefully how the universe responds to our transmission of frequency, we have also acknowledged that this is nothing more than what has been discerned in the past as the power of prayer. When we personally express our prayers to god or a divine entity, we are only in essence transmitting our frequencies to the universe in an instant through all time and space. Our request for favor, our gratitude, and our grievances are all being simultaneously heard. And by law, we must be acknowledged and given to us a personal answer. Even if we are an atheist or agnostic, we can still take to heart that we can command the universe to make what we want happen as if we were powerful gods ourselves. Did not Christ's consciousness give evidence to this statement?

"For truly I say to you, if you have faith the size of a mustard grain . . . nothing will be impossible for you. . . . [W]hoever tells this mountain, 'Be lifted up and thrown into the sea,' and does not doubt in his heart but has faith that what he says will happen, he will have it happen" (Matthew 17:20, Mark 11:23).

This may be controversial and hard to accept, but the laws of physics tells us that it is so, and it will continue to be proven by present and future empirical evidence. I also dare to say that the past statement has been proven behind the scenes, but like powerful secrets, it will only be revealed to those who are privileged.

I have also acknowledged that I have been using the reference of "universe" and "God" as parallels but never suggesting that they are

JULIAN VALDERRAMA

one and the same. This is where theological philosophies may start to be interpreted, and I do not feel adequate or equipped with enough experience or knowledge to say otherwise. But let's consider for a second this question: Is there a conscious creator outside these mechanisms integrated in the fabric of time and space?

Like a sort of infinite genius who wanted to replicate his consciousness to care for life and thus created energy, frequency, vibration, time and space. A creator who completely integrated in us the ability to create in our lives just like himself, for our own pleasure and expression of that life.

To illustrate this concept further, could we suppose and imagine for a second: an ingenious man who successfully creates a financial empire, where he successfully delegates and replicates positions of duty and movements to accomplish what he wants, all the while putting it together to be self-sustaining. In essence, is that exactly what God had done? Or are we just plugged into a massive computer matrix that responds and reacts to every form of input and output of personal energy? The question then must be acknowledged; is the creator the founder of the enterprise or matrix, or is the creator those things in themselves? I guess whichever way we try to look at it, we cannot currently get a real answer. At least I am not personally aware of an answer. I believe atheists and scientists got it right in the sense that a complex mechanism must have a creator. Thus if we find a toothpick in the middle of nowhere, like a desert, we would understand that a thing as simple as that toothpick must have an original creator. But the other side of the coin is that since the creator is infinitely more complex than the creation, then who created such complex creator? The question also applies to scientists who believe it was the universe that created us; but then the same argument would stand: The universe in its infinite complexity created us, then who created the universe? If it's a thing that created us through blind chance, then who created the universe through blind chance? And thus the question will repeat itself, like a never-ending flip of the coin where you will always get either heads or tails, and no other answer is possible. Like the weird illusion of infinity when we look at a mirror while holding another mirror in front of it, reflecting itself ever forward through infinity. The argument is valid, since we cannot know for sure what is the answer. Therefore we should not create a hang-up, as if to say, "Since there is no answer, I cannot live out my life."

We can only deal with the facts. So whether you believe in a creator of the universe or the universe as God himself, it does not matter. This is because our prayers will always be answered and we are always transmitting energy vibrating at different frequencies. Whether our transmission comes from our DNA, our brain or mind, or our entire consciousness and energetic blueprint, we know for a fact that vibrating is exactly what we do. Thus we know precisely what we can improve upon. This is why I personally believe in Nikola Tesla's statement that we have the moral obligation to achieve immortality, for it is an aching need in our world. Death is the ultimate enemy, and we must not let it win. This is the will of God or the universe, as you must take your pick.

This takes us to this next powerful concept, which I must admit I have personally experienced at least once, and it has given me happiness beyond belief.

## Letting Go of All Decision Making

How can we suggest to leave out all decision making? We are not implying that you should leave out all thinking to someone else, but like the opening scripture suggested, we must acknowledge the unsearchable power of the known universe. The scriptural reference has given us some powerful suggestions. In my opinion, it is the secret of secrets. Why? Because once we acknowledged that the infinite universe is all there is as the apex of creation, then we can ask it to examine and decide an infinite outcome for our best possible scenario of experience. Or if you are acknowledging that the creator in the heavens knows what is best, then it is our moral obligation to ask him to create through us as well and help us search for and live out the best outcome.

To illustrate, let's consider that Mike wants a mate and a loving, fulfilling relationship. There are three potential choices he can go about making the selection:

First: In his limited knowledge, he examines his prospects. He thinks of all the attractive potential mates in his immediate vicinity: work friends, friends of friends, friends of family members, people at social clubs, bars, the gym, etc. He may have written the list and narrowed it down to the best twenty. At which point, he may decide to start dating one, two, or three at a time. He would have to go through much work, examination, and observation to see and decide who would be the best choice. I believe this is how most people go about choosing their mate, and there is nothing wrong with that. But it is not the best at all.

Second: Mike, in his limited knowledge, acknowledges that he doesn't know what he doesn't know and therefore decides to leave the decision up to the universe, or God, to choose the best from the twenty prospects. Very wise indeed, since it would save him an inordinate amount of time and effort to try pick one all by himself. The universe then goes to work, and in an instant examines each of the twenty individuals' energetic blueprints and comes to a conclusion that Jasmine is a much better vibrational match for Mike than the other nineteen. What did God or the universe examine? What questions and details did the universe consider that were relevant to the selection process?

Considering that a million different outcomes could possibly exist, then the universe in a much higher realm examines every possible scenario with each individual. The universe examines qualities, likes, dislikes, parents, family members, friends, goals, dreams, thought patterns, intentions, past, DNA impressions and patterns, possible future outcomes, etc. The entire energetic blueprint is examined in connection with Mike's blueprint, and the best choice thus has been selected—Jasmine.

It could be that Mike is an intellectual and needs support in the organizational skills department. Thus the universe observes that Jasmine is a clean and organized person who dislikes others trying to rearrange her immediate space, and therefore she is picky about how, when, and where everything must get done. This would complement Mike's qualities. On the other side of the coin, the universe examines that Jasmine lacks basic common sense, confidence, and study habits that would improve her social life and career. Thus Mike, in his great intellect, knows exactly what books she should read and helps her develop the skills and confidence that she needs to improve other aspects of her life.

There is truly an infinite amount of details that must be considered that, with our limited conscious awareness, we could not possibly even come close to considering. The universe will examine past and future, length and width, height and depth, and will absolutely make the best choice. The best part is that it will make the decision in an infinitely faster way than ourselves could. And is not time more valuable than gold itself? As fascinating as we may find the second way to achieve what we want, it is still only second best.

Third and best way: Since we have acknowledged hopefully thus far that we do not know what we do not know, then it is the best course for Mike to not even consider the twenty people on his original list. Why? Because he doesn't know what he doesn't know. But what he does know is that he knows someone or something that knows best. God or the universe is left with some very limited options when he was asked to examine only twenty out of all the possibilities in the whole planet!

Maybe five months from now, by improving Mike as person, the universe can match his frequency to Veronica, whom he will bump into at the subway station once Mike's training has been completed. Thus he will be the best person he can currently be to become Veronica's mate. Or maybe at some point or another, Mike will travel to a distant country where he will meet the best possible choice from all the outcomes. What Mike should do from the beginning is ask for a mate that the universe or God thinks is the best one possible for him. This releases all pressure and stress and allows the infinite universe to determine the best possible outcome that will make Mike and his mate the happiest. That is true wisdom.

> *Trust in Jehovah with all your heart and do not rely on your own understanding. In all your ways take notice of him, and he will make your paths straight.*

> —Proverbs 3:5-6

Remarkably the scriptural reference emphasizes this concept as the only way to successfully live out our lives.

> *Do not become wise in your own eyes. Fear Jehovah and turn away from bad. It will be a healing to your body and refreshment for your bones.*

> —Proverbs 3:7-8

JULIAN VALDERRAMA

Can we really see the dangers of taking decisions in our limited knowledge? I believe we see it every day in this world, with all of its pain and suffering. Consider the following teaching:

"I well know, O Jehovah, that man's way does not belong to him. It does not belong to man who is walking even to direct his step" (Jeremiah 10:23).

These words at this point should resonate with us in the sense that we are not really forfeiting all self-determination, but that the best way to live is by choosing to be the best we can possibly become. Since we have an infinite source of wisdom at our disposal, why waste trying to consciously make all decisions by trying to weigh all the factors? The best part is that we are, in essence, still making the decision and delegating the hard part of the work to someone much better equipped to make such decisions. That in itself is the best decision.

*Humble yourselves, therefore, under the mighty hand of God, so that he may exalt you in due time, while you throw all your anxiety on him, because he cares for you.*

— 1 Peter 5:6-7

*Commit your way to Jehovah; rely on him, and he will act in your behalf.*

— Psalms 37:5

*Do not be anxious over anything, but in everything by prayer and supplication along with thanksgiving, let your petitions be made known to God.*

—Philippians 4:6-7

*Commit to Jehovah whatever you do, and your plans will succeed.*

—Proverbs 16:3

If we have considered that the best collective decision humanity could decide upon is to achieve biological eternity, then how could we ever hope to reach such point if we do not rely on such source of wisdom and power? How could we possibly become successful to find such answers to such a huge problem and challenge as death is, if we do not decide to surrender our decision making to this much higher consciousness? Ironically the scriptures do promise "life everlasting" on the earth for those who do make such a choice. But just like in the movie *The Matrix*, anyone can choose to just take the blue pill and wake up each day believing whatever we want to believe. But it takes real courage to take the red pill.

This gives way to a powerful cognition and discovery—the secret to opening unfathomable riches and wisdom. The activating of our own personal legend.

## Your Personal Legend

The phrase is coined from a book entitled *The Alchemist* by Paulo Coelho. In an interesting turn of events, this book came to me to fill the gap on some questions I had in my personal application of these concepts and knowledge through trial and error. "When the student is ready the teacher will appear"—it is a teaching that we will continue to develop us as we live out these concepts found in this book. Although an interesting fictional story, various concepts found in this book describe valid parallels that will help us integrate. One of them is referred to as our "personal legend."

It is certainly encouraged to the reader to pick up this book as a source of reference. It is not only entertaining, but as we read it, we will continually find nuggets of gold that we can apply in our lives to help us achieve our own personal legend.

So what is a "personal legend"? According to the book, it is "one great truth, that whoever you are, or whatever you are, or whatever it is that you do, when you really want something, it is because that desire originated in the soul of the universe. It is your personal mission on earth."

I don't personally believe in predestination as if we were predetermined to live out someone else's version of our lives, as if we were just puppets with strings attached with no will or force of our own. We must have self-determination and free will if we are made in the image of God, or for that matter, the universe. We are 100 percent in control and responsible for everything that happens in our lives. Everything begins with choice, including our surrender of our decision making to the universe, which we already established as a personal yet powerful decision in itself.

I believe a better definition of our personal legend is found in the following text: "Find exquisite delight in Jehovah, and he will grant you the desire of your heart." (Psalms 37, 4) I feel it is a great parallel to Coelho's quote of the definition of our personal legend. I like to take away the mystic air and bring things down to earth with simple definitions and basic common denominators for most people to understand such concepts. We could even say that it says, "Find your greatest joy in the universe, and it will grant you its final outcome."

The literary and scriptural references denote to the idea that the thing which we most desire was given and hardwired into our essence, our own personal consciousness from the beginning of our lives. If we have already accepted as fact that our desires already exist in the matrix or field of infinite energy not defined by time and space, and if we also realize and accept as true that the universe or God knows the best outcome in relation to our desires, then by definition, we must also accept that the universe or God has already made the choice as to what would be the best possible life we could live out personally. It is like a hidden treasure just for us, waiting to be discovered before the founding of our personal lives. It is a treasure in the form of a desire that was designed to bring us on a journey that would convert us into the best version of ourselves. A result or mental picture that would call forth powerful forces within us to take us to places that otherwise would not happen ever unless we decided to pursue our personal legend.

I believe this is the true definition of destiny. Destiny is only a treasure designed by the infinite intelligence of God, hardwired into our being, which we could choose to pursue anytime we decide to do so. It is like an inheritance projected to be given to us once certain requirements are fulfilled. Since only God could best make such decisions, then it would only mean that once we begin the journey in the pursuit of our personal legend, then and only then will we progressively experience the best feelings for us, the best people for us, the best things and possessions for us, and the best spiritual, mental, and physical wealth we could possibly experience.

But like all knowledge, our experiencing the best will only continue to produce more desire for the best of the best. This process will continue through infinity. I believe Nikola Tesla experienced such feelings as he was unfolding and living out his own personal legend. It is obvious he must have experienced incredible joy and fulfillment. How can we know? His legacy and legend to this day continues to touch us in very real ways. Any thought of not continuing to progressively experience such life was a nightmare to him. Is that not why he could express and call for the need for youth and immortality, since such vision was in his mind constantly and was vividly conceived? He himself was aching for it.

The biblical reference does dedicate an entire book to contemplating this idea. King Solomon had written the book of Ecclesiastes explaining what his incredible wealth and success had given him. Consider what he expressed in his conclusions:

"I explored with my heart by indulging myself with wine, all the while maintaining my own wisdom; I even embraced foolishness to find out what was the best thing for humans to do during their few days of life under the heavens. I undertook great works. I built houses for myself; I planted vineyards for myself. I made gardens and parks for myself, and I planted in them all sorts of fruit trees. I made pools of water for myself, to irrigate a grove of flourishing trees. I acquired male and female servants, and I had servants born in my household. I also acquired much livestock—cattle and flocks—more than any of my predecessors in Jerusalem. I accumulated silver and gold for myself, the treasures of kings and of provinces. I gathered male and female singers for myself, as well as what brings great pleasure to the sons of men—a woman, yes, many women" (Ecclesiastes 2:3-8).

You would think he was the happiest man that could have ever existed, but this was his following conclusion:

"But when I reflected on all the works that my own hands had done and all the hard work that I had toiled to accomplish, I saw that everything was futile, a chasing after the wind; there was nothing of real value under the sun" (Ecclesiastes 2:11).

JULIAN VALDERRAMA

But why would he conclude that everything he accomplished was so empty and meaningless? Why did he not appreciate the inheritance he would leave to his future generations? Why did he not show gratitude for the great prosperity he had brought upon himself and his nation? The answer:

"Then I said in my heart: 'What happens to the stupid one will also happen to me.' What, then, did I gain by becoming excessively wise? So I said in my heart: This too is futility." For there is no lasting memory either of the wise one or of the stupid one. In the days to come, everyone will be forgotten. And how will the wise one die? Along with the stupid one. So I came to hate life, because everything being done under the sun seemed distressing to me, for everything was futile, a chasing after the wind" (Ecclesiastes 2:15-17).

King Solomon was not necessarily a narcissist nor negative in nature, as if always looking for the dirt in life. But his reflection is that he loved his life but hated the fact his final outcome would be just like everyone else. He was having such personal and constant enjoyment in his life by continuing to create everything he desired, that the prospect of death made everything seem futile and "distressing." He highlights this point on the next few verses:

"I came to hate all that I had worked so hard for under the sun, because I must leave it behind for the man coming after me. And who knows whether he will be wise or foolish? Yet he will take control over all the things I spent great effort and wisdom to acquire under the sun. This too is futility. So I began to despair in my heart over all the hard work at which I had toiled under the sun. For a man may work hard, guided by wisdom and knowledge and skill, but he must hand over his portion to a man who did not work for it. This too is futility and a great tragedy" (Ecclesiastes 2:18-21).

Let's reflect on this thought. Since our growth can and would grow through infinity, then death is our ultimate enemy. It must be done away with. The prospect of death takes away value from our desires and even our own personal legend. Consider that even the scriptural reference promises of a time when "the last enemy, death, is to be brought to nothing" (1 Corinthians 15:26). The nature of the universe is infinite;

therefore, its will in its infinite intelligence is eternity. It is in our nature and consciousness to want to live forever and create forever. It is our deepest desire to unfold our personal legends through infinity. Nikola Tesla revealed it in his works and comments about life.

## Activating Your Own Personal Legend

We have talked about what is the best and fastest way to achieve; it is by turning our decisions and desires to the universe or God. We also talked about how we all have a personal legend that is hardwired into our very essence. It is a gift passed down to us as an inheritance for us to enjoy the best life has to offer. But how can we know for sure what our own individual personal legend might be? Also, how can we begin to pursue it to the point of fulfilling and arriving at its destination? The answer is simple:

"Keep on asking and it will be given you, keep on seeking and you will find, keep on knocking and it will be opened to you. For everyone asking receives, and everyone seeking finds, and to everyone knocking it will be opened. Indeed which one of you, if his son asks for bread, will hand him a stone? Or if he asks for a fish, he will not hand him a serpent, will he? Therefore, if you, although being wicked [negative] know how to give good gifts to your children, how much more so will your Father who is in the heavens give good things to those asking him" (Matthew 7:7-11).

Activating our personal legend is as easy as a request from a son to his parent. We may decide to ask of God or the universe to reveal to us the means to pursue our personal legend. Or for those who may not readily pray to a higher being, then we must know that we must make a personal declaration to the universe that we are now activating that which we desire in our lives, as it is hardwired into our energetic blueprint. Once we do, we must begin to persistently ask and demand of it under this general intention:

"Specifically whatever you* think is best in connection to my deepest, most innate desires and the ability to follow through." (*Here, *you* is the universe or God.)

This is a general idea of the prayer or personal declaration: to trigger the progression to what must begin to be unfolded before our very eyes.

This will activate our own personal legend to give us what has been chosen to be the best for us as individuals. On a personal note, my personal request was to Jehovah God, the God of the Bible. I realize that he would know better than I would. I wanted to create a life of freedom and prosperity for myself and my wife. I did not know whether I should start a business, begin a new career, or go back to school. I did not know what the best outcome should be, or what could the best way or course of action. I wondered, how could I ever really know which direction to take and realize the shortest, quickest route to a place where such feelings would be real in my life?

I am not saying that you should pray or ask Jehovah personally, but you sure are welcome to give it a try, and you may be surprised with the kind of answers you would get. Either way, you know your own personal circumstances much better than I ever could, and therefore you must take this information through your own cognitive reference and decide what you must do. You are encouraged to come up with your own conclusions, and that is very important to your personal discovery of your personal legend. The choice is up to you. One thing is sure, though—your request must come from a place of full faith and total reliance on the power of such infinite intelligence. As such, we must surrender all pride and fear and let our personal legend be naturally revealed to us. How will we know? It does not matter because the universe knows how to let us know for sure, beyond a shadow of a doubt, that we have been heard and that it will progressively redirect us on the right course.

At such point, we must refer our awareness and perception continually to the PCES and all of the natural evolutionary events that will turn us into that which we must become. They are there not to make us stumble, but to redirect and shift our energies to progressively raise our individual frequencies to match the thing or place that ultimately belongs to us—our own personal legend. The irony is that the universe will only reveal the way in which we must go, but it will never show us what *it* is that we will receive. It will be an enigma to us that which has been created and reserved for us.

What do we mean by not knowing what it is? Through a series of PCES, our desires may begin to unfold into a movie. We could end up down the road with a picture in our mind where we live in our dream home, driving our dream cars, going to our dream vacations. It may include a mental movie of ourselves with scenarios of being successful in some career, business, or endeavor. Either way, we will begin to notice that we are being nourished and bombarded by all these potential scenarios of what our lives could become in ways that we could never have imagined before. The enigma is that we won't know until the last second when we have arrived at our destination. So just like Joseph who went from a lowly prisoner one day and was then literally transformed into a leader in one of the most powerful nations of that known world the next day, so it must happen to us the same way. Why?

## The Matrix Trilogy

The best way we can think to illustrate this concept is by referring to *The Matrix* trilogy. If you have not watched them, I encourage you to do so. If you did in the past, I encourage you to rewatch them, so that, just like rereading a book, you will get new cognition and realizations that will continue to propel you to your ultimate desire.

In the movie, the character known as Neo finds himself constantly waiting on instructions from a guide referred to as the Oracle. It was only a few times that he had certain feelings that made him act courageously regardless of seemingly insurmountable obstacles. This was first illustrated by the climactic scene where Neo decides to rescue his mentor Morpheus from the agents' room. He was to go through a military building and finally meet up and fight three superhuman agents. It was considered a suicide mission. Neo just left it up to a belief that he can do anything and everything.

In the second movie, Neo finds himself in a situation where he felt perplexed. He had all this power and ability but did not know how to ultimately fulfill his personal legend: to end the war between the machine world and the human world, to liberate mankind from bondage and slavery. In this movie, an enthralling conversation takes place between the Oracle and now the fully awakened Neo, who is "the One."

If we desire to fully integrate the lessons found in this chapter, the entire series gives cognitive points of references that will help us really draw out the lessons and make them part of us. In this conversation, Neo explains to the Oracle that he has been seeing Trinity, his love, falling from a building in a series of recurring dreams. The Oracle asks if he sees her die. Since he does not see Trinity die, the Oracle explains to him that, "absolutely no one can see the end result of choices or decisions we do not understand."

Neo asks whether it was up to him to choose whether Trinity would die or not. Surprisingly, the Oracle explains to Neo that he was not here to make the choice because he had already made that choice. He was only there going through the motions to understand why he had already subconsciously made that choice.

This conversation gives light to the essence of the concept of our personal legend. It could be said that we have already made the choice of what we ultimately want because it was given to us since the founding of our lives, or our birth. Once we decide to pursue it, we cannot see the result in our mind's eye because we do not understand it, nor can we comprehend what it could possibly be. God's judgments are unsearchable, and his riches unfathomable.

Scientifically, if we did know, our consciousness would ultimately just get in the way of its ultimate fulfillment. Why? Because if its ultimate outcome were to be specifically defined and shown to us before its fulfillment, our limited minds would just convince us of its impossibility, and therefore, we would begin to transmit a frequency opposite to that dream. We would steal God's dream and gift to us. In essence, we would create resistance, and our powers of perception would just collapse the wave function of the dreams' collective energy and would ultimately dissipate it. To prove this point, consider another scriptural reference that emphasizes the essence of this teaching.

## Gideon and His Three Hundred Men

The story of Gideon is found in the book of Judges, chapters 6 through 8. This story is remarkable because it highlights the will of God and his desire to improve our personal lives. In this story, the nation of Israel is conquered by the nation of Midian. The Israelites become heavily oppressed and decide to search and ask for God's hand to get them out of this situation. God decides to appoint a young man named Gideon. Gideon is shown as a lowly worker in his father's winepress, full of doubt and disbelief in himself. "But Jehovah said to him: Because I will be with you, you will strike down Midian as if they were one man" (Judges 6:16).

The real focus of this story is found in chapter 7. Gideon is appointed by God to lead an army of about thirty-two thousand men. They were about to face the Midian army, which were 120,000 men armed with swords. They were outnumbered; for every man they had, the Midianites had four. The enthralling event was before the battle. At this point, Jehovah decides to instruct Gideon to inform all the men in his army that those who had fear would be allowed to go home. God had explained to him that even though they were outnumbered, they were still too many. Jehovah wanted to prove his power in their behalf and did not want them to conclude that it was their strength in numbers and their personal faith and courage that would bring them success. At this point, twenty-two thousand men chose the easy route and left Gideon with only ten thousand men.

Jehovah, surprisingly still wanting to prove his power, lets Gideon know that they still have too many men present for the battle. In a strange test, they are instructed to go and drink water from a spring, where he separated the men who lapped the water from those who bent their knees to drink the water like dogs do. Only three hundred used the palm of their hands to lap water, and so they were chosen to battle. So first, they were outnumbered four to one, then they became outnumbered twelve to one. And now with only three hundred men, they were outnumbered four hundred to one.

Obviously no matter how much faith, power, training, stamina, desire, and willpower these three hundred men had, they were not going to beat an army of 120,000 men. Once they won, they could only attribute all success to the power of God and nothing else. They would have no choice but to acknowledge that such force existed outside themselves that could make such accomplishment. The same implication must be referred to Joseph's ultimate best outcome. No matter how much training, skills, or faith there was in his heart, there was absolutely no way he could have gone from being a lowly shepherd to second in command for the most powerful nation of that time on his own merit and power of transmission. All credit as such must be given to its rightful source.

This is good because it teaches us that we can ask for a personal miracle in our lives. We can ask for that outcome that has been decided from the beginning of our life that would instruct us of such personal force. It will allow us to see the finger of God right into our personal life by pursuing and making active our own personal legend. The privilege to see and experience such a powerful outcome in our lives can only infuse us with unbelievable godlike power. We would have no choice but to become the "sons of God."

What will the power of God turn us into? What lessons and skills would we acquire as we are refined in the alchemy of the universe? Could we all learn how to eradicate illness, disease, and unnecessary pain and suffering? Could we establish a peaceful society under a new system of things where everyone could prosper and live in constant ecstasy and bliss? Would we not be able to eradicate death, as promised by the scriptural references?

## A Small Autobiography

At this moment, maybe the reader may be wondering about the author of this book. Has the author of this book experienced the finger of God in his life? Has he finally reached the final destination and acquired his own personal legend?        Well, that may depend on the time and place. Obviously you are reading my collection of thoughts to this point in time in my life. It is now March 5, 2015. I am sitting in my tiny living room with my computer hooked up to my TV, typing what could be a successful book or not. It is 11:48 p.m., and my wife of eight years is upstairs sleeping in our bed with our new baby who is only seven months old. Both are suffering from a common cold and are in the process of recovering.

To this point, I can tell you I have gone through some rings of fire, and I am becoming a better person for it. My recent PCES are telling me to focus on this book and nothing else. My wife's TV shows and movies present men who are writers and successful publishers. The most recent movie we watched is called *Lucy*. In this movie, the character, through some unfortunate event becomes a powerful being who begins to acquire hidden knowledge, and the ultimate lesson for her was to pass it on. It made me feel like the universe was telling me to pass on the information I have been learning from incredibly successful individuals by sharing my own perspective in connection with quantum physics and how it relates to scriptural reference.

My most recent audio trainings were recordings of a gentleman describing a system that could help anyone achieve their dreams. One of those listed potential dreams was the possibility of someone engaging in writing a book. The last book I read was *The Alchemist*. Interestingly, it describes the author as someone who grew up being trained to become something he did not really want to be, but he ended up finding his affinity with writing.

There are probably hundreds of experiences that have continued to speak to me, trying to redirect my energies into writing a book. The irony is that I have never written anything substantial aside from some papers in college that were completely rejected because I failed to follow some instructions. And that was over ten years ago. But the second I gave in to the idea and decided to write, I thought, *Wow . . . I have never been so excited about a project in my life until now.* Information is continually being poured into my mind, and all I do is type. I am not struggling to write the pages of this book nor have I stressed about it, as if to say that my imagination was running out. But then my energies were redirected.

Suddenly my energies were influenced to focus on an educational project I had been struggling to finish for the last two years. But I realized it was because I was only trying to force the matter to its completion. To this point, before writing chapter 8 of this book, I did not know what else to write. I didn't fret or worry about it because I knew I was being redirected to finish my educational project. But then I arrived at a point where, at one of my Christian meetings, a personal acquaintance would approach me on a regular basis and tell me excitedly about a book that he thought I should read. I was curious because I knew the universe was trying to tell me something, that there was a lesson I had not yet grasped and needed to fully integrate. After some weeks, I was finally able to get ahold of the book: *The Alchemist* by Paulo Coelho.

This helped me integrate the lesson on PCES and the concept of our own personal legend. Not that everything I am writing was originated from that book, but there are certain ideas and concepts found in this book that, through discernment, I was able to integrate with previous acquired knowledge and understanding. This resulted in this final concept as it stands now. I immediately began to think about how it related to the scriptural reference, successful individuals' personal stories, and quantum physical laws. So like a puzzle being completed, those whole pieces created an even bigger picture, fitting together perfectly in a master puzzle. The big picture was finally revealed. The answer to questions that I had agonized for the past four years finally came to light. As a student, I was ready to receive its lessons, and thus the teacher appeared to me to tell me about this powerful lesson in life. Moreover, the title and the content of this chapter was put together.

The interesting phenomenon is that the information is being poured into my mind and I am just typing away. I had not conceived each sentence or paragraph or ideas before I started to write. But it was my decision to write this chapter based on a picture of concepts that is progressively helping me now to begin to integrate these lessons in this chapter. I almost feel like it is somebody else's words I am typing. In essence, I am teaching myself new lessons of life that I had not grasped previously. I am mesmerized by the beauty of this process, and I can see that Jehovah is teaching me.

So to answer the question whether I currently have my own personal legend, as I reflect on my present, the answer is no—not yet. But I know I am being trained and refined like gold. I am learning lessons that will guide me and refresh me as I continue to fulfill my personal legend to its final completion, and how excited I am to experience it. Maybe as you are reading this book, many years may have already passed; I may, at this point in time, be already living my own personal legend. And through your own set of PCES, you are now reading this book because you must now activate your own personal legend. Maybe you prayed for guidance or information that would empower you forever and help you acquire your heart's desires. Maybe this book is now speaking to your innermost profound being.

But then again, maybe I am just being dramatic and self-centered— the decision is yours to make. We have all heard the phrase: you can bring the horse to the river, but you cannot possibly make him drink the water. It is up to you whether or not you will take to heart these lessons. As the Oracle explained to Neo, "As soon as you step out that door, you will remember that you don't believe in any of this fate crap. You are in control of your own life, remember?"

We must take to heart such counsel. We are at cause over our own environment and we vibrate our energetic blueprint 24/7 whether we believe it or not. We will continue to affect our immediate vicinity with our own personal imprint, and it will continue to reflect back to us what we give it. Do we like what we see? We can change it if we don't. But it all starts with the choice to do so—nothing else does. Neither the universe or God will make us change anything. The choice is always up to us, period.

I wish to now conclude this chapter by emphasizing that a process is now taking place that will restore what was supposed to be our current reality: life eternal and eternal youth is just around the corner. How can I say that such is the case? Because there is a blueprint to immortality. The next three chapters will cover that.

An Introduction to Part II of *Blueprint for Biological Immortality*

In this section, it will be discussed precisely through expert reference what it would take to create a real shift in people's minds. As mentioned before, Nikola Tesla emphasized that inexorable agents present in the collective consciousness of the world prevent a quantum leap forward from taking place. In the previous chapters in part 1 of this book, we examined how, as individuals, we can ascertain the power of our minds and grasp our innermost abilities to acquire our desires.

Since it is our moral obligation to do so, for the exercise of faith is always present, thus we either exercise faith that we can have, be, or do whatever we want, or we exercise faith that we cannot have, be, or do whatever we want. There is no middle ground, and our nature proves this is true, for we vibrate at every instant of Planck time the exact blueprint of what we are. The laws of magnetic force will continue to perpetuate our predominant projections of energy.

In the next chapters, it will be plainly shown that the biblical reference, in light of true social and political science and quantum physics, shows what prevents us from achieving a world of peace and security. Universal policy will be examined and how, in the future, the inexorable agents that prevent the current paradigm of things ruling this world from changing will be radically modified by new thought. Agents from outside this world, a.k.a. aliens, are coming, not to obliterate the world, but to wipe clean the current corrupt matrix reality.

We will no longer put up with the present state of affairs anymore, but before we do experience such reality, we must qualify and align ourselves to universal policy and exercise our free will and individual sovereignties to make the energetic exodus to freedom from modern-day Egypt and its corrupt practices. So like applying for new citizenship to benefit from the prosperity of a better country, we must exercise our brain transmission of frequency to conquer what is currently disqualifying us from entering that future world. Universal diplomacy is now being implemented from the government of the universe to help citizens of this planet to apply for residence and acquire its most unfathomable reward: biological immortality on a new paradisal Earth.

Nikola Tesla's dream for a world where biological immortality, beauty, and youth does, and will absolutely exist.

# CHAPTER 9

# Blueprint for Immortality: Part I

*The way you see people is the way you treat them, and the way you treat them is what they become.*

—Johann von Goethe

T HE TITLE OF this book absolutely suggests that the human genome has every building block and potential to maintain its existence throughout eternity. By examining how the universe works to its most minute detail, we continue to observe that its nature does seem infinite. In reference with our entire essence, since we are connected to this infinite consciousness, when we examine the ramifications of the nature of infinity, then such data easily help us to conclude what kind of existence our lives must become. Although Napoleon Hill never discussed the aspects of the possibility of eternal life, he did emphasize the desire to see our world united in peace and security.

Napoleon Hill has been an outstanding source of information who continues to create indescribable success in those who decide to take on his lessons and integrate them into their personal lives. So much so was the case, he describes in chapter 12 of his original work entitled *The Law of Success* an interesting action plan for the ramifications and stipulations—a blueprint, if you will—of exactly what needs to occur in order for such scenario to play out in our world. But why should we even consider Napoleon Hill's plan for world peace?

We should consider that Napoleon Hill has been one of the most avid students of natural law and success philosophy as they relate to mankind's consciousness and the power of our essence. So just like this book, his most famous works, such as *The Law of Success* and *Think and Grow Rich*, emphasize that the principles contained therein are solely based on laws of physics and not opinions or plain guesswork. So just like scientists depend on mathematicians to discover and reaffirm theoretical laws of physics, so do we depend on proven principles of life for us to have integrated ability to understand such laws as we learn to live by them and learn how to apply them in our lives to create desired results. We can say that, in essence, we are doing our best to become masters of natural law. We must study and pass the bar exam based on the laws of the universe to graduate and become proficient at interpreting such laws. We owe it to ourselves and our loved ones.

Can we see why and how Nikola Tesla, as a master student of natural law was able to conceive the idea of a future society where people have discovered the secret to immortality, youth, and beauty? His shining example as a master student and interpreter of the laws of the universe has allowed us to experience life faster and better. He has given us one of the more expensive and valuable resources known to mankind: time. Every conceivable technology came to be thanks to his ingenuity. Not that he must be attributed credit for every piece of tech, but that his influence and knowledge has touched the lives of those who have originated probably every piece of technology we know about today. So just like an integration is built upon another, we are now experiencing technology that is mind blowing due to Tesla's first integrations of scientific knowledge.

The opening quote in this chapter gives light to a powerful insight in relationships and the laws of physics and how they must be applied when we come in contact with other human beings. Since the way we relate to people is influenced powerfully by our preconceived ideas, whether we developed them through social heredity or our DNA bloodline, our perceptive powers may be distorted to the laws of physics. Thus, some drastic changes must take place at the root of people's lives. Napoleon Hill made many comments that align with the universal principles that must be implemented, like the way a surgeon must apply emergency medical procedures to maintain the life of a terminal patient. This does not mean we must agree with every word he ever said or wrote, but that we should also use discernment and find practical applications.

As such is the case, we can also consider successful examples of those who have applied these principles to create relative peace and security among the populace. Is there such an example? Absolutely! But before we mention this seemingly insignificant group of people who have achieved tremendous success in relation to world peace, let's discuss what exactly must begin to happen within the populace to get the ball rolling on this fantastic idea.

There has got to be a predominant shift in people's minds at the core of their very beings and replicate and permeate the ether with its blueprint transmission. Thus, like stacked dominoes, one will continue to knock against the other progressively to reach the final outcome. Therefore each successive event must take place before the next event occurs.

## The First Key to the Door to Immortality

*I wiped the slate of what I believed to be my previously gathered knowledge and to unlearn much that I had previously believed to be truth.*

—Napoleon Hill

It is obvious here that Hill came to some serious discoveries about his thinking. He realized that just like completely reformatting or resetting the drive of a computer, he had to remove all corrupt data that did not align with the positive consequences of the practical application of universal law for the betterment of his personal life. For example, a person who believes is superior to others for whatever reason may form the habit of looking down on those who may not have achieved their personal success. An extreme negative example may be that of Nazi Germany. Their feelings of superiority did not influence them to give of themselves to improve their society and other people's lives, but instead they decided to remove from existence those people they deemed unworthy through obscene, gross, and immoral actions. Their pride and ego devastated the lives of millions of people's well-being and happiness through a horrendous world war. The world is still feeling the consequences of those past actions.

What if they would have decided to implement all those resources and their mental canon to creating technologies to improve the world, exercising the Golden Rule. Could they have learned how to eradicate illness and disease at least to a certain extent? Could they have learned and implemented educational systems in their world that would have propelled their most common people to incredible success? And instead of subverting other nations' sovereignties through war and invasion, could they have invaded other countries with positive education and technological advancements throughout the world? How would have the law of attraction helped repay such giving once those services were rendered throughout the world?

It would be wise to scrutinize our mental patterns, behaviors, and beliefs to see whether they are creating in us positive and loving habits. What if the most foundational principles of belief of every individual were to govern the mind of the populace in such a way that at every moment of the day, we would ask ourselves, "How may I be of service to others?"

If we were to see others under the light of how we can produce value for them, what kind of person would they become?

What was the result of Napoleon Hill's personal application of these laws and how they shed light to the nature of his most prevalent beliefs?

> *I found most of my views on these subjects without support by even a reasonable hypothesis,* much less sound *facts* or reason.
>
> —Napoleon Hill

The Foundational Laws of Immortality

Are there really such laws or principles that we can live with to eventually achieve biological immortality? Yes, for by understanding the most basic laws or principles that govern the physical universe, such knowledge will help us to know and give us the discernment as to what must be our most prevalent thoughts. Once we perpetuate this knowledge through our very being one person at a time, then we would have no choice but to get there. Let's consider strongly the following foundational principles of life:

JULIAN VALDERRAMA

*Foundational Law of Immortality #1:*

"We must love God with your whole heart and with your whole soul, and with you whole mind."

*Foundational Law of Immortality #2:*

"We must love our neighbor as ourselves."

This is not religious dogma or biased stubbornness based on religious lies. These are the most foundational building blocks of life as they stand to create the most wonderful life we could possibly acquire. Nikola Tesla emphasized that his driving force was, in essence, these principles. Let's consider this thought carefully for a second. He said:

"The desire that guides me in all I do is the desire to harness the forces of nature to the service of mankind."

Here we see the driving force behind all his success, which is founded on the foundational laws for immortality. He was able to harness the forces of nature to create; thus, we see the physical manifestations of his creations till today. But how specifically was he able to "harness such forces" into practical value? The following quote may shed light on the conclusion:

"The gift of mental power comes from God, divine being, and if we concentrate our minds on that truth, we become in tune with that great power" (Nikola Tesla).

The key is to be "in tune," or to match and resonate to the frequency of the power of God and the universe. How? We must exercise *love* for God and those who reflect his power, those who are made in his image. But how can we show love for God?

"For this is what the love of God means, that we observe his commandments; and yet his commandments are not burdensome" (1 John 5:3).

Interestingly enough, the scriptural reference emphasized that we show love for God by observing and living by statutes or decrees based on laws of the universe. As stated before, since we learn about God through creation, then our behavior must conform and "resonate," or must match the frequency of vibration of those energetic laws of the universe. We must tune in, as suggested by Tesla, by concentrating or focusing intensely our powers of perception to those truths. They are all physical laws based on love. But then the question arises: What is love? Napoleon Hill referred to it, quoting Jesus, as the Golden Rule. We all know or are at least familiar of the concept: that we must do to others in the same way we want others to do for us. Nikola Tesla had love for others since he stated that he wanted to service mankind. He loved neighbor as himself. Thus he fulfilled the universal laws of immortality.

We must, as individuals, create and transform our entire mentality to align with the Golden Rule to match the energetic blueprint of love. We must examine carefully like Mr. Hill to bring into submission every thought and belief we may have and test them to see if they are fireproof. In essence, do they align with and match the same resonance of the love for God and love for self and neighbor?

This places the moral obligation in us to ask ourselves about our personal philosophies of life—where they came from and where we got them. And if they do not align with these building blocks of life, the foundational laws of immortality must suppress that which does not support them. Love then will destroy or burn up any agreements or man-made preconceived notions that do not perfectly align with these principles.

*If a law is unjust, a man is not only right to disobey it, he is obligated to do so.*

—Thomas Jefferson

*A just law is a man-made code that squares with the moral law, or the law of God.*

—Martin Luther King

*Any law which violates the inalienable rights of man
is essentially unjust and tyrannical; it is not a law at all.*

—Maximilien Robespierre

The essence of the Golden Rule is applying and exercising our inalienable rights without taking away or overstepping the inalienable rights of others. This is love of neighbor, for our right to do anything ends when our desires or actions interfere with the rights of others. Then in reality, the Golden Rule takes us even further into exercising our inalienable rights to build on our neighbor's inalienable rights and enhance other people's experience of life. The human genome has natural laws that govern its continuance of existence. They include the right to life, since it is a gift from our creator. Our right to life includes anything and everything that adds value and quality to the individuality of the life of each person in existence. Thus if any of our life's current and existing beliefs take away others' quality of life, happiness, peace, joy, love, kindness, goodness, or self-control, then it is the law that our right to experience such things must become eroded and diminished. When we fail to uphold the highest law, we will become more alienated from the source of life: God.

But then the opposite is true, for as we exercise the Golden Rule and show love by observing how the laws of the universe will improve our lives once applied, then we will continue to draw in closer and match the vibration of the field of life. This, in fact, is the love of God by definition. For when we learn to harness the natural laws of the universe and show ourselves love first by improving our personal lives, then and only then are we truly empowered to really help others and fulfill the second part of the law and show love for neighbor. Jesus said that we must remove the rafter in our own eye before we can remove the straw in other people's eyes. Once we remove the rafter from our own eye, then we will clearly see how to remove it from others; we will see exactly what is holding them back from achieving success and essentially what is holding us back personally as well. We must realize that most of the time, other people's negative traits are just a reflection of our bigger shortcomings, and when time comes when we clearly accept that and take responsibility, we will know how we must acquire skills and use our abilities to "wipe the slate of what [we] believed to be [our] previously gathered knowledge and unlearn much that [we] had previously believed to be truth" (Napoleon Hill).

As Napoleon Hill suggested, we must start and renew our mind. He said, "We must become self-aware of how and where we acquired our philosophy of life in general. That we may trace our prejudices and our biases to their original sources. That you may discover, as I discovered, how largely you are the result of the training you received before you reached the age of fifteen years."

We can observe that both commandments are in unison. Thus when we show love for God by exercising our mental capabilities to learn of the laws of the universe and how to aptly apply them in our lives, we will have no choice but to experience personal gratification. When we harness these laws to the service of mankind as Tesla did, then we will apply the Golden Rule in its most optimal level, and it will drive us to heights of achievement comparable to Nikola Tesla himself. Exercising foundational law of immortality #1 will allow us to fulfill foundational law #2, and vice versa. Refer to chapter 5 for the best course of action to persevere and put into practice these laws. We suggest that we read and reread this entire book and these concepts, along with the other recommended references, so as to enforce our fulfilling the law.

These laws of nature, as they are interconnected to our essence, must progressively be ingrained in us and program our entire human genome to affect every aspect of human life. It must start with us as individuals, then as communities, towns, states, countries, and then it must permeate the whole world. The question and obvious statement is will we really achieve biological eternity by just fulfilling the Golden Rule? The truth of the matter is that our taking these laws and applying the Golden Rule in our lives is but one key of an entire set of keys to be able to open up the secret to immortality and youth.

The Second Key to the Door to Immortality

*The nations of the world will subordinate their individual interest to those of the human race as whole.*

—Napoleon Hill

*In the final part of the days, the mountain of the house of Jehovah will become firmly established above the top of the mountain. And it will be raised up above the hills, and to it the nations will stream. And many peoples will go and say: "Come, let us go up to the mountain of Jehovah, to the house of the God of Jacob. He will instruct us about his ways, and we will walk in his paths . . . He will render judgment among the nations and set matters straight respecting many peoples. They will beat their swords into plowshares and their spears into pruning shears. Nation will not lift up sword against nation, nor will they learn war anymore.*

—Isaiah 2:2-4

As long as it depends upon us as individuals, we must exercise our moral obligation to know that the laws of physics call for the end of violence. We have all heard the famous comment by Jesus, that those "who live by the sword must die by the sword." Interestingly it seems that the future promised by Isaiah, he observed a world already in existence where people were eagerly learning the law and principles of the universe which will ultimately render justice among the nations where war was no longer an option or even a consideration. This may sound farfetched to many, but as mentioned before, the systems described in chapters 5 through 8 will help us keep score where we stand in relation to where we should consider wanting to go, for they are founded on the laws of the universe. They are also connected to the foundational laws for immortality, for the triad of knowledge says it is a possibility; therefore peace, security, and immortality are in fact a reality.

*By forcing upon the minds of the young of all races the fact that war is horrible and does not serve the interest of the individual engaging in it or the group to which the individual belongs.*

—Napoleon Hill

It must be personally and collectively accepted to establish moral law in our hearts, and not just a suggestion, to know that any volunteering of our energies and abilities to the cause of learning war is devoid of any real benefit. What we focus on expands, and its consistent transmission of energy from those who decide to engage will continue to perpetuate that vibration's essence. That person will only reap misery and pain—all fruitage of violence and war. The consistent offering of such energies will be sent into the ether toward its final outcomes. People will be influenced to think, feel, speak, and act out violence. Feelings such as anger, vengeance, rage, and hatred have strong, energetic streams that amp the power of desire. If those desires are pictures of people learning how to combat and wage war against others, then the likelihood of those creations becoming a reality are a certainty.

A system (which already exists) thus must be established firmly to convince not only young ones, but all kinds of people of all races and nationalities to hate war and abstain learning from it. This system of learning is so successful in having convinced in the minds of young and older, that individuals who have acquired this knowledge, have risked and suffered imprisonment for conscientious refusal to draft in their respective countries' military programs. They are willing to give up nationalistic dogmatic views of war and willingly sacrifice freedom, time, and energies by exercising their inheritance of natural law to disobey unjust laws, such as obligatory or compulsory military service in the nations of the world. These have truly beaten their swords into plowshares.

The people who make such a stand against serving in the military of their respective nations allow for a real positive energy frequency to be transmitted and thus influence a powerful shift that will enforce what we are looking to achieve: the establishment of world peace and security. What would happen if the congregations, churches, synagogues, also schools, colleges, and universities made it a prerequisite for membership and admission to vow to never engage in conflict using arms and weapons?

There is one organization that is successfully doing just that today. Its members pledge to fulfill many of the quintessential common denominators that must take place before the world experiences world peace and security.

*Any plan to abolish war, to be successful, depends on the*
*successful coordination of effort between all the churches and*

JULIAN VALDERRAMA

*schools of the world for the avowed purpose of so fertilizing*
*the minds of the young with the idea of abolishing war that*
*the very word "war" will strike terror in their hearts.*

—Napoleon Hill

This organization has successfully implemented the procedures as described through chapters 5 through 8. All of its members must qualify and make pledges to persist and insist on this success system. As we previously discussed, this success system integrates the use of books, audio material, meetings, workshops and seminars to perpetuate a goal or dream by building a person up. These societies have been progressively integrated around this systematic approach to learning, enforcing the concept of world peace and biological immortality. Its members also continue to build and integrate their relationships solely to those who are like-minded and limit their contact with those who are not in agreement, thus they will be more successful in implementing prolonged collective transmissions of frequency that must continue to take place. Their recognition for each other and support of each other does not know nationalistic boundaries, and thus their membership has grown and continue to grow throughout the world.

All of its members are taught and required, before acceptance, to make a vow to honor these laws and principles and to uphold them. Far from perfect as they exercise their potential, they are consistently implementing honestly and genuinely:

*This appeal must be made by organizing and highly*
*emotionalizing the people of the different nations of the*
*world in support of a universal plan for peace, and this plan*
*must be forced upon the minds of the oncoming generations*
*with the same diligent care that we now force upon the*
*minds of our young the ideal of our respective religions.*

—Napoleon Hill

The powerful emotion that is permeating this organization, is making millions of its members to volunteer incredible amounts of energy and time, even forsaking personal desires and goals temporarily for the bigger picture. They exercise their moral obligation under the Golden Rule to go to people's homes and talk to people at work or in public places to try to disseminate these instructions for others to implement and replicate. Millions of people all over the world are readily accepting this hope as future reality—peace and security under a prosperous new world, where everyone will enjoy "the exquisite delight in the abundance of peace" It is all a promise supported by universal policy that will bring about the fulfillment that we are now supposed to experience. This is the will of the universe, and we are now seeing this tremendous force perpetuate the minds of the people involved in this movement. Once examined, we may come to realize that we are at the threshold of the fulfillment of this promise. This organization is reflecting what Napoleon Hill knew must happen before we would be able to see this worldwide peace:

> *If the organized religions of the world, as they now exist, will not subordinate their individual interests and purposes to that of establishing universal peace, then the remedy lies in establishing a universal church of the world that will function through all races and whose creed will be based entirely on the one purpose of implanting in the minds of the young the ideal of worldwide peace.*

> —Napoleon Hill

This society and all of its individual members are focusing their energies and their thoughts, emotions, words, actions, and habits to align with the will of universe. They have decided and continued to enforce their entire destiny around this concept of universal peace and security where everyone gives recognition to the universal principles of the Golden Rule and the foundational laws for biological immortality. We previously examined that whatever reality we wish to create in our lives can only become a reality as long as we perceive the laws of the universe, and when applied consistently, they can bring such reality into existence through our matrix of particles defined by time and space. Thus Napoleon Hill was forced to acknowledge: "The majority of the people of the world want peace, wherein lies the possibility of its attainment!"

Millions of members within this organization not only want and desire its final outcome but have come to the realization of its absolute certainty and future fulfillment. Its energy has continued to call out progressively for just over a hundred years in connection with this promise, where we will see action from the nations of the world, where governmental sovereignties will surrender their pre-conceived negative notions; both individual citizens and collective national governments to the fulfillment of this promise. They will have no choice but to comply to the validity of force that these laws of the universe are looking to fulfill collectively, for that which does not match the will of the universe must be removed from existence. If it didn't, then chaos and destruction of the collective consciousness of people would continue to create everything wrong we see today, which will not only ultimately destroy us as a race, but it will permeate the universe. The infinite intelligence that governs the laws of the universe cannot tolerate this gross and willful ignorance.

This is why people must awaken their sense of justice and come to the awareness that there is something really wrong with the current matrix reality and its system of things governing our world. Nikola Tesla said, "Let the future tell the truth and evaluate each one according to his work and accomplishments. The present is theirs; the future, for which I really worked, is mine. I do not regret that others have stolen my ideas, rather than why they haven't their own." We must ask the questions with candid self-examination. Have our current lives prove positively the exact representation of the valid truths we have personally acquired, or would our life prove that we have no idea what we are doing? This must be examined closely, for our lives are the current result of the then created future results of our past truths we have exercised. The laws of nature are telling us that what we are today is only the result of what we have continued to believe and thought about in the past. So if we have readily accepted this truism as individuals, then we must know that this is a fantastic principle for which we can guide our lives. Should we then not consider the big picture of our world and its history and see how miserable we have failed?

This present organization that has shown tremendous unprecedented success to achieving some steps in the direction to creating biological immortality have accepted this fact. Therefore, all of its members have surrendered preconceived notions and ideas that did not line up with real principles that work in our life. Leaving behind practices and past lives, they have adopted present real-life working principles. They have given up religious dogmas and stubborn bigotry, including life styles and attitudes that permeate the negative results of this world. In a harmonious brotherhood, the current membership has agreed, under contract, to accept the higher truths. They have progressively fulfilled yet another piece of the puzzle as Napoleon Hill emphasized:

"All denominations [must] formulate a working agreement under which the combined strength of organized religion will be used as a means of forcing a higher ideal upon the minds of the members."

In addition, it must be emphasized that the agreement must be enforced through highly emotionalized individuals. Women have been known to have high emotional energy, and thus can take action and act in harmony more readily than men can. We have all been able to examine that women's nature is to nurture and give of themselves with tremendous ambition and energy, thus we know that this is how they experience fulfillment in their lives. Throughout this organization, it has been plainly shown that the membership that complements women under this system have taken the lead to spreading this message all around the world to nurture people's minds to these universal truths. Yet another parallel from Napoleon Hill that should be accomplished:

"The task of bringing about this alliance of the churches in support of the world of universal peace must rest upon the female members of the church for the reason that the abolition of war promises advantages that may be prolonged into the future and that may accrue only to the unborn generations."

This statement thus fulfills yet another unprecedented requirement that needs to take place as result of a collective women force. Emotion is the most powerful force to drive a desire to its completion; therefore the female emotion does empower this movement drastically more than anything else that could make it happen. "Jehovah gives the command; the women proclaiming the news are a large army" (Psalms 68:11).

*Emotion rules the church, and the church is the only organization that rests solely on the power of emotion. The church is the only organized factor of society that has the power to harness and direct the emotional forces of civilization because the emotions are controlled by*

*FAITH and not by reason! And the church is the only great organized body in which the faith of the world is centered.*

—Napoleon Hill

The Third Key to the Door to Immortality

Shifting the current matrix paradigm to that of love

Let's regress for a second. Here it is not being suggested that you, the reader, should become part of this organization, nor was this book written with the purpose to sell you a set of religious dogma. It is not suggested either, that you, the reader, should change personal preference if you already have some kind of affiliation to a congregation, denomination, or club. There are too many factors and circumstances that play out in people's lives to give such an opinionated remark. Napoleon Hill's idea, in his chapter on tolerance, was to infuse confidence in a set of action steps that are founded on the laws of physics —the blueprint, if you will—that is certain to propel us into world peace and security. They are common denominators of thought attached to very specifically defined principles and laws of nature taking place in time and space and the planet's collective reality.

We must be reminded that the emphasis by Mr. Hill was that people must surrender their will and most basic beliefs to align them to the ideal of peace and security. The premise that war is horrible and must be completely done away with is obviously a desire for most of the populace. So realizing what this blueprint calls for is that everyone should at least consider surrendering first the beliefs and dogmas that are not in alignment with the laws of the physical universe for the benefits of the planet as a whole and the biggest minority: the individual. Also, the foundational principles and workings of the concept and word *church* or *congregation* should be considered and examined to learn how they can and will potentially accomplish this paradigm.

For example, to the large portion of the populace, the word *church* has an extremely negative connotation, even more so than when Mr. Hill wrote the *Law of Success*. The word *church* has been defined as a place where people with a common interest in a deity will come together to "worship." These words have become confusing misnomers, and thus their more essential meanings have been obscured. As it stands today, many religious organizations are besmirched due to reports of corruption and moral hypocrisy among its leaders and its constituents. Many of these reports absolutely have strong and clear evidence, and therefore people are turned off by them. Also, people's awareness that many religions organizations will foment and stir up strong emotions and abuse such power for the sole purpose of acquiring exorbitant amounts of money can be appalling and turn many away. Many people are disillusioned with religion in general.

But let's consider and break down some of these words to really see what they mean exactly. Let's specifically examine the words *religion*, *church* or *congregation*, and the word *worship*. The most basic and foundational meaning for the word *religion* is "a pursuit or interest to which someone ascribes supreme importance." Other definitions have added to it descriptions such as "a particular system of faith and worship." We already defined the word *faith*, but we can see that the first definition of the word *church* is more accurate in its most basic terms.

Let us examine the word *religion* as "a pursuit or interest to which someone ascribes supreme importance."

With this, we can say that a person who expresses importance of family closeness and support is a form of religion. We can also say the same that when an individual expresses the importance of integrity and honesty and their exercise must be allowed at all costs, then we can say that the individual is expressing their religion. On the other hand, a person who expresses his will to exercise and engage in habits or hobbies for personal gratification essentially is also expressing their religion. The point is that regardless of a person's opinions of what is important to them, when they are being exercised, in essence they are expressing their religion. It could be said that I am currently expressing my religion, for I find these principles to be of supreme importance, thus this book you are now holding in your hands came to be.

Can we say that, in a way, we are expressing our opinions and interpretation of what we consider to be our moral laws? Let's suppose we are in agreement concerning this statement, then we can consider these personal moral codes and compare them and put them to the test in the light of the most powerful law: the Golden Rule. We must use our

JULIAN VALDERRAMA

discernment and consider every possible outcome based on our moral law to see whether it stands against the foundational laws of immortality, mainly love for neighbor and self.

For example, we can say that a person who develops liver cirrhosis due to overdrinking failed to uphold the second law—or at least, love for self. But if the individual has family and children, then should we ask whether the illness will become a burden to them? Will spouses and children have to sacrifice time, energy, and resources to care for a person who may be terminally ill for lack of personal dignity? What about the pain and sorrow they cause to those who will be left behind prematurely? Thus one religion based on a personal moral code can, in essence, be against the most fundamental laws of the universe. The Golden Rule most be reflected in the light of our religious beliefs regardless of where they came from. Therefore it must be our moral obligation to unlearn, as Napoleon Hill did, every preconceived notion of knowledge, belief, cognition, habits, or suggested wisdom that does not pass the test of the Golden Rule, regardless of where they come from. The laws of nature demand it.

## Church or congregation

The most basic foundational definitions when examining the words *church* or *congregation*, denote the idea of a group of people assembled for religious worship. An even more fundamentally defined term for the word *congregation* is a gathering or collection of people, animals, or things. So we can say that a church or congregation is a collection of people who express their opinions to what is most important for them to pursue, for they ascribe supreme importance to those ideas. Then if we were to define this even further, we could say that a church is "a collective vibration of consciousness vibrating together a set of specific energetic blueprints of frequencies, based on its most quintessential imprint." Therefore we must ask, is the imprint of such frequencies positively based on the most foundational laws of the universe and both foundational laws of immortality? Will these collective vibrations help us as individuals and as a human family to attain what is supposed to be our most basic nature: biological eternity? But let's take this definition a step further by asking the question "What, then, is worship?"

*Worship*: "Honor given to someone or thing in recognition of their merit."

No matter how we define the word *worship*, when we break down the most common denominator of its definition, this archaic definition of worship highlighted above will be at the base of all of them. For example: one definition of the word *worship* is "the feeling or expression of reverence and adoration for a deity."

Other definitions: "The acts or rites that make up a formal expression of reverence for a deity, a religious ceremony or ceremonies." "Adoration or devotion comparable to religious homage, shown toward a person or principle." The words "feeling of expression of reverence, adoration, religious homage," etc., all these definitions carry the idea of showing due honor that is given to someone or something for their own deserved merit. The origin of the word *worship* denotes the idea of worthiness, acknowledgment—all synonyms of the word *merit*. The word *merit* is defined as "the quality of being particularly good or worthy of praise or reward." To illustrate: there is a famous quote that says that in life only two things are certain, death and taxes. We all pay taxes; it is what is due to the government. Whether your local government uses such moneys for good or not, that is not the point. But the fact is that the government demands taxes out of its own volition and merit. It is what is due to it. It is a form of recognition, as taxes, by definition, are a "form of honor that is given in recognition of merit or credit." Another definition for *credit* tells us that it is "public acknowledgement or praise, typically that is given or received when a person's responsibility for an action or idea becomes apparent."

For example, a husband may decide to give his wife a rose and a card as a form of thanks for being a great mother to their children. Certainly he feels that she should be given proper "worship," for he feels like she deserves honor and recognition for being a nurturing mother to their children. Maybe a mother decides to give her daughter proper "worship" by giving her a shopping spree for excellent academic performance, as the daughter also deserves proper honor and recognition out of her own merit. A different scenario may occur. Let's take taxes again as an example. Regardless of how we may feel about paying our taxes to the government, we are rendering proper worship, for the government must be recognized and given its proper honor for their merit and services rendered. We may all be familiar with the famous remark by Jesus in reference to taxes: "Pay back, therefore, Caesar's things to Caesar, but God's things to God."

Spiritually minded people may object by saying, "But it is God who deserves the highest form of worship." While that may be true, does such a statement explain what that really means? What does such a belief really mean in its most fundamental definition? Can we suggest that God, as the creator of the universe with its most fundamental laws, is deserving of the highest form of recognition by law? Then like taxes, how can we properly honor him? The question then calls for knowing exactly what type of taxes we are to render to God. If we could ask him personally, how would he respond? The biblical reference points to the love of God as the highest law, for it tells us: "For this is what the love of God means, that we observe his commandments." (1 John 5/3)

So we must ask: What are the most fundamental and highest laws that we should observe so that we may exercise principal love for him and fulfill that first law? I believe we already went over those laws. Let's carefully consider these quantum laws of the universe to access the mind of God, for as Albert Einstein and Nikola Tesla emphasized, we must learn the mind of God and focus our most essential energies to the harnessing of such source of energy.

*Foundational Law of Immortality #1:*

"We must love God with your whole heart and with your whole soul, and with your whole mind."

*Foundational Law of Immortality #2:*

"We must love our neighbor as ourselves."

So God defines the observance of his highest laws as the highest form of worship or recognition that we can give to him. Therefore the observation and application of the most quintessential physical laws of the universe, in the light of the Golden Rule, as being the highest good for mankind, period. Then we can say that the highest form of worship or honor we can render to God is *for us to become a collective vibration of consciousness, vibrating together a set of specific energetic blueprints of frequencies, based on its most quintessential and vertex vibrational imprint: love.*

I don't know how much deeper we can possibly go to define love, worship, and true religion, or for that matter, church. For if we become what we think about, then we have the moral obligation to become love. We must learn to align our every thought, emotion, word, action, and habit to the apex of creation: love.

This has to be strongly considered at least if we are to succeed in achieving biological immortality, if not true worldwide peace and security.

What could be the result of such a paradigm shift on our current matrix of particles of energy defined by time and space? Will we be able to collectively vibrate so high, that lower-frequency manifestations such as illness and disease will just disappear on their own? Will we transform our energetic blueprints, based on our most prevalent thoughts, to command every action we take to be that of a loving nature and thus eradicate any possible outcome for war or the slightest form of violence? Will we ever be able to sustain this collective consciousness of vibrational energy long enough to create real, physical manifestations and create the desired shift?

The answer is no, we won't. At least not on our own, even as a collective family, the entire human genome. How can we possibly say such a statement after trying to build up credibility and faith on the concept of peace and immortality? This is as if we're saying, "Just kidding—it is impossible." While it is true that we will be able to achieve a measure of peace through these principles and laws, our nature has been fundamentally corrupted which must be reengineered into something new. We mentioned previously that there is an organization that is absolutely applying these principles and is progressively fulfilling the law, but it is far from perfect. Their effort to exercise love and permeate the ether by affecting our current matrix reality is absolutely being integrated into its fabric in time and space. But this will in no way achieve us immortality on its own, but it will, with certainty, push the world to achieve a measure of relative peace and security. This is why the scriptural reference points to a time where people will willingly and eagerly want to learn these laws. Why? The answer take us to the fourth key to the door to immortality to finally open.

# CHAPTER 10

# Blueprint For Immortality: Part II

The Fourth Key to the Door for Immortality
A Golden Rule Society Under One World Government a New
Trilateral Commission Under Christ Consciousness

"Public opinion, through the aid of an able organizer
and leader who will organize and direct the efforts of a
golden rule society, the object of which will be to move
the President and Congress into action." - Napoleon Hill

Let's define some titles of official responsibility as they stand today:

- Plenipotentiary: a person, especially a diplomat, invested with the full power of independent action on behalf of their government, typically in a foreign country.

- Ambassador: an accredited diplomat sent by a country as its official representative to a foreign country.

- Minister: A head of government, generally used to achieve, convey or administer something.

- Christ Consciousness: In this instance the writer is portraying these words to mean precisely, not the rulership under an accepted perceived individual deity, but a conscious mass awareness, a master mind if you will, that can create a 'Golden Rule' society. A new generation of people must grow up in our world that have and continue to fully integrate these universal principles with the awareness and desire to create and bring about 'the secret to immortality, of eternal beauty and youth,' as Nikola Tesla envisioned. But as he explained, it is inexorable agents that are preventing the mass consciousness, or the thinking and present awareness that is preventing us from making this quantum leap. These energetic webs will resist the change or the force of this new knowledge. But that it is time and persistence that will gradually modify human thinking.

TO CLARIFY THIS point, we must now become aware that the energy matrix program known as Christ Consciousness can essentially operate under any one individual at any point in time in the space time continuum. This is why many avatars have been recorded to appear at certain points through our historical record to distribute reminders of universal policy. Through the past 200 years this influence is becoming more obvious.

To illustrate we can consider that the physical universe works as the hardware of a massive computer. Within all its components there are software programs that run and facilitate the practical functions of such computer. If a virus were introduced, there are search programs or executive programs that will establish code to remove or rewrite codes for optimal operation of the computer.

The Christ program in essence has always existed and will continue to exist in order to help the universe's main frame to run our reality simulation as smoothly as possible. This allows for the players of this game to make progress so not one of the 'sheep of the fold' gets lost forever. So when these terms are used within this book, please be aware that it is always in reference to a consciousness or a software program that helps to direct our steps in the proper direction; prosperity and abundant life. In essence the universal policy is enforced through its components to help prevent mass software disruption.

### Plenipotentiary of Christ Consciousness?

The key words of this definition are connected to the stipulation that a single person, or group of people, have invested in them full power for independent action on behalf of a government. Therefore, people may be given the honor by their respective leaders to represent them when they are sent to use diplomacy when dealing with other representatives of others countries. Diplomacy is defined as 'the profession, activity, or skill of managing international relations, typically by a country's representatives abroad.' The most basic understanding of the word diplomacy is; 'the art of dealing with people in a sensitive and effective way.'

Then the question does come up and is worthy of examination in the light of the laws described thereof. Is the center and focus of the entire bible's message, that of following the pattern of Christ Consciousness, a representation worthy of replication? Why? Most of the world is at odds with universal policy or the natural rulership which can potentially create the foundation for a golden rule society. It is preventing or resisting the creation of a government with true leaders and representatives for this world that would help establish this movement.

As you read this book and apply its principles you will be met with overwhelming amounts of evidence proving that this world is controlled and manipulated by powerful forces beyond our ability to grasp under our present matrix of awareness. Thus Jesus was forced to respond to a governor: "My Kingdom is no part of this world. If my Kingdom were part of this world, my attendants would have fought that I should not be handed over to the Jews. But as it is, my Kingdom is not from this source." (John 18/36)

As we examine the scriptural references, we can see that Christ's consciousness was never of this world, but was sent as Plenipotentiary; invested with tremendous power to speak on behalf of an outside paradigm or government that it came from. For what? "Now there is a judging of this world; now the ruler of this world will be cast out." (John) Strong and powerful diplomacy is now being put into place and exercised by foreign powers. The Christ Consciousness operating through Jesus has come to conquer per say by infusing trust and power in its ability to supersede this world's social systems. He is also not doing it out of his own merit, but his power and authority as a plenipotentiary is strongly supported by the most fundamental laws of the universe and their originator.

Essentially, it is the energetic program that acts as a force to help individuals come to the apex awareness of their creative ability, or Christ Consciousness. There have been many through history who have displayed this awareness and their teachings, like these principles, are timeless.

Unfortunately we have been robbed of our perceptive powers through the energetic manipulation of our connection through both fields of energy defined, and not defined by time and space. So whether it is through our immediate five senses, or covertly, through the manipulation of wave frequencies in the air, our thoughts are being influenced to conceive that there is nothing more but this world.

These ministers are not coming here to destroy unjustly and indiscriminately populations of innocent people, but that ultimately will establish a take over by fulfilling the promise: "In the days of those kings the God of heaven will set up a government that will never be destroyed. And this government will not be passed on to any other people. It will crush and put an end to all these governments, and it alone will stand forever." (Daniel 2/44) In chapter 11 we will discuss how a foundation was helped to be established precisely on the 4th of July in the year 1776. The Declaration of Independence was a reflection of universal policy and in the last few centuries it has been undeniably demonstrated the positive impact that this government has brought upon the world.

The time is now to disconnect from the negative input and output these world's rulers are trying to progressively shape us into. We must align ourselves to the laws of the universe as described by empirical evidence so we may unplug by developing habits of behavior that will prepare us to "qualify" to become members of that coming true 'New World Order.' In fact we can become collectively an energetic blueprint that vibrates so high that our matrix awareness of particles defined by time and space will be shaped gradually 'and modified by time' to the reality which will work for the foundation to create this desired and most needed paradigm shift; 'A Golden Rule Society under a One World Government.'

So like citizen rights and privileges may be given to potential residents, we must either exercise our will to qualify for those future benefits, or continue on the despondency of this world with its negative patterns of behavior, ultimately finding ourselves disqualified and unfit from such promised new world. At which point we may never attain life eternal, peace and security. But like a cancerous body, we will just rot away and be either isolated without remission, or just completely removed from the entire body of energy. The worst case scenario is if we find ourselves fighting against those who wish to establish universal policy. Then the question we must each personally face; for when we are faced with these positive forces and observe a take over, whose side we'll we find ourselves taking?

The word Christ or Messiah, is closely related to the word plenipotentiary. The word Christ or Messiah means anointed, or chosen if you will; as someone nominated by a higher authority to be a successor or as a leading candidate for a position of responsibility. It is an appointment into an office of power and authority. Likewise when the context of the scriptural reference emphasized Jesus as being the Messiah or Christ, for by this reference we learn of his invested power to fulfill the universe's will to align our creative reality to its most fundamental laws, then we can see that his appointment was to a powerful position of governance and diplomatic influence.

Ambassador and Minister Under Christ Consciousness?

An ambassador uses diplomacy and goodwill to build relations with countries in which there is open diplomatic relations. For example; Jesus operating under the influence of Christ Consciousness, in his most basic essential pattern of behavior, has fulfilled diplomatic responsibilities in connection with the scriptural reference. Let's compare the responsibilities and duties of an ambassador as described by the U.S embassies' code, for the role of an ambassador is described as the following: "In most countries with which it has diplomatic relations, the U.S. maintains an embassy, which usually is located in the host country's capital. The U.S. also may have consulates in other large commercial centers or in dependencies of the country. The chief of Mission, with the title of Ambassador, Minister, or Charge d'Affaires -- and the Deputy Chief of Mission head the mission's "country team" of U.S. Government personnel. Responsibilities of Chiefs of Mission at post also include:

1.  Speaking with one voice to others on (country's) policy--and ensuring mission staff do likewise--while providing to the President and Secretary of State expert guidance and frank counsel.

Christ Consciousness as operating program through Jesus ambassadorship was proved as he focused his attention on universal policy; laws and principles defined by the most essential laws of physics. His prime role when on earth was to essentially construct consulates for the people to be in contact with the pre-established organized embassies. For what purpose? Congregations that would uphold the master mind of likeminded individuals, whose sole purpose became to replicate the disciple making work throughout the then known world. The congregations would integrate what was then known as the Hebrew scriptures with the newly founded edification of Jesus.

This organization's purpose would center on the idea that of a coming new world where 'God's will be done as it is heaven also upon the Earth'. Congregations, or embassies were to be established among every nation that is considered sovereign. Its constituents were to replicate the policy established by this representative from this foreign government, and thus warn people of its coming influence for failing to uphold the universal laws of justice. Thus Jesus ministry was closely and mainly patterned to the subject of government; the kingdom of God and its establishment upon the earth.

2.  Directing and coordinating all executive branch offices and personnel.

The various established congregations or government consulates had an inner circle membership or a governing body of members also called elders. This governing body were the earthly founders and main representatives of that main ambassador or plenipotentiary; whose job dictated to leave and report back to the mother land on the progress of the mission. These were known first as the 12 envoys. It was a cooperative liaison of direct mediators for newly converted members of the establishment for the new government councils or ecclesiastical building assemblies; churches or congregations. We could have just as easily describe that Jesus and his disciples founded the Christian church, but unfortunately these terms have become misnomers to most people of the world and have become devoid of true meaning. But by helping to emphasize that just like governments will establish embassies throughout the world to establish influence, so in the same manner through a series of actions and active common denominators, the authority and influence of now appointed Plenipotentiary influencing planet Earth, has been propagated as well through a parallel commission. Thus friendly relations have been established legally without having to use force of invasion, or covert means of creating coup d'etat to create a take over.

This ensures that people's lives are protected where chaos and civil war is averted, as a result of diplomatic requirements. In this manner people are influenced through the use of a propaganda machine or a system for the proper dissemination of policy. The laws of justice call into account that 'the inexorable agents which prevent a mass from changing suddenly its velocity would likewise resist the force of the new knowledge until time gradually modifies human thought.' (Tesla) Or as illustrated by a the dialogue in 'The Matrix,' 'we must understand that most of the peoples lives are so inert and hopelessly dependent on the present system, that they will fight to protect it.' They act as enemies of universal policy but they don't have to be, and could become viable subjects and supporters of this upcoming new establishment.

So the renewed terminology can restore powerful recognition by helping people understand and grasp that words like church, minister, and pastors in reality are timeless titles and tools that help to uphold the highest law of the universe; the fundamental laws for immortality. They are closely related to government appointed officials and public servants, for their roles have parallel responsibilities and their buildings uphold the same ideals.

The executive branches of the world's governments enforce the law. The legislative branches have the power to make laws. Finally, the judicial branches of governments help to interpret the law. In like manner these governing bodies within these consulates, helped to interpret and enforce the already established law; the natural laws of the universe. This ensures the propagation of foreign policy to the masses as it is still currently happening today. This dissemination of knowledge and policy is helping millions qualify to become members of the new global information network under the new governance lead by this new plenipotentiary or new prime-minister; Christ's Consciousness and the quintessence of the one who upheld the role of Jesus.

These entire systematic structures of government and its policies help to fulfill the following roles and duties of an ambassador:

3. Cooperating with respective country's legislative and judicial branches so that (respective country's) foreign policy goals are advanced, security is maintained; and executive, legislative, and judicial responsibilities are carried out.

4. Reviewing communications to or from mission elements.

5. Taking direct responsibility for the security of the mission -- protecting all (respective country's) personnel on official duty and their dependents.

6. Carefully using mission resources through regular reviews of programs, personnel, and funding levels.

Under the current paradigm of control and governance, this world's government establishment only exists due to the proper application of public funds; mainly taxes. The governments are required to properly use these funds for the entire mission and propagate its sovereignty. In a similar manner constituents under this new Christ Consciousness program encourage new potentials into alignment, and thus the new system of diplomacy was financed mostly by funds volunteered by those who accepted the new promised establishment. The kingdom of God then was upheld by its new members high in mind since not only did they have to pay taxes under their already established home country's government, but also would set aside any extra funds to support the new arrangement. Their energetic resources once sacrificed, helped them to qualify progressively to become citizens of the new kingdom. Jesus was quoted as giving this instructions:

> "Also, I say to you; <u>Make friends for yourselves by means of the unrighteous riches, so that when such fail, they may receive you into the everlasting dwelling places</u>. The person faithful in what is least is faithful also in much, and the person unrighteous in what is least is unrighteous also in much. Therefore, if you have not proved yourselves faithful in connection with the unrighteous riches, who will entrust you with what is true? And if you have not proved yourselves faithful in

connection with what belongs to another, who will give you something for yourselves? No servant can be a slave to two masters, for either he will hate the one and love the other, or he will stick to the one and despise the other. You cannot be slaves to God and to Riches." (Luke 13/9-13)

The fast growth of this new arrangement was driven forward by volunteered funds, rather than by compulsive taxes. For the laws of physics tells us that what is focused on and nurtured consistently must expand, and that whatever we put out must come back to us. This process then would re-enforce this newly established consulates to fulfill the authority of the plenipotentiary, for anything that was sacrificed for the new program had to come back to its members in the form of more benefits and resources. Then a momentum cycle would ensue and take over like a massive snowball effect, thus exponential growth took place in a relative short time. Like a massive pyramid network, the policy would appropriately be applied and upheld high for the sake of the mission statement and its vision:

"In the final part of the days, the mountain of the house of Jehovah will become firmly established above the top of the mountain. And it will be raised up above the hills, and to it the nations will stream. And many peoples will go and say: "Come let us go up to the mountain of Jehovah, to the house of the God of Jacob. He will instruct us about his ways, and we will walk in his paths...... He will render judgement among the nations and set matters straight respecting many peoples. They will beat their swords into plowshares and their spears into pruning shears. Nation will not lift up sword against nation, nor will they learn war anymore." (Isaiah 2/1-4)

Is it plausible to accept as fact that the role of the United States as diplomatic power and influence, is a foreshadow of what the world could become? Is it not obviously observable that the diplomatic system of the U.S constitution has created a nation of 50 states, united peacefully under the universal policy of God? Have not many nations been 'instructed about his ways and walked in the same pattern of governance creating the same positive outcome for themselves? Have not the 50 states, which could easily had become individual countries, beat their swords into plowshares and their spears into burning shears? Have not these 50 nations as states put away their swords and learned war no more?

Is it then not also plausible to accept the fact that even though the whole planet is still divided, that the unanimously decision of the world's governments to establish the same government world wide could create the same results? Has not in fact this quantum leap been aptly demonstrated that principles found within the U.S. constitution helped to bring the mountain of God to be firmly established above the top of the mountain, raised up above hill like nations? Have not nations streamed and continue streaming into the United States and nations like it, for they offer unprecedented freedom? For as defined by the U.S constitution, has not the modern world now prospered beyond the understanding of past generations and other nations, in contrast to those who do not uphold universal policy?

In chapter 11 we will explore these questions and how universal policy and influence from providence, or Christ Consciousness, was a force that helped to make the world a quantum leap of progress. A movement where we saw the world lifted from the abject mental and physical poverty to a world of unprecedented never before seen freedom and abundant prosperity.

There is absolutely one more concept that must be considered. This new vision cannot be fulfilled by just having and able rulership with power and authority sitting on a figurative throne per say. Neither can the success system of a powerful master mind and its replication process be the key to everlasting life and youth. This final key in its most basic components has three parts: its leader, the system, but the third part has to do again with more 'inexorable agents that prevent a mass from changing suddenly.' Why? Jesus explained it plainly:

> "Nobody sews a patch of unshrunk cloth on an old
> outer garment, for the new piece pulls away from the
> garment and the tear becomes worse. Nor do people
> put new wine into old wineskins. If they do, then the
> wineskins burst and the wine spills out and the wineskins

are ruined. But people put new wine into new wineskins, and both are preserved." (Matthew)

The first and final set of inexorable agents;
the error of our quintessence

This concept relates to an obscure fact in which there may be much debate. But by using enough deductive reasoning and examining as many facts as possible, then we can narrow down the determination of the nature of concepts. For example; if we look at our physical bodies we have examined that it breaks down from body parts, to cells, cell parts, to molecules, then atoms and finally energy. So we can say that our body is nothing but a form of collective energy. Obviously we know all there is to know to the point of realizing; this is what we know so far. So like everything that has been discussed up to this point in this book, these concepts will continue to be expanded upon much deeper into the future as more scientific understanding of the physical universe continues to unfold.

What we mean by the error of our quintessence, is that our most basic component that makes us aware, the 'I' is fundamentally flawed. This is most likely the reason we age and die. What is it being implied by the word concept of the awareness of the 'I'? This is in connection with the question that progressively is being continued to be asked by the general populace throughout the millenniums: Who am I? What am I? Why do I function? Why am I aware of me? How can I know I am unique and not just some robotic replica? These are all common questions that deserve an answer, for it is questions like these that makes us different from the animal kingdom which operates through mainly instinct. The answer to these questions will help us to define who we really are to its most basic definitions.

The movie 'Avatar' and 'The Matrix' give powerful descriptive illustrations of these concepts and we are encouraged to consider these movies as points of strong reference.

# Are we our body?

Can we say that we are our biological body? Let's ask; does it sound correct when we say, I am my arm or do I 'have' an arm? Am I my brain or do I have a brain? Am I my heart or do I have a heart? We all know deep inside that we are not those things because we know we always point to those things as personal property. It is the same idea when we think of things like, my couch or my TV. We say; 'I have a house', 'I have a car'. So in the same way we say we have ownership of those things, therefore, we own our body. It is scientific fact that our body renews its cells about every seven years, at which point we have a whole new body. But we are very much still aware that we are still ourselves, and our awareness of our quintessence is still intact and therefore we know we are the same person.

"And Jehovah God went on to form the man out of dust from the ground and to blow into his nostrils the breath of life, and the man became a living person." (Genesis) The scripture does seem to suggest that the first man was not a living person, or his record of life did not start but until the 'breath of life' was infused into the body that was to complement Adam. Body and energy were needed to complete that life and create Adam. For even in the scriptural reference it is emphasized that twice the life of Jesus, his quintessence or consciousness was 'TRANSFERRED' into a new body, a physical and then spiritual one, operative bodies under the their current matrix of energy. So the answer?

## 'We are not our bodies'

### Then,.. are we our thoughts?

There is a statement that has been coined by Rene Descartes where he said, "I think, therefore I am". This denotes also to the idea that our quintessence is not our thoughts. Since we also refer ourselves as having thoughts, then our ability to have thoughts, memories, concepts and mind pictures including every conceivable form of thought, helps us to discern and conclude that probably they are also only our property.

We can illustrate it by examining the concept of choice. Let's suppose that a woman is being courted by two men from two different countries. One is Mark and the other one's name is Jay. One lives in England

and the other one is from Australia. Brittany has a choice to decide to move to either Australia or England to further develop one of the relationships. Or maybe both men decide to move close to her vicinity to establish potential relations. Scientist are stipulating that there is the possibility that at a quantum physical level Brittany can and will make both choices since they are both potentials. As if our decision making abilities were just an illusion, and the second we have a choice to make, then our life is progressively splitting into an infinite amount of choices based on an infinite amount of potentials. They are suggesting that our lives continue to create an infinite amount of parallel universes, one where Brittany decides to be with Mark, and the other parallel universe where she decides to be with Jay. Therefore it is emphasized that her quintessence, or the things that makes her; 'Brittany', her consciousness and quintessence is also split into an infinite amount of times.

But this implies that we are nothing but empty vessels defined by our internal natural response to external output. Just a collection of memories based on experiences being accumulated to the point of death. We must come to understand that once Brittany decides to go to England to be with Mark, or be with Jay in Australia, or even stay home; her entire course of future memories and experiences will become completely different from the other potential choices. But regardless of her decision she will still be Brittany and her quintessence would be intact.

We can illustrate this concept further this way as well. Let's suppose that like using the copy and paste tool in a computer writing software program, we could copy our body and entire memory bank up to this point. You go in a machine; capsule A, and then the technology copies and pastes you on the other side into another machine; capsule B. You both come out of each capsule and examine there is an exact replica of you on the other side. But you realize he or she is no longer you. This is because you will both go on to make different decisions based on their personal quintessence and bodies defined in time and space. Both consciousness could not sustain the exact time and space for there is two of you now. Essentially not the same person. So like identical twins, triplets or quadruplets being born, they are essentially different people. All of them will go on to develop a complete set of different experiences, people and circumstances. Their memory banks will be much different even though they have the same looks and bodies. And even though they may see perfect replicas in front of each other, they each know and are aware of each other's quintessence, their own personal awareness of the "I". We know we are all unique.

> "His spirit goes out, he returns to the ground; on that very day his thoughts perish." (Psalm)

> "Then the dust returns to the earth, just as it was, and the spirit returns to the true God who gave it." (Ecclesiastes 12/7)

The Hebrew terminology emphasizes that in these contexts, after the physical body returns to the dust, then the spirit or breath of life comes out or goes forth to where it came from; God. But in connection with all this data, then can we conclude that we are not our thoughts, but that our thoughts are only a result of what we are? The reader may decide out of his own volition, for it is a concept that must be clarified, for the universal laws as defined by the field of quantum theory do give ample evidence that our particles that complement our body, do split and infinite amount of times based on all the potential up until now. For even the scriptural reference does emphasize we certainly are not our thoughts. For if we stop thinking the moment we die, then are we the spirit itself that goes out and goes back to God? I think so,.. but lets examine further evidence that:

## 'We are not our thoughts'

### So,... are we spirits?

There are some interesting dichotomies that give clear understanding of the possibilities of the answer to these questions when we examine certain stories and word contexts in the scriptural reference. One is found in the story of Jesus resurrecting his friend that had already been dead for 4 days. In this account we find Jesus explaining to his companions that he was to travel back to "awake his friend Lazarus for he had gone to sleep." He was obviously talking about his death. Throughout the context of the accounts that describe Jesus' ability, Jesus knew he could have healed him from a distance for he already had done that with others. But why did he not cure his friend before his death? The story gives tremendous data and perspective to what is possible. Many people believe that people go to heaven when they die to live in eternal bliss. Certainly if this is the absolute truth then surely Lazarus as Jesus close friend, would certainly have gone to heaven to live in eternal bliss. For 4 days he must have been in total ecstasy and happiness. (Luke 11)

But the account by definition tells us that this is far from the truth. Since Lazarus had been dead for already 4 days, then could we say that he was already watching his own body rot from heaven? Was he already enjoying the companionship of other relatives or angels and experiencing joy and perfect happiness and satisfaction? If that is true then Jesus did something out of character, because he decided to pull him out of heaven to put him back into his body back to live a life full of pain and misery in comparison. Obviously this was not the case, for Jesus had in actuality resurrected him. Lazarus was dead; meaning asleep as he illustrated, conscious of nothing at all.

> "There is hope for whoever is among the living, because a live dog is better off than a dead lion. For the living know they will die, but the dead know nothing at all... (Ecclesiastes 9/5)

> "The dead do not praise Jah; nor do any who go down into the silence of death." (Psalm 115/17)

"For the Grave cannot glorify you, Death cannot praise you. Those who go down into the pit cannot hope for your faithfulness." (Isaiah 38/18)

So up to this point we understand that even though we may not be conscious of anything at all when we die, we do also understand that something that makes us unique as individuals comes out and goes back to God; our spirit. Is our spirit our quintessence, is it who we are? The scriptural reference suggest to us that it is true. Another definition for the word spirit describes this word as; a quintessence of a highly refined substance or fluid thought to govern vital phenomena. Vital phenomena then is translated as an energetic object of a person's perception; what the senses or the mind notice. The Greek terminology denotes it as the thing appearing to view. It is the uniqueness and powerful phenomena of the power of observation connected to us.

To illustrate, in the Matrix movie, Neo is explained and trained to do whatever it takes to survive. For when their minds were hacked-in into the computer matrix program, and were killed in the process while experiencing the Matrix reality, they themselves would die in the real world. "The body cannot live without the mind." (Morpheus) Therefore a mind cannot live without a body.

Jehovah had responded to Adam after stealing property that was not his, the forbidden fruit; 'for dust you are and to dust you will return.' This cannot possibly mean that we become a big fat 0 in the space time continuum, but just like Jesus did to Lazarus, we are just waiting for a future resurrection.

"Do not be amazed at this, for the hour is coming in which all those in the memorial tombs will hear his voice and come out, those who did good things to a resurrection of life, and those who practiced vile things to a resurrection of judgement." (John 5/28,29)

"And I have hope toward God, which hope these men also look forward to, that there is going to be a resurrection of both the righteous and the unrighteous." (Acts 24/15)

This adds a powerful insight to the validity of our unique quintessence and God's ability to resurrect us. For if our quintessence becomes non existent, and God decides to create a new body just like ours in full detail with every memory and possible neural-pathway, then how could we know it is us and not just a replica of us? Certainly once such a person is recreated, they will know to be us because he or she has no choice but to know it is us. But it is not us for our quintessence is gone, and it is just a new quintessence being infused into a replica of our mind and bodies. So just like the illustration of the machine replicating us, the second person is an entirely different being and essentially not us. Like a burning candle flame just lighting a different candle, but essentially not the same candle nor the same energy force.

This makes a strong suggestion that also our entire energetic blueprint is also recorded into our spirit. Thus if we die and then are resurrected, our asleep spirit can be infused into a new body and become a living operating being again. A new body then can have our original quintessence that we received when we were conceived.

But let's regress for a second, since we also do not want to be dogmatic about anything here, for it is plausible we are somebody else when we leave our present identity. Lazarus identity may be just that; an identity. To illustrate, scientific research has explained to us that energy can never be destroyed but that it only changes shape. Spiritual philosophy has explained to us that we are made in the image of God. God has always been conceived as eternal, not having a beginning or an end. God has been described similar to the forces of the universe, ever present everywhere or omnipresent and omniscient. Quantum mechanics and its laws describe that us as energy are spread thin through all time and space, in essence omnipresent but we are just not aware of it.

This could mean that our present identity is just that, a set of people, circumstances, events and situations that we identify with. But that it is possible to experience a different identity through an infinite amount of different people, circumstances and events defined from birth to death, obviously not just one birth and one death. More research on this could give evidence to the powerful awareness of what many spiritual and ancient manuscripts have taught, that we can reincarnate and come back and experience a different identity if we feel we are done with the present one we are experiencing.

So why fret so much about biological immortality if we are eternal beings anyway? What is the purpose for myself as the author, writing this book, and bringing this message to you now reading this. Ultimately I would love to be a catalyst, or at least an influence to move humanity into the awareness and the plausibility of biological immortality and the expansion of our species as a force for good throughout the planet just like Tesla had in mind.. But why? So humanity can come to be in a place where we can choose to have, be and do whatever we desire without the fear of death. Where death is a conscious choice and not a circumstance forced upon us. Why? Because I agree with Nikola Tesla's observation of our nature, that eternal beauty is the aching need of humanity. Why? Has it not been our observation over that of our personal lives to be defined by various forms of enslavement? Have we not observed how our selves and loved ones live out our lives defined by despondency and unhappiness, and the experience of feelings of overwhelming disempowerment?

## In conclusion: We are our spirit (probably)

Earlier we pointed out to Jesus statement of not putting new wine into an old wine skin for it would just burst open and the new wine would be wasted. This means that unfortunately that just like our entire energetic blueprint is recorded in our quintessence, then putting our quintessence into a new body would just re-create and replicate the same outcome, death. Our every negative pattern whether inherited or developed through our life time, will permeate the newly formed body's energetic field and deteriorate it. For the low frequency of our negative programing is damaging and destructive. This gives powerful emphasis that our nature is flawed and must be repaired or cleaned out.

In this book, it is the author's absolute intention to build objectivity and restore truth from the scriptural reference. For the following connection of the previous information of our essence, supports the next axiom as it is supported heavily by everything previously discussed throughout this book. It has been suggested that a close examination of the entire biblical reference should be considered in the light of the newly discovered laws of quantum physics to create posterity. For what? To give at least circumstantial evidence that this widely accepted spiritual reference, does have basis in reality as a source of viable information without leaving room for prejudice.

This is not to say that everything in it is clear in connection with its various stories and large selection of reading material. But that just like the laws of physics have been timeless, so does the many of the principles found within have been shown to be timeless as well. Also, I am acknowledging that many of the so called laws of God or principles found within these various accepted spiritual references, no longer fit into the description of what quantum mechanics has shed light to be universal policy for the creation of a Golden rule society. We must also acknowledge that many books and publications may go out of print in just a few years, but the bible has survived millenniums for its practical value. But, we must also acknowledge that it has been used as a tool for control and repression, and because of its misuse and dogmatic approaches by many so called representatives of God it has wreck much havoc on humanity through past centuries. The quintessence of the one who identified as Jesus in the New testament warned of what would happen to his message by stating the following:

> "The kingdom of the heavens may be likened to a man who sowed fine seed in his field. While men were sleeping, his enemy came and oversowed weeds in among the wheat and left. When the stalk sprouted and produced fruit, the weeds also appeared. So the slaves of the master of the house came and said to him, 'Master, did you not sow fine seed in your field? How, then, does it have weeds? He said to them, 'An enemy, a man, did this.' The slaves said to him, 'Do you want us, then, to go out and collect them?' He said, 'No, for fear that while collecting the weeds, you uproot the wheat with them. Let both grow together until the harvest, and in the harvest season, I will tell the reapers: First collect the weeds and bind them in bundles to burn them up; then gather the wheat into my storehouse." (Matthew 13/24-30)

## What did it all mean? He explained:

> "The sower of the fine seed is the Son of man (Christ Consciousness), the field is the world. As for the fine seed, these are the sons of the Kingdom, but the weeds are the sons of the wicked one, and enemy who sowed them is the Devil. The harvest is a conclusion of a system of things and the reapers are angels. Therefore, just as the weeds are collected and burned with fire, so it will be in the conclusion of the system of things. The Son of man will send his angels, and they will collect out from his Kingdom all things that cause stumbling and people who practice lawlessness, and they will pitch them into a fiery furnace"

It is important to acknowledge that there may be times where universal policy demands that the prosperity of those who uphold it, be protected from those who do not uphold the highest forms of principle.

> "A man who stiffens his neck after much reproof, will suddenly be broken beyond healing. When the righteous are many the people rejoice, but when the wicked rules, the people groan." (Proverbs 29/1,2)

People may fret, and dispute the validity and integrity of religious organizations, but it is the fact that people still uphold respect and honor for the New Testament's general positive instruction. As we may find most of the time that the only reason religious organizations become widely criticized, it is due to their failure to uphold to what they claim to represent and practice; principles of good found in many of these scriptural references. Religious organizations' failures, does not in any way take credibility away in the book's reputation, but that just like a mirror, we can contrast its teachings to the validity of people's claims to practicing its principles, whether collectively or individually, for the biggest minority is the individual.

We also want to acknowledge that specific beliefs about so called holy scriptures, and who God is, have been detrimental to the well being and progress of humanity. Beliefs such as:

– Holy Book X or other scripture, is the one and only inspired word of God ever.

– That people's perceived gods or authorities are the only true and inspired authorities and completely infallible.

These beliefs have been a force against the laws of nature and universal policy, what makes things work for a peaceful and happy species. More wars have been campaigned in the name of gods, angels and demons than any other reason in history. More freedom and prosperity has been destroyed in the name of gods and Devils than anything else in history. The dark ages was an absolute testament that biased dogma is destructive to principles of liberty and freedom.

But what does the general credence in these historical spiritual references have anything to do with the fourth key to immortality.

As suggested before, the author is absolutely not in any way desiring to be dogmatic about anything on this book. New studies in the field of science or technology could completely squash and discredit this entire philosophy. But it is highly unlikely, for we are basing it mostly on empirical evidence and established facts in the field of science. Therefore, if we thus far have accepted that laws of quantum physics and principles of life as clearly defined throughout the scriptural references, then we have to consider the probability that every story and account, or at least most of them found within, are viable and have had basis on reality.

This brings us to the story of Adam and Eve the supposed first human couple. Who were they? How did they think? How did they feel? How did they act? Is it true that they introduced such a thing as "sin" into their entire genome? What exactly is sin? To bring clarity to the story or allegory, we must realize that this entire account is teaching us about energetics and laws of the physical universe as they operate in connection with us. But first it must be acknowledged that the story of Adam and Eve could be one of four perceptions.

1. An illustration to explain specific perceived notions about life.
2. A story highly edited and made to be believed without question for control and manipulation.
3. A myth or story that factually took place but was heavily distorted to fit preconceived notions of how life started on the planet.
4. A myth or story that factually took place but currently only symbolizes our memory of the first version of the human species, but obviously more than just two were created.

I am heavily inclined to suggest to the reader that all four perceptions are factually true. But so as to not deviate from the main point, these topics will be discussed and explored more heavily in a future book.

We know for a fact that humans have lived more than 6000 years. Archeological and scientific research has proved beyond a shadow of a doubt that this is the case, and for that reason a debate will not be started here. Exact mathematical equations have proven that the universe is 13.772 billion years. There are billions of stars in our milky way galaxy with trillions of planets orbiting those stars. There are also trillions of galaxies that form clusters of galaxies which form super clusters. And within those galaxies ever more stars and bodies that could complement planets with intelligent beings and civilizations like ourselves. To believe within this premise that we are the only creation to exist or have exited ever, or that we are the only physical intelligent species God created ever in this massive ever expanding universe is but absolute and resolute ignorance.

It is also written that everything that has happen will happen and has already happened and will happen an infinite amount of times, this is the foundation of our creative ability. Thus yours and our individual lives exist currently because in essence it was programed into the universe to be so from its foundation. Our life as it stands now has happened because its possibility was already programed into its matrix. So when we deny the undeniable overwhelming evidence of intelligence outside of our sphere is like denying that the law of gravity exists. This fact then allows for questions like the following to come up: Have we been visited by intelligent life forms in the past? What about now? Are we being observed or manipulated by them? Are all the scriptural stories of beings coming down from heaven with great power and ability, just the limited description about highly advanced beings through the perception of ancient and limited civilizations? Thus, did they claimed them to be God or the gods? This is highly complex and more of it will be explored on 'Blueprint for Immortality book II'.

## Sin and Imperfection

This topic will be explored under the following premise. If we have been taught by our past generations that we were born in sin, what is the definition of sin? Thus, if sin exists, then did God create it? If we are inclined to say that God did not create sin then does that mean something can exist that God did not create and thus he has no control over it, for he did not create it? Would that indicate that if this were to be true, that God then is not all powerful? But if we are inclined to believe that God created everything including sin then he also created what we have perceived to be evil, bad or negative. For if the laws of physics stipulate that everything that can happen will happen, then must we not conclude that God also created the laws of physics that allow for what we perceive as negative things to occur and thus the foundation for true free will?

This topic also must be discussed under this second premise. For if God created the myriads of possible universes with all its stars and planets, and thus the laws of physics explain that everything that can happen will happen, then, we must conclude that there must be other intelligent beings outside of our sphere of universal influence. Thus original sin is not what we have made to believe without question.

For if God created sin and imperfection, then its possibility is fully integrated into the fabric of space and the matrix of both particles defined by time and space and particles not defined by time and space. Were it otherwise, it could not be. Then, does that mean that these other civilizations outside of our sphere of influence are also prone to sin and imperfection? Is it possible for these beings to sin against God? For then we would have to ask, have and did other beings sin against God across the universe? How many times? How many different civilizations have sinned? And do they all have their own so called 'lord and savior.'?

Then under this premise, to believe, that in this infinitesimally small point of time and space in contrast with the rest of the universe, what we now call civilization on Earth, is the only place where evil or sin has been is but a silly notion. If it were true then this would have to mean that everywhere in the universe but planet Earth is paradise. Of course common sense let's us know this is far from the truth.

These conclusions then forces us to acknowledge one obvious and glaring truth; that it is extremely unlikely that the gods described in the various texts such as Yahweh, Jehovah, Allah or Jesus as the only true God and only God. But that they are most likely highly advanced beings from outside of our sphere of influence or planet Earth. Essentially, Genesis chapter one describes an extremely vague and primitive description of how the Universe came to be. But that Genesis chapter two suggest gods as planting the Garden of Eden and recreating already established life on Earth. It describes a point in time infinitesimally small in contrast with the life span of the physical universe. The Genesis account is but a small premise to describe the influence of beings outside of our globe in essence establishing dominance and rulership thereafter.

This book is not written to debate historical accuracy of spiritual books, but it is the choice of the author to convey context for the principles contained within. It is all designed to expand or stretch the reader's mind to a new perception evidently being demonstrated through empirical evidence. What empirical evidence? The author would suggest the reader to search online viable sources that refer to the 'ancient astronaut theory.' For what purpose?

## The True Definition of Sin and Imperfection

This will helps us to see that is not sin against God that brings destruction but negative thinking and using our creative ability to harm ourselves and others. We can perceive also for every action there is an equal and opposite reaction and that for the world of the relative, our world, to function as it stands God did create all its components. Completely understanding that our quintessence is marred or not, and whether our very consciousness is corrupted or not, will help us know where we stand in relation to being able to put together the final key to immortality.

We defined that faith is in essence thinking about what you want with positive assurance, and that fear is also in essence thinking about what you don't want with assurance. We either have faith that we can have or achieve something with certainty or we have faith that we cannot have or achieve something with certainty. One is positive and the other is negative. One is a high frequency and the other vibrates much lower. The question then does come up as to the nature of our collective frequency? If at some point in creation we existed as beings with absolutely no negative thoughts yet introduced into our essence, then our exercise of prolonged vibrations to such nature of thoughts must have been almost impossible.

We do know it was absolutely possible, for as we know from Newton's third law of motion; that 'for every action there is an equal and opposite reaction', then the following text shows how this law was allowed to operate in our individuals lives as it respects to our free will:

"Thus Jehovah God made to grow out of the ground every tree that was pleasing to look at and good for food and also the tree of life in the middle of the garden and the tree of the knowledge of good and bad."

There is much debate as to the exact ramifications of both trees, but one thing is certain; one promised life and the other one promised knowledge. How do we know? The story explains that once the couple decided to take from the tree of knowledge of good and bad, God responded like this:

> "Jehovah God then said: 'Here the man has become like one of us in knowing good and bad.' Now in order that he may not put his hand out and take fruit also from the fruit from the tree of life and eat and live forever." (Genesis 3/22)

The emphasis is clear, the possibility still was even acknowledged by the caretaker of this garden, that they could live forever by eating of the fruit from the tree of life. We can stipulate that the fruit might have been infused with energetic properties that would allow the human body to continue in its fortitude forever as long it was persistently nourished by the tree's fruit, but we certainly don't know for sure. This may also suggest that their bodies were also made in a way that would progressively decay like everything we find in nature, but that as long as they were able to partake of the tree of life they would be able to live indefinitely or for much larger periods of time.

Regressing though, we must acknowledge in the same manner, thus far as we have perceived it is highly unlikely that the person known as Jehovah was in essence the God of creation. But most likely Jehovah is the name that represents a group of beings representing themselves as our gods, managers or ministers from outside our sphere of influence, planet Earth.

But we can come to this conclusion by seeing the facts, mainly that sin and death are fully integrated into physical universe, thus a way to perpetuate for an individual's life to exercise free will by living with the choice, to die or not to die. But that with the tree of life, we could exercise our will power to continue to live forever until we would become able to access God's essence within us, for God is in all things. Therefore it is only a matter of time before we become aware of life within us. We are energy and energy cannot be destroyed but only change form.

Adam and Eve then are described as beings not allowed to partake from the tree. The result then was a creation of degenerative negative frequencies ultimately deteriorating their entire energetic blueprint to their own detriment, also an inheritance for their progeny for centuries to come. Our entire quintessence was doomed from conception because the energetic patterns from our first parents heavily programed their quintessence. Our manipulated DNA frequency was then programed with extremely low vibrations and thus programed our entire existence with habits of fear, greed and betrayal; all original frequencies generated by the brain transmission of what became their most prevalent thoughts. Any hope to gain biological immortality is now funded on the hope of getting access to the tree of life, for it would perpetuate our existence and life. Then we would have all the time in the world to exercise faith and develop stronger patterns of behavior much more positive than the garbage that has been handed down to us, a joke of an inheritance of sickness and death. So where is the tree? Enter; "Prime Minister of the Universe. Jesus, under the influence of Christ Consciousness said:

> "Let the one who has an ear hear what the spirit says to the congregations. To the one that conquers I will grant to eat of the tree of life, which is in the paradise of God." (Revelation 2/7)

It is the Plenipotentiary and main Ambassador, and now Prime-Minister of the government of our universe, that has complete authority and access to the 'Garden of Eden" and the "Tree of life". Timeless symbols of what is absolutely possible for humanity to accomplish. But what does he mean by; 'to the one that conquers I will grant to eat"? And more significantly where is the paradise of God?

The following scripture does shed clear insight to where the tree of life currently resides:

> "I have to boast. It is not beneficial, but I will move on to supernatural visions and revelations of the Lord. I know a man in union with Christ who, 14 years ago-- whether in the body or out of body, I do not know; God knows--was caught away to the third heaven. Yes, I know such a man--whether in the body or apart form the body, I do not know: God knows-- who was caught away into paradise and heard words that cannot be spoken and that are not lawful for a man to say." - Paul of Tarsus (2 Corinthians 12/1-4)

Here again the scriptural reference gives emphasis that our quintessence can be either pulled from, or most likely stretched from; the current vibrational body house.

The visions were either in the body or out of the body. Or it also suggests that his spirit or quintessence was caught (stretched) away, in the body or out of the body. Either way the context leaves no room for any other possibility, but that it was his experience of such phenomena only determined by one or the other; in the body or out of the body.

With this in mind the fact that his experience could have been out of body, suggests that his awake quintessence was literary in the immediate locality of paradise as it stands within time and space. On the other hand it also suggests that, if his experience was in the body, then his visions were of the literal paradise. It could be stipulated that like a telescope that uses quantum properties, such technology could allow us to observe the distance between the interstices of the dimensional field constructed and defined by the energetic spectrum of light. For example; the scriptural reference tells us that the Garden of Eden was somewhere close to the Euphrates River. Let's suppose that we, somehow knew exactly where the Garden used to reside. The reference tells us that paradise is currently on the third heaven. If we were to vibrate as high as that plain field, then it would be the law that we would find ourselves traveling between the interstices of energy that divide the dimensional fields. It has been previously mentioned, scientist are suggesting of the possibility for parallel universes. In essence we would be traveling through time and space both vertically and horizontally under the same point. Although we disagree that our quintessence could not possibly be defined by just choice, this does not mean that the particles of energy that exist in duality that compose the entire universe do not have their parallel counterparts. The laws of physics defined by quantum mechanics does explain that this is true.

Particles of energy can be influenced to vibrate higher or lower based on external influence. As such is the case we can deduce slightly that if we live in the lower levels, say energetic heaven negative 'ten'; then we would only have to vibrate high enough to access the 'third' heaven. In essence we either climb the steps or take an elevator that will take us from base floor number ten to the third. But as mentioned previously, it is Prime Minister of the universe or Christ Consciousness who holds authority, and he will only give access to those who qualify; those who have conquered. We must align our creative abilities to universal policy.

(To clarify this point, we must now become aware that energetic matrix program known as Christ Consciousness can essentially operate under any one individual at any point in time in the space time continuum. This is why many avatars have been recorded to appear at certain points in our life to distribute reminders of universal policy. To illustrate we can consider that the physical universe works as the hardware of a massive computer. Within all its components there are software programs that run and facilitate the practical functions of such computer. If a virus were introduced, there are search programs or executive programs that will establish code to remove or rewrite codes for optimal operation of the computer.

The Christ program in essence has always existed, will continue to exist in order to help the universe's main frame to run our reality simulation as smoothly as possible. This allows for the players of this game to make progress so not one of the 'sheep of the fold' gets lost forever. So when these terms are used within this book, please be aware that it is a reference to a consciousness or a software program that helps to direct our steps. In essence the universal policy is enforced through its components to help prevent mass software disruption.)

How do we conquer? What do we conquer? Do we need training to conquer? These and more are good questions, for as a minister he can qualify us to receive access to the tree of life and finally attain biological immortality.

Hear What the Spirit Says to the Congregations

Another way of saying this is we must take in instruction and training as a prerequisite by plugging into the system of replication created and established by the quintessence or operative consciousness of Jesus or others who taught and emphasized the same teachings while on Earth. These systems of training were propagated through the consulates or embassy buildings that represent the universal government or christ consciousness. It is the foreign entity that Jesus represented as its Ambassador or Plenipotentiary. These are terms that describe the nature of his office and public service as he implements and executes universal policy as defined by the universal laws. We must be instructed of his authority and the spirit that operates for those who exercise the universe's most fundamental laws. This is the only way to conquer.

Conquer what? We must conquer the world's influence in our mind and its negative inputs as defined by the collective quintessence of the lives of the entire populace. It is the entire blueprint of energy that permeates the programming of peoples spirits; the negative feedback of who they are as they influence the collective brain transmissions of the populace. This entire energetic program propagates through the matrix of particles of energy defined and not defined by time and space. Jesus explained it in simple terms: "I have said these things to you so that by means of me you may have peace. In the world you will have tribulation, but take courage! I have conquered the world." (John 16/23)

Other scriptural references give even more insight as to what conquering the world means:

> "For this is what the love of God means, that we observe his commandments; and yet his commandments are not burdensome, because everyone who has been born from God conquers the world. And this is the conquest that has conquered the world, our faith." (1 John 5/3,4)

> "I have fought the fine fight, I have run the race to the finish, I have observed the faith." (2 Timothy 4/7)

> "I am writing you, little children, because your sins have been forgiven you for the sake of his name. I am writing you, fathers, because you have come to know him who is from the beginning. I am writing you, young men, because you have conquered the wicked one. I write you, young children, because you have come to know the father. I write you fathers, because you have come to know him who is from the beginning. I write you, young men, because you are strong and the word of God

remains in you and you have conquered the wicked one"
(1 John 2/12-14)

"Furthermore, the world is passing away and so it
its desire, but the one who does the will of God remains
forever." (1 John 2/17)

Observing and living up to the physical laws of the universe is doing the will of God, for as we observe and live up to them with positive goals in mind we will always fulfill the Golden Law. Our service to others to improve their lives by creating in other people's lives desirable circumstances will allow us to exercise the quintessence of moral law. Our persistence will continue to help us maintain integrity as we uphold the fundamental laws for immortality. Loving others as we love ourselves will help us to continue exercising our faith, our ability to sustain positive frequencies for prolonged period of times to reprogram our spiritual nature.

But one more thing is required from Prime Minister of the universe; the reprogramming of our DNA and the reformatting of our spirit to the point where we could access life within us. Our quintessence must be reset from its inherent negative programming that has been passed down through generations.

We will now examine how the matrix program known as Christ Consciousness has used its trilateral commission as; Plenipotentiary, Prime Minister of the Universe and its Ambassadorship to gradually modify the vibrational blueprint of our world for the better. For its programming continues to modify human thoughts so its inexorable agents that prevents us from making the quantum leap to eternal life may be removed.

Prime Minister; Administers Life

"If the dead are not to be raised up, 'let us eat and drink, for tomorrow we are to- 'die.'" (1 Corinthians 15/32)

This short and simple sentence defines the entire axiom of what is stipulated to be all religious faith. For if it is a lie that the quintessence of Jesus, acting and influenced by Prime Minister, was not resurrected, then any belief in biological immortality is also a lie. But as we have examined the laws of physics as stipulated by quantum mechanics, these allow room for the plausibility that Jesus was indeed a real life time character who was infused with incredible powers of will. His advanced technology was able to control weather, heal illnesses in an instant, even raise up dead people. A close examination of Prime Ministers' energetic vibrational imprint by observing the nature of his thoughts, words, actions and habits of response and initiative, can give us ample evidence of his authoritative legal disclosures. This includes the seemingly impossibility of his personal resurrection.

But why would he have to give up his life to help us attain eternal life and for that matter forgiveness of our so called 'inherited sins or errors'? Why would the universe or God need a scape goat to supposedly forgive or just forget about seemingly serious errors committed through our lives? Why does the life of a sinless person with a clear quintessence free from fear, have anything to do with the ability to just forgive the conscious negative vibrations that dominate people to live in fear? Are we just not victims of unfortunate circumstances and situations?

## Our Inheritance; A Debt Sentence

The words; 'sin' and 'forgiveness of sin' have now become misnomers. Why? Because in reality what we owe is taxes. We have failed to give proper recognition to the highest authorities of the universe, mainly natural law and universal policy, for it is required to live in harmony with them for a life of prosperity and peace. Since our entire energetic blueprint vibrates and permeates all time and space, then such vibration of light also reaches the source. But are we paying back with illegal monies? Is our entire nature an improper application of the laws of the universe?

We already discussed the nature of true worship. It is nothing more than giving the proper merited recognition that someone or thing deserves. We realize that the proper recognition of God is to follow and observe its most fundamental laws of the universe. They are mainly closely connected to absolutely persevering in the Golden Rule including loving God. Hard cash is used as legal tender, it is backed up by the acceptance or recognition that money has value based on its wide and excessive circulation. We all must pay taxes for if we don't we will pay a higher price with our property or even our freedom.

Then how much more the energetic taxes we must pay to the creator? Jesus did emphasize that this was absolutely the case when it came to the nature of our so called sins. On the famous 'Lord's prayer he said when considering God in prayer; 'Forgive us our debts, as we also have forgiven our debtors'. He also gave an illustration:

> "That is why the kingdom of the heavens may be likened to a king who wanted to settle accounts with his slaves. When he started to settle them, a man was brought in who owed him 10,000 talents. But because he did not have the means to pay it back, his master ordered him and his wife and his children and all the things he owned to be sold and payment to be made. So the slave fell down and did obeisance to him, saying, 'Be patient with me, and I will pay back everything to you.' Moved with pity at this, the master of that slave let him off and canceled his debt." (Matthew 18/23-27)

Interestingly, the king canceled the slave's debt. The slave was hopelessly in debt with absolutely no means of paying the king back. The story of Adam and Eve, it seems, was used to illustrate to us that negative patterns of behavior can be passed down and thus create a continual cycle that creates pain and suffering from generation to generation. By pulling away our vibrational focus from God as the source to our perspective focus, we take away what rightly belongs to God but mainly to ourselves. Failing to uphold universal policy is a decision. These decisions also program our future and our unborn potential progeny so that their energetic frequency of vibration would then be set on auto pilot to vibrate away from the source once conceived. Failure to pay taxes was then perpetuated into the human genome. Thus we have become hopelessly in debt, for we could only cancel our debt with our lives. This is why the scriptural reference explains that the wages sin pays is death.

If we think about it, when we are personally offended by others, we feel hurt or under appreciated for we have not received the proper recognition of the value our lives. We know we have value and are worthy of respect and love, for that is how we are made. When we fail to receive that from others, or we fail to give that to others, the stipulation teaches us that we in fact become indebted to them when we offend, or them to us when we are offended. We demand retribution with interest unless we decide to cancel such debts. That is why it was emphasized in the illustration of the king and the slave that we should just as easily forgive others failures to give us proper recognition in the same way that God had done the same by bailing us out of our debt. For if we fail to do so, then our debts will just be reaffirmed in the same manner that we have reaffirmed the debt that we may feel others owe to us. In essence we must accept the fact that any perceived damage is self created mainly from a subconscious level. By acknowledging that we create our own reality we can begin to manifest better situations and patterns.

For just as easily as the King can forgive large debts, then how could we owe anything to someone who owns it all. Why would a King who has it all require more?

So by accepting that the universe just naturally responds to our energetic patterns of programming, then we know that it is only by asking for forgiveness for any perceived damage in us or outside of us. For example a baby who lived during World War II could not have consciously created or consciously chosen for the out break of World War II. But everyone in the planet had a slight negative vibratory frequency that added to the collective creation of a second World War. But what could possibly be in a new born baby and by connection the whole world that could collectively create such violence?

We must remember that the nature of energy will manifest into physical reality when it reaches critical mass. Then the war is an obvious mirror reflection telling us that there is a little bit of violence, intolerance and bias in all of us. So when we hear reports of war, murders, violence, kidnappings and other perceived evils we must accept responsibility that it is a reflection of negative energetic patterns in all of us, as individuals and collectively. We may exercise our mental abilities and pray that we be cleared of such internal code, in essence ask for forgiveness.

Our only hope for progress from such degenerative coding, is for God to cancel our debt by committing to his legal disclosures. The nature of these disclosures will guide us back to paying back our debts by accepting the proper government bail outs that are being rendered. The key is we must qualify and accept the new government program that will absolutely cancel our debts. Thus Christ Consciousness can and will always provide what is necessary for the assurance of life. Life is and will always be, life always will find a way. This is God's guarantee that we will never be lost in within the universe's programing forever.

## Legal Disclosure for Loss of Property

We have been made to consciously make decisions to legalize by our own consent and free will, to make and create our own laws. Since energetically our choices affect our quintessence, our ability to rely on the pre-established Plenipotentiary already ruling throughout the universe was made void and canceled. No longer citizens of that universal kingdom, the human race was and has always been at the mercy of those who have chosen exile and separation from that arrangement. Thus the human dream in connection with the universal policy in relation to mankind's future plans was severed.

We became lost property and potential value for the kingdom of the universe. This made for a legal disclosure or decree, a new arrangement for a way back to regain what was lost: "the quintessence of mankind fully restored to its original purpose." This new legal disclosure then was progressively revealed through the centuries for those who were deemed potentials. These potentials would prove their desire to return to the source by doing their best to uphold specific instructions given at epochs. Our entire historical reference is in essence a transcript of the positive and negative consequences of those who have submitted to universal policy or not; it is a progressive demonstration of the application of diplomacy by the will of the universe as defined by the laws of physics. The scriptural reference explains that it is the will of God that would reveal this legal disclosure.

Through a series of legal disclosures, which were made legitimate by envoys sent to transfer information to those potentials, the answer was revealed. Through these procedures legal agreements were made between potentials and envoys by the legal authorities entrusted to the representatives of the universal government. As orders were recognized and carried out by the candidates, then further instruction was further passed down for progressive fulfillment.

For the most part the Hebrew scriptures denote the emphasis of the positive and negative results, the outcomes that singular and collective prospects of the kingdom experienced as they 'faithfully' carried out the universal policy given to them, or when they failed to do so. These legal disclosures gave specific instructions that would eventually return to the source those who listened; the potentials would be brought back in time to the original state of affairs that was supposed to originate and perpetuate the human race.

The results and benefits of plugging into the universal policy were described in the preceding chapters. It is encouraged to the reader to reread Deuteronomy 28/1-14 to get the essence of what was supposed to become the collective reality of its benefactors.

Tremendous benefits thus needed to be perceived by potentials from the Kingdom of the universe to remake and refute the already wired previous decision. Transactions of purchase and exchanges of goods needed to be implemented on the lost property in order to recoup what was considered loss. So like a business investor who sees potential on a business going bankrupt due to incompetent management by previous ownership, progressive restoration and investment would have to be made to save the business concept. In this case, mankind needed some serious change of management and ownership to one that was more competent and able. This is where the role of Prime Minister had to come in, and his office had to funnel and siphon valuable resources and energies to bring about this radical change upon the human race.

No expenditure has been held back for even the value of the lives of the many avatars operating has been put into contract under legal disclosures. Willingly, like a seriously committed business man, Prime Minister gave up everything to ensure the success of his trilateral commission for the fulfillment and completion of the project. So what is the result that is being kept in mind by the highest forces of the universe? "What is mortal man that you keep him in mind, and a son of man that you take care of him? (Psalms 8/4)

We don't know for sure for it would certainly take an eternity to progressively experience what is the real value of a human life. But what we do know for sure is what that legal disclosure has progressively revealed to us up to this point:

"With that I heard a loud voice from the throne say: 'Look! The tent of God is with mankind, and he will reside with them, and they will be his people. And God himself will be with them. And he will wipe out every tear from their eyes, and death will be no more, neither will mourning nor outcry nor pain be anymore. The former things have passed away." (Revelation 21/3,4)

"For the vision is yet for its appointed time. And it is rushing toward its end, and it will not lie. Even if it should delay keep in expectation of it! For it will without fail come true. It will not be late." (Habakkuk 2/3)

It is the absolute promise that the Christ Consciousness matrix, as it continues to operate through chosen individuals through time will culminate in that final vision for mankind and will be fulfilled. So just like Nikola Tesla envisioned the secret for immortality, youth and beauty; so has also this scriptural reference denote to us carefully throughout, all the way to the conclusion of its extensive record. Thus when we choose to accept the full value of our repurchase or reinvestment, then our personal individual lives as potentials of the new kingdom will prosper like a fully renovated business enterprise. It may sound bizarre for humans to be referred as corporate entities, but even the present system of things of rulership has deemed all human life exactly that; corporate property.

The legal disclosure is a guarantee through the universal policy established by God and by its highest constituents of government. The legal procedures have been implemented, and the payment for the proper exchange of goods has been ratified by the highest courts of justice. The decree by the authority of God has been put into effect and it has no choice but to transform the particles of infinite possibility to become what God originally envisioned. It must come true period. It will ultimately be up to us to finally qualify to become citizens of that government. Plenipotentiary will then establish a foundation for a peaceful takeover of this old world bringing tremendous benefits to all who align their quintessences to universal policy.

## The Final Axiom: The Reengineering of our DNA Genome

Billions of people have paid the cost of fear and negative thinking with their lives. Everyday millions of people still do. Whether is timeless death due to illness, disease, pain or accidents, they are all a co-creation of the collective human genome. We do not qualify to receive and eat from the tree of life for if our quintessence were to continue vibrating negatively we would continue to create chaos and misery and we would become a destructive black hole of negative energy for life. We would progressively become the antithesis of light particles, and like matter being clashed with anti matter we would only become a neutralizing force for creation. The law is we must die for we are essentially corrupted energy in vessels of fear and a destructive force to life.

But as we were promised through the various legal disclosures, our debts have been canceled through Prime Minister's resignation and dissemination of the code found in his quintessence. For what purpose? To bring potentials back to perfection, for perfection is only defined by the ability to know that a tool or thing is being used properly according to the purpose it was created to accomplish. Perfection is only relative to the instruction manual that ensures the proper use of a creation. Creations' instructional program is defined by the laws that are relevant to our present, and so when we come to become in disharmony with it, we become faulty products and must be recalled to the source. It is stipulated by the warranty that at the point of discovery of faulty equipment, immediate repair and restoration must be implemented. It is also true that due to misuse, equipment can become damaged beyond repair and as such it is scraped for its remaining usable value. This absolutely can happen to us and thus our identity could become beyond repair and thus we can just come back to the source for original reformatting. At that point we may lose the personal identity we presently identify with.

As we may recall, our entire genetic code including our neural pathways vibrate into the ether and permeate the interstices of energy of particles defined and not defined by time and space. Christ Consciousness while on Earth through many avatars has thus far vibrated its entire genome and resonated his entire codified vibrational blueprint. The ether must have been completely saturated by the high frequency of the nature of such beings. Thus we can get closer to accessing powerful concepts, cognitions and discoveries that we can integrate into our quintessence for the proper application of the laws of the universe. For as we exercise our will to align ourselves to the universal laws, by law of magnetic attraction, the powerful attractive forces will bring in like minded thoughts ultimately bringing us closer to Christ's Consciousness. In essence we will progressively vibrate higher and the ability to act on fear will be also progressively be removed from our consciousness, for even our spoken words will always be marked by positive reflection.

> "For we all stumble many times. If anyone does not stumble in word, he is a perfect man, able to bridle also his whole body." (James 3/2)

On the other hand if we fail to appreciate this provision and bailout, then we will become universal junk. Rejecting repair will only separate us even further from the apex creation through the space time continuum. The world of peace and security will continue to be beyond our grasp for its resonance of existence will continue be beyond our current vibrational point. This will be true for us whether in the body or out body. But as potentials the entire human race has been repurchased and given an another chance at doing it right this time:

> "Do not be amazed at this, for the hour is coming in which ALL those in the memorial tombs will hear his voice and come out, those who did good things to a resurrection of life, and those who practiced vile things to a resurrection of judgement." (John 5/28,29)

> "Your dead will live. My corpses will rise up. Awake and shout joyfully, You residents in the dust! For your dew is as the dew of the morning. And the earth will let those powerless in death come to life." (Isaiah 26/19)

> "From the power of the Grave I will redeem them; From death I will recover them. Where are your stings, O Death? Where is your destructiveness, O grave?... (Hosea 13/14)

JULIAN VALDERRAMA

"Martha said to him: 'I know he will rise in the resurrection on the last day.' Jesus said to her: "I am the resurrection and the life. The one who exercises faith in me, even though he dies, will come to life." (John 11/24,25)

"And I have hope toward God, which hope these men also look forward to, that there is going to be a resurrection of both the righteous and the unrighteous." (Acts 24/15)

"For if we have faith that Jesus died and rose again, so too God will bring with him those who have fallen asleep in death through Jesus." (1 Thessalonians 4/14)

These scriptures quoted, strongly suggest of the possibility for our quintessence to brought back to life. It also suggests that there will come a time when we will get the opportunity to exercise faith in our abilities so as to perpetuate our personal identity.

So that's it. There is absolutely no hope for mankind to access biological immortally if there is no technology to access people's quintessence and bring them to a newly created body. And even if we were able to transfer our quintessence into new bodies through new technological means, our negative quintessence will continue to become worse and destroy life around us, if universal policy continues to be rejected. Our very presence would become destructive to what is good. Our ability to access and reset our quintessence to perfection based on our free will depends on our ability to access the tree of life. We must become aware of highly evolved consciousness that may direct us to access it. All scripture quoted here is to emphasize that the possibilities for immortality, its existence are not beyond plausibility, thus we could create a situation where we could recreate ourselves to be in a place and time where we won't depend of others to access the so called 'rivers of life' or 'trees of life.'

"And he showed me a river of water of life, clear as crystal, flowing out from the throne of God and of the

Lamb down the middle of its broad way. And on this side of the river and on that side there were trees of life producing twelve crops of fruit, yielding their fruits each month. And the leaves of the trees were for the curing of the nations." (Revelation 22/1,2)

## Tying it all together

The catch is we must qualify and accept the bailout. How? We must align our lives to the most fundamental laws of the universe. This is how we must conquer so when the time comes where Prime Minister is given full authority and influence over Earth's affairs we can qualify to receive citizenship. We must submit to the universal policy implemented and now soon to be enforced. Will its programming give us access to the tree of life then?

We must plugin into the educational systems previously discussed. We must read books, listen to audio material, and attend meetings on a regular basis with like minded people that re-enforce universal policy and governance in their own lives. We must continue to affect our thoughts, words, actions and habits back to source so we can qualify to eat from the tree of life. No one will do it for us. We are the ones that must conquer. The choice is up to us.

# CHAPTER 11

## Identifying Christ's Consciousness And The True; 'New World Order'

"In the days of those kings the God of heaven will set up a kingdom that will never be destroyed. And this kingdom will not be passed on to any other people. It will crush and put an end to all these kingdoms, and it alone will stand forever." (Daniel 2/44)

A T THIS POINT, the reader may have already considered that there is certain validity to the scriptural reference. We have discussed how laws of physics as they are described today through quantum physics, have been described as laws or principles of life throughout history by past and present spiritual leaders and philosophers. These teachings are timeless and continue to create magnificent success by those who have used them. We have also seen how these 'tools' per say, do also have a double edge sword. Our negative patterns have a drastic effect in our lives and other peoples' lives. It shifts the universe to continue to mimic and mirror back to us as what we fear; what we don't want. The continuance of such negative thoughts' vibration permeate the matrix through the fabric of space, and such thoughts finally bring unnecessary pain and suffering to the source of resonance or those who choose such broadcast of energy.

The universe will make us pay for those thoughts the way a parent will inflict punishment for misbehavior. We can either accept that discipline and correct our thinking and continue to perpetuate thought patterns of a positive nature, or we can continue to wallow on the negative until we pay the ultimate price; our lives. We have all seen the illustration of three monkeys, one covering his eyes, the second covering his ears, the third his mouth. The inscription relates the thought, 'see no evil, hear no evil, say no evil." Timeless council for those who will understand the powerful mind and how our creation is firmly established based on our habits of focus. But also we must be fully aware to identify a bucket of shit. If it looks like shits and if it smells like shit, then it must be manure, and manure can be used as fertilizer.

Unfortunately we have seen the authorities of this world create horrific acts of violence and oppression throughout time. The books of history are filled with examples of massive wars between nations. Just during the last 100 years more people have died in conflicts between nations than all the deaths caused by the collective known wars in the past. We have seen World War I, World War II, the 'Cold War', and now the war on terror. People are more fearful about their lives than ever before with no knowledge of how to break free. The nations are bewildered as to what to do.

There are reports of central governments and nations creating a coalition; an alliance for combined action of governments in the world. The purpose? A call for a new world order where the world is controlled by one central world government. A governance by a group of elite members of society, where national boundaries are no longer recognized. People are skeptical but these plans have been clearly inscribed in the Georgia guide stones. The address is' Guidestone Road Northwest, Dewy Rose, GA 30634. Ideas of one world currency, one world religion, one world social system overwhelm the internet and other sources that emphasize the idea of a drastic change.

One of the more disturbing ideas from those who desire to establish this new order of things, is that they wish to keep the world's population under 500,000,000. Considering that the world's population is over 7 billion, it is an understatement to say that they are trying to create a situation where mass genocide will take place. Of course this is far from what universal policy requires, for love and love of principle would never consider or require such drastic and extreme measures to create a world where equitable living where peace and security are the norm.

Under universal policy a government of peace and security will be firmly established among the potentials who choose to align precisely their collective vibrational lives to enforced suggested laws of universal policy. This will progressively qualify us for the perpetuation of the life of our quintessence on to eternity. Life everlasting will absolutely be given to everyone who submits to the new legal disclosures from the government of the universe enforced by Christ Consciousness.

Some questions do arise. Who really rules the world? What forces are behind the curtain? What does the current scene or system of things governing the world have anything to do with our personal desires? Has Christ Consciousness reveal to us what can create a one world government where truly the entire globe can prosper from universal policy? Yes, this infinite consciousness has revealed it through a series events that have made the world create a massive quantum leap of positive progress never before seen in history. What created this change? The United States' Declaration of Independence.

## Was the U.S Declaration of Independence, and by connection the constitution, inspired of God?

To answer these questions we must contrast the quintessential energy of the Declaration of Independence, its Constitution and the principles for which it stands. For these documents and the minds that inspired them were created to uphold universal policy. We will examine how these principles found within correlate to the triad of knowledge and our foundational principles that can create our quantum leap to biological immortality as envisioned by Nikola Tesla. It is all connected to precise scientific laws that can ultimately open our way for a global governance where humanity can prosper under the mantle of energetic principal love. A government under Christ Consciousness influencing the master mind or collective mind of the masses. To recap let's review the essence of this book:

The "Triad Of Knowledge"

"If the genius of invention were to reveal tomorrow
the secret of immortality, of eternal beauty and youth,

for which all humanity is aching, the same inexorable agents which prevent a mass from changing suddenly its velocity would likewise resist the force of the new knowledge until time gradually modifies human thought." ____Nikola Tesla

"Truly I say to you that if you have faith the size of a mustard grain, you will say to this mountain; 'move from here to there' and it will move and nothing will be impossible for you."____Christ's Consciousness

"Whatever the mind of man can conceive and believe, it can achieve."____Napoleon Hill

Also let's be clear about the foundational laws for life and personal creation:

### Foundational Law for Immortality 1:

"We must love God with your whole heart and with your whole soul, and with you whole mind."

### Foundational Law for Immortally 2:

"We must love our neighbor as ourselves."

So through natural research of spiritual principles, success philosophy and scientific data; we can define life's highest laws as the highest form of recognition that we can give to God and each other. Therefore it is the observation and application of the most quintessential physical laws of the universe in the light of the golden rule as being the highest good for mankind, period. Then we can say that the highest form of worship or honor in recognition for life's merit that we can render to God and life is:

For us to become a collective vibration of consciousness; vibrating together a set of specific energetic blueprints of frequencies, based on its most quintessential and vertex vibrational imprint; 'love'.

If thus far you have agreed with these statements then let's contrast them to the spirit of the Declaration of Independence and its principles for which it stands. But what is the declaration of independence? Why was it written? What does the Declaration of Independence factually say? And why are these questions important and relevant to us as individuals? What do they have to do with the triad of knowledge and Tesla's vision and call for the secret to immortality and eternal beauty? And how does it relate to our global ability to create a one world government where life, liberty and the pursuit of happiness are in fact guaranteed under universal policy? How has it influenced our creative ability? How will it continue to impact our creative ability?

Also does the fact that as we readily examine these principles as they are obviously highlighted through these documents, thus can we conclude Christ Consciousness was positively imprinting its spirit into the words. Are they in fact inspired words?

These topics will be examined in light of the Principles highlighted through the book: "A Miracle That Changed the World, the 5000 Year Leap" by W. Clean Skousen.

## 1ST PRINCIPLE

### The Only Reliable Basis for Sound Government and Just Human Relations is Natural Law.

As emphasized previously in this book, as the author I do not wish to be perceived as dogmatic, the reader is of course encouraged to read for themselves the Declaration of Independence and come to their own conclusions. You may notice that the essence of the document highlights all the principles we have been encouraged to put into practice. We will now examine exact sentences or highlights from the document that pinpoint the essence; universal policy guided by the principle of the Golden Rule. In this chapter the author has made the attempt to clarify the archaic but eloquent wording of what was said through the writings of the Declaration.

# 1ST Paragraph of the Declaration of Independence

"When circumstances force people to separate officially from their current governments who assume to rule over such people, it is by the same God given authority as evidently demonstrated through the laws of nature; God's laws that they do so. It is these laws that gives the people under such government, the power to speak of the reasons explaining their decision for official rejection of such authority. Natural law demands that such decision be respected"

Here we can clearly take in that the writer of the Declaration of Independence had in essence the Golden Rule in mind. For no one has the authority to govern another without the consent or the agreement of the second party. Why? For if we decide to forgo our ability to create our own reality by releasing our individual sovereignty to an outside source, we may be in essence giving our freedom away and empowering another with it.

Tesla had emphasized that we can attune our mind to receive instruction or information from the store house of knowledge from the universe. We can resonate with the mind of God to solve any challenge and care for our own lives. For if God is for us who will be against us?

"The gift of mental power comes from God, divine being, and if we concentrate our minds on that truth, we become in tune with that great power." Nikola Tesla

We have established that everything we could ever want to accomplish can be accomplished by exercising our mental faculties through the power of faith or knowing that whatever we choose to experience is in fact already ours. This means that we can, in essence, have God in an instant give us the answer to any question or request. Therefore why would we pass our power to do so to others?

We risk the limited perception of others to decide what is good and what is not good for us, and in the name of security we may begin to give up our freedom and our inalienable rights; our God given rights.

These principles are founded in natural law through the laws of quantum mechanics. It is eternal and universal, for if you were to live in another part of the universe the same rules would apply to your entire energetic structure. Since these laws are intrinsically connected to us, the writers of the Declaration were then forced to acknowledge that our rights are nonnegotiable for giving them up would cause chaos. This is because doing so would surmount to creating a belief that contradicts our nature and our creative ability.

Giving away our freedom of thought is tantamount to giving away the essence of who we are. Our thinking ability and our precise exercise of that power is what helps us create our own desired reality.

"Thinking ability will keep you watch over you, and discernment will safeguard you,.. Safeguard practical wisdom and thinking ability," (Proverbs 1:4/3:21)

## 2ND PRINCIPLE

### A Free People Cannot Survive Under a Republican Constitution Unless they Remain Virtuous and Morally Strong

"When the righteous are many the people rejoice, but when the wicked rule the people mourn." (Proverbs 28/2)

## 2nd Paragraph of the Declaration of Independence

"We hold these truths to be obvious, for all men are created equal, that they are endowed by their Creator with certain nonnegotiable rights; life, liberty and the pursuit of happiness. That to secure these rights, people create systems of government for the people. This means that the power is given to the government by the choice of such people under their freewill, and not under duress or violent force."

It is interesting to note that the original governmental structure that was first established for the people of Israel in the Old Testament, when carefully studied, we notice that it was close to what we now call a Republican Constitution. It is also interesting to note that a time came when the nation desired to have a King, a single ruler system or monarchy that would rule over them. They were warned of the oppression they would suffer under such Kingdom if they insisted on establishing such rulership:

> "This is what the king who rules over you will have the right to demand: He will take your sons and put them in chariots and make them his horsemen, and some will have to run before his chariots. And he will appoint for himself chiefs over thousands and chiefs over fifties, and some will do his plowing, reap his harvest, and make his weapons of war and equipment for his chariots. He will take your daughters to the ointment mixers, cooks, and bakers. He will take the best of your fields, your vineyards, and your olive groves, and he will give them to his servants. he will take the tenth of your grain fields and your vineyards, and he will give them to his servants...... the day will come when you cry out because of the king you have chosen" (1 Samuel 8/11-18)

In contrast they already had a system of governance that allowed them to prosper where the power was decentralized similar like the power is decentralized under the government in the United States. This was aptly demonstrated when at the suggestion of his father in law Jethro; Moses was to appoint leaders and divide the nation and its power structure. Under this government Moses was but as a Prime Minister as opposed to a Monarch with absolute power. Moses had progressively been taught to share power among other leaders throughout his service to the nation of Israel. (Exodus 1813-27)

The decentralization of power will always be preferred since it allows for a master mind to be created which amplifies collective power. This in turn allows for a powerful broadcast of frequency for the common good of its constituents of such government. It is about power-with and not power-over. By giving away power the law will empower, but what we fail to give we lose, for it is by giving away that we experience more.

This is why we have always been encouraged to share what is good with those who do not have.

It is also evident that these writers of this document had in mind a collective morality or beliefs that acknowledge the rights of others; mainly a person's right to living life under freedom and happiness. But what could we say is the highest form of morality? I believe Nikola Tesla said it best.

> "The desire that guides me in all I do is the desire to harness the forces of nature to the service of mankind."

Using our creative abilities is harnessing the forces of nature. It is carefully defining what serves us and what doesn't serve us, which is ultimately defined on what we next desire to have, be or do. Our desires truly shape our world for everything begins with a thought. Knowing this gives us the moral obligation to be the best version of us we can currently become. Jesus was quoted saying that a lamp is never hidden but is put in places where everyone can see so that the light may be shared. Darkness is a symbol for nothingness and if we could not see or discern light we could not create for there would be no relative concepts. No ups or downs, no lefts or rights, no ins or outs.

First and foremost this point must be highlighted. For it is the physical manifestations that demonstrate simply whether something is working or not. The United States' Declaration of independence was a powerful massive change in the affairs of the this world. History has shown that generations of people were ruled from tyranny to tyranny with brief superficial periods of true prosperity and abundance.

The United States government is a republican constitution where we thus far have seen the best progress. In just over 200 years the world has finally made tremendous progress in light of scientific discoveries which were made possible by the mantle of principles of life and liberty. Having the freedom to pursue our dreams through industriousness and personal ability is necessary for our continuous progress and personal evolution for our ability to continuously supersede our current levels of belief. When we experience the satisfaction of setting up a goal or dream and then create it, our faith and knowingness of our abilities increase. Thus we build stronger foundations to create bigger or better. This can be stifled by governments who may be manipulated into creating a sea of rules and superficial laws that may drown who we are.

We must be careful that those who refuse to align their interest to universal policy not usurp or manipulate power, thus the writers were forced to say:

> "That whenever any form of Government becomes destructive of these ends, it is the right of the People to change or to scrap it, and to place newly more efficient Government that continues to protect its foundation which is based on such nonnegotiable personal principles mainly safety and happiness."

And what is the best way to make sure these natural God given rights are protected? And how can we make sure that our creative abilities are not stifled by dogma or bias tyranny? What can guarantee that the populace continues to uphold the principles that allow for freedom and happiness?

I believe it is defined by the principle of persistence. To continue to do the right things long enough and consistently without let up. But to also whenever possible to continue to transcend such principles so as to inspire more freedom and happiness whenever possible. Thus the following principle must be put in place:

## 3RD PRINCIPLE

The Most Promising Method of Securing a Virtuous and Morally Stable People is to Elect Virtuous Leaders

It is imperative that the population be educated into these principles and laws. Educational systems must continue to be refined and put in place by people approving the current governance. We live in a world where entertainment and distractions could dull our perceptive abilities and give way for others who may not have the best intentions and take advantage. In the other hand the following statement must also be acknowledged:

# 3<sup>rd</sup> Paragraph of Declaration of Independence

"Common sense and awareness must be used by the people of the government in place, to not allow brief opinions or short term visions and causes to drastically change the government away from protecting those rights."

We must strongly consider that as individuals not to be fickle. We cannot become so dependent on what the government may or may not do, afraid of every possible preconceived bias and evil conspiracy. To live in fear is counter productive and we may actually shift our experience. We cannot let our emotions or imagining run wild thinking that the government somehow is the enemy and think we are in danger when there is no evidence of it.

We must take full responsibility for our lives and periodically check and be proportionally involved in such affairs. Public officials are that, public servants, and as such we can always use the grievance system through master mind gatherings. But it will always be wise to direct our thoughts and treat and think of our government to what it could become. This may paradoxical and hard to perceive but the laws of physics tells us it is true, for we will experience what others do to us because we judge them as so, in fact our decisions of who others are will make them manifest those qualities in our perceptive reality. We must treat people as if they were living to their full potential and not as they currently are. This will direct our energies and their energies. The thing we focus on will be influenced to change based on what we perceive and decide our outside influences are.

To illustrate imagine wife A perceives that her husband is distracted and quite because he may no longer love her anymore. This is wife A exercising fear through her mental faculties. Husband B then becomes more and more preoccupied with other things but her wife. He may be thinking about work, and the future of the family mirroring in essence his wife's insecurities, for he is also consumed with thoughts of fear draining his energy leaving little room for family time. But this does not mean he doesn't love her. As wife A continues to believe the thought 'program'; 'my husband no longer loves me,' this creates in essence a force field around her that prevents her husband from showing love. She is the creator of her reality. His thoughts may be enforced and as a result he may want to participate in other activities such as TV, sports or hobbies to relax and break from the exhausting exercise of fear. This is perceived by wife A as neglect. But Husband B is doing this because he may want to restore his mental peace so he may have the energy to be with family, but it is not possible because there are now two incongruent programs in their field.

Husband B will battle to show love and thus wife A will perceive that as exactly what she believes; not being loved. Wife A's belief about her husband may escalate to he doesn't love me because he thinks I am annoying, or there is someone more attractive, or he regrets marrying me, etc. This negative energy as it escalates depletes her and him literally zapping positive energy from their life force. Thus it would become a self created nightmare whereas both parties, unless they become fully aware of their creative abilities and how it influences each one, these programs will continue to progressively create more havoc on their relationship. This may be why statistics say that first marriages have more than a 50% chance of failing. And that second and third marriages have even greater percentages of failing. This is because the negative patterns of behavior are then brought to the next relationship. This applies to our personal relationship with money, authority figures, bosses, systems of thought but more to the point and relevant to this chapter, our government.

So let's make the agreement to think, and speak of our governments as competent, able, virtuous with the best intentions in mind but not allowing our happiness to dissipate if we perceive the government as failing. We have the moral obligation to collectively create the best governance this world can potentially offer. But at the same time let's not give up our freedom for a false sense of security provided or promised by government. For if we believe that security is an expectation as opposed to a given then we will collectively create a train of experiences challenging our security, thus we will perpetuate the state of being known as 'security expectation.' Thus we will always be in expectation, in need of it and will live our life in insecurity perpetually.

> "It is observably true that it is man's habit to endure
> suffering for as long as they can instead of removing the
> cause of their suffering. But that when such suffering

persist and gets worse then finally people will look for the cause and should remove the cause of the suffering"

4th Principle

Without Religion the Government of a Free
People Cannot be Maintained

"Politics are the divine science,… what is to become of an independent statesman, one who will bow the knee to no idol, who will worship nothing as a divinity but truth, virtue, and his country?" John Adams Founding Father

As we progressively expand on the fact that principles of love and life are founded on very precise laws, then we have no choice but to conclude that politics is our spirituality demonstrated practically. It is our religious beliefs that determine our spirituality or the force of our spirit as defined by our mental agreements of what is true. This in turn demonstrate our politics for they are deeply rooted in our spiritual beliefs. So what exactly did the writers of the Declaration of Independence have in mind?

"..the Founders, therefore, is a group of very independent, tough-minded men whose beliefs were based on empirical evidence and the light of careful reasoning. Even their acceptance of things which are not seen, the existence of the Creator— were based on observable phenomena and precise reasoning.

The well known psychologist Abraham Maslow, in his book titled The Third Force, concluded after extensive testing that a mind-set based on a spectrum of well established beliefs, such as the Founders possessed, definitely produces a higher quality of human behavior and more positive adjustment to the stresses of life.

No Doubt Cicero would respond to such a conclusion with the observation that these results should have been expected. Beliefs based on reason and self evident truth bring a human being into harmony with natural law and the eternal realities of the cosmic universe" (The 5000 Year Leap, pg73)

These paragraphs were fully quoted to the credit of the writer of the book; 'The 5000 Year Leap' to emphasize the harmony of the idea of fully integrating our personal religion in alignment with universal policy as defined by the principles of love and the Golden Rule. Once these principles are continually introduced to the masses and future generations it will in fact produce another quantum leap that will not take 5000 years but as Nikola Tesla said:

> "The day science begins to study non-physical phenomena, it will make more progress in one decade that in all previous centuries of its existence" This is why he was also forced to acknowledge and say: "If the genius of invention (science) were to reveal tomorrow the secret of immortality, of eternal beauty and youth, for which all humanity is aching, the same inexorable agents which prevent a mass from changing suddenly its velocity would likewise resist the force of the new knowledge until time gradually modifies human thought."

Spirituality and success philosophy guided by science and the study of the laws of our physical universe must be fully integrated into the world's religions so as to transcend human dogma and bias. It will progressively be introduced but it will happen just like German philosopher Arthur Schopenhauer said:

> "All truth passes through three stages. First, it is ridiculed. Second, it is violently opposed. Third, it is accepted as being self-evident."

Also this philosophy will only be accepted through the following phenomena:

> "A new scientific truth does not triumph by convincing its opponents and making them see the light, but rather because its opponents eventually die, and a

new generation grows up that is familiar with it." (Max Planck)

There are absolutely more principles that govern the constitution and reflect the spirit of the Declaration of Independence, but these will be discussed in later publications for more emphasis that we are in urgent need to re-emphasize its principles to the populace mainly the United States.

## Modern Day Egypt; As Above, So Below

Referring back to the story of Moses in chapter 1, we discussed why it was a big deal to Jehovah the god of the hebrews to prove his power over the Egyptian gods. For it was not in essence Pharaoh who had the power, but like a puppet being manipulated by higher frequencies, it was the higher ranking angels in opposition to Jehovah who had full control. It was truly a battle of the gods with its obvious physical manifestation of their vibrations as they manipulated that events' energetic matrix reality. It was nothing but all malleable particle mass ready to be transformed to whatever they saw fit for such mass to become. It was all particles of energy defined by time and space being reshaped as these gods saw appropriate. It is highly likely that technologies were used to make these so called miracles happen, but we are not certainly sure of it. For this reason I feel that the events described in the Old Testament and dealings with Egypt, represent an appropriate symbol of our current paradigm.

But are these tyrannical governments still ruling from the higher dimensional realms? Is the struggle of the gods in the so called heavens a direct reflection or our current struggles. Is the current power struggle in today's world a result of the physical manifestations of the will of the gods ruling from their respective thrones? Is there in essence a modern day Egypt` where we have now become their slaves where we are but pawns in their hands to do whatever they like as demonstrated by the violent picturesque in the Old Testament and other holy books?

If so then doesn't that mean that we may have the collective ability to call for the acceptance of Christ Consciousness to influence our minds, so that in turn we may influence positively those who may have oppressed us from these higher realms?

One thing is clear; the negative consciousness operating in the minds of this world must be cleared if we are to have a chance at peace. On the offset of this chapter we quoted a text describing that the God of heaven would establish a government that will never be destroyed. Then it will replace opposing forces that may resist a one world government under Christ's Consciousness rule. This will force a bigger exodus where large masses of people will be liberated from the modern day Egypt into a truly peaceful world. Whether it is literal beings or figurative forces being stopped, this process will give us way to finally truly create the collective world we are yearning for. With what results?

"The righteous will posses the earth, and they will
live forever on it." (Psalms 37/29)

The promise is that as we continue to exercise our freedom and align ourselves to universal policy under this new government, we will continue to progress to the point of resetting our quintessence to finally our original place. No longer corrupted by the unfortunate inheritance from past generations, we will be able to exercise our complete free will and creative powers and conquer the fear patterns that have been perpetuated through the ages. Thus we will finally be able to qualify to get free access to the tree of life and live forever. As the true owners of Earth, we will finally fulfill our purpose which is to care for our home and the animal kingdom.

Some people may ask won't the earth become overpopulated? This is impossible for as we raise our vibration and creative abilities we certainly will be able to inhabit other known worlds throughout the universe. And even if that was not the case would we not be able to access higher dimensional earth realms and populate those worlds as readily and easily as this one? The laws of physics that govern the earth's field of energy allow for an infinite amount of parallel earths to exist, and as such we can perpetually continue to inhabit earth infinitely. The idea that we will live on earth and live forever upon it is no longer an impossible notion.

"The earth remains forever" (Ecclesiastes 1/4)

Sources continue to fill people's minds that the earth might be destroyed through a nuclear holocaust, or that a comet of epic proportions could completely pulverize the planet. Others believe the we may all be destroyed by some evil alien agenda, and certainly in a very literal way that is exactly what the scriptural reference has been emphasizing when it describes the end. The only difference is that those who are currently holding power of the current state of affairs governing this world; absolutely want to convince us that they themselves are the ones that are benevolent and the good guys who desire our best interest. They just forgot to tell us that they cannot and do not want to give us life because they themselves are dying. What we know for sure is that it is not going to happen like movie moguls wants us to believe. Spiritual forces are absolutely coming but not to destroy the planet and every inhabitant indiscriminately, but they are coming here to help fulfill universal policy.

It is Plenipotentiary's intention to establish the real new world order, where people will prosper and achieve biological immortality. The government of the universe has the will to save the literal planet from the destruction being implemented by the negative collective vibration of the human race, but it will not do it for us. We must accept and be aware of the instruction that is being given to us, essentially we may have to come to terms that nobody is coming to save us and that the calvary is us.

Our very negative patterns of behavior threatens the very order of the entire physical universe and our corrupt vibrational outputs will not be tolerated for much longer. Life must go on, life will always find a way. A drastic change must be implemented to preserve the human race as a species. The Earth will also be restored and built into a universal paradise.

"He will swallow up death forever, and the Sovereign
Lord will wipe all the tears from all faces." (Isaiah 25/8)

The future power structure of universal policy will bring about a drastic reset on our entire energetic matrix of particles defined by time and space. As we examined before, fatal accidents and natural disasters are only the proper physical manifestation mirroring back to us that there is something very wrong with our current mental paradigm. All cause of untimely death will be done away with because the PCES that create all kinds of death can only exist under the present lower vibrational realms. They are creations and physical manifestations of the improper use of our imaginations as fear gets encapsulated into our very essence.

Under the new power structure through powerful instruction, further understanding of the universal physical laws will be described in practical terms for all to apply and reverse the cause of our permanent negative output of energy. By developing new neural pathways; integrations of accurate knowledge of universal policy, we will progressively resonate higher until we qualify to manifest and be able to partake of the tree of life that is in the paradise of God.

With eternal life as a natural resource, infinite life will make it almost impossible to experience pain or suffering. For whatever challenges we may face, feeling and knowing that we have acquired infinite time and space will equip us mentally to deal with them perfectly. But what will be the physical manifestations that will prove that we are progressively moving in such direction? Are there milestones that we can look forward to experiencing?

> "At that time the eyes of the blind will be opened, and the ears of the deaf will be unstopped. At that time the lame will leap like the deer, and the tongue of the speechless will shout for joy. For waters will burst forth in the wilderness, and streams in the desert plain." (Isaiah 35/5,6)

> "They will build houses and live in them, and they will plant vineyards and eat their fruitage. They will not build for someone else to inhabit, nor will they plant for others to eat. For the days of my people will be like the days of a tree, and the work of their hands my chosen will enjoy to the full." (Isaiah 65/21,22)

Once the Prime Minister of the universe comes to take over the current power world order, the time will come when the powerful rulers of this world will not acknowledge its authority, for it is their personal authority and power that is being threatened.

Just like an Ambassador who uses diplomacy, Prime Minister and Plenipotentiary will bring about powerful changes and benefits to the human race, thus showing that universal policy will only bring the best benefits to those who act in accordance with Universal Policy. In harmony with the illustrative description; nations will readily acknowledge the mountain of God being raised on top of every visible governmental system, subjects of their world's governments will readily see that the benefits are better under the new power structure. To illustrate; it is known that there is a consistent flux of immigrants from third world countries that decide to move their livelihoods to more prosperous nations. Hispanics throughout the America's will sacrifice everything at a chance of a better life in the United States of America. Third world countries in Africa have also seen massive numbers through the years move to Europe in search of the same prospects. They do this because they realize these countries can offer something better.

It could be that they are leaving due to corrupt officials becoming parasites and destroy the value creation of the common people. Maybe incompetent rulership wastes resources in weapons and other dead end items that cannot create the necessary advantages and needed basic necessities of life. People may be in constant fear of kidnapping for the ransom of what little resources they may have. Maybe crime cartels oppress people with mass criminal activity by stealing and forcing commoners to become addicts to drugs and addictive substances. Parents may leave their respective countries to protect their children for fear that they may be caught on a vicious cycle of different forms of slavery such as forced prostitution and drug addiction.

And even if some people manage to create a life style where they have a measure of prosperity in these areas, their families and resources are in constant threat of being taken away from those who are envious, greedy and parasitical.

In the same manner, promises by this new government by its visible physical manifestations will prove that Plenipotentiary's rulership under universal policy is better. Thus many will be given ample opportunity to become kingdom citizens of that government to benefit from provisions.

This will force many of the Kings of the Earth to acknowledge their incompetence to their personal rule and their higher dimensional masters' authority. How? Because those who submit to universal policy and exercise their mind to align their energetic blueprint to that of the laws of the universe, automatically qualify for the kingdom of the universe.

The following will be some of the physical manifestations of the kingdom of the universe when in place as well as some its citizenship benefits:

"All the kings will bow down before him, and all the nations will serve him." (Psalm 72/11)

"So he will startle many nations. Kings will shut their mouths before him, because they will see what they had not been told and give consideration to what they had not heard." (Isaiah 52/15)

"At that time you will see and certainly become radiant, and your heart will throb and overflow, because the wealth of the sea will be directed to you; the resources of the nations will come to you." (Isaiah 60/5)

"And she will certainly become to me a name of exultation, a praise and a beauty before all the nations of the earth who will hear of all the goodness that I bestow to them. And they will be in dread and will tremble because of all the goodness and peace that I will bestow on her." (Jeremiah 33/9)

I believe in a very literal way the United States has benefitted in the way that these scriptures suggest, a result of its acceptance and persistence of universal policy as defined by the Declaration of Independence and the Constitution.

Nikola Tesla lived to create better and transcend this world, for his creations were known to be created for the ultimate benefit of mankind. Tesla wanted to give a system that would provide clean safe energy that everyone could freely access. His vision of a world where the secret to immortality, youth and beauty was not farfetched nor far from probability, and he knew it.

These realities already exist under the government of the universe and the fabric of space. Its reality exist because we already are able to perceive it in our imagination, which is evidence suggesting its

JULIAN VALDERRAMA

plausibility. We must remember that it is our absolute will to create it, our collective consciousness, is what will bring it into our reality. Our imagination creates and brings it into reality. It is up to us to raise our collective vibrations to match such frequencies. We must either expand or digress, grow or die. For if once we see those real physical manifestations in our real physical world and still stubbornly decide to support those who oppose the upcoming take over of universal policy, our erratic quintessence will remain in us and we will not qualify to receive the citizenship to that government. We would become outsiders, outcasted to still depend from those so called kings of this world to provide. Like a plague, conditions will worsen for it is the collective vibration that must continue to match those people's fear programs.

What will be the end-result? Although parasitical classes of people from this world may stubbornly decide to fight for their cause, for they hopelessly depend upon that system, their world outside of this new arrangement will continue to live progressively under the same arrangement. There will be two world orders, the first and most prosperous will be the government of the universe established on earth by Prime Minister, where those who qualified to become citizens prosper and have gained access to the tree of life. The second is the perpetuation of this old world with the parasitical beings who may rule from behind which may be currently in control of this world. We then will have the choice to either submit to the new power structure of universal policy or decide to continue without the support of the new established paradigm.

The nature and ability that must persevere in us, is to be able to apply and live up to universal policy, for it is the struggle and the fight for our mind that we must win and conquer. This will allow us to become part of a prosperous new world. We will see that we will have become a people without military arsenal for we will become a people who were trained to 'beat their swords and spears into creative tools for the benefit of others and to learn war no more,' since all resources under universal policy from God will be used for the benefit of its citizens.

The fact that this future global paradigm under Plenipotentiary has prosperity, gives an enticement of the still prevalent mentality of those who chose the hard way; complete independence from Universal Policy and its universal rulership. Meanwhile qualified potentials will have made the Earth into the kingdom of God physically manifested, a reflection of our God given consciousness. We will also perpetually learn to use the full power of our mind to create and expand our realities. But at the same time those who refuse such change may want to still use their creative ability to resist the change. Who would do so? Those who lose out from losing control of the status quo, which as we may have already observed only benefits those who have monopolized power and control instead of sharing it.

## The Issue of Our Sovereignty Settled

Everyone living then will be faced with a test; will we choose exile or will we become permanent citizens of universal policy? By that time there will be absolutely no doubt as to what the laws of the universe are and how they relate to love. There will be also no disbelief in Plenipotentiary's ability to use his power for the benefit of his subjects under his governmental rule. Prime Minister will have fully helped us to clear and reset that erratic nature of our quintessence by teaching us to download the energetic code disseminated by the perfect example of beings who reflected perfectly such code as they were living their life while on earth. Our ability to think, feel, speak and act as Jesus or many other avatars who exemplified Christ Consciousness is based on our ability to learn to download data from the ether by matching the frequency of those vibrations. We will in fact, be able to download the Christ program; the exact nature of a perfect human being into our quintessence.

Thus, if the entire universal field of energy, vibration and frequency including time and space was originated through this single powerful consciousness, then while it was on earth, there is the probability that this entire "Matrix" of knowledge was therefore integrated carefully close to the universal access of the human mind and the consciousness surrounding the species. We must but match the frequency of those vibrations to access all the secrets of the universe and its creation. The potential for growth and experience staggers the mind.

Christ's Consciousness may even help us to become aware of the knowledge that originated the point of singularity, a point of energy smaller than an atom where all the infinite energy that we see in the universal field came from, including all the energy that is yet to be discovered; the big bang. This gives ample room for the possibility, that according to the latest data in science in harmony with scriptural validation, there exists the probability of us potentially being able to do the same thing at some point in the distant future. Could we then create powerful universes of energy with their own intelligent beings made in our image? Do not mark my words to heart but remember what the triad of knowledge says:

"If the genius of invention were to reveal tomorrow the secret of immortality, of eternal beauty and youth, for which all humanity is aching, the same inexorable agents which prevent a mass from changing suddenly its velocity would likewise resist the force of the new knowledge until time gradually modifies human though...If you want to find the secrets of the universe, think in terms of energy, frequency and vibration."____Nikola Tesla

"Truly I say to you that if you have faith the size of a mustard grain, you will say to this mountain; 'move from here to there' and it will move and nothing will be impossible for you."____Jesus

"Whatever the mind of man can conceive and believe, it can achieve."____Napoleon Hill

Provided we have become aptly trained and qualified to receive such privileges of power, anything is possible. Where will we be as individuals when these things begin to take place? So even if we find ourselves on a neutral ground from such spiritual wars by still maintaining and sticking to our independence from Universal Policy, such decision could cost us the highest price. If we decide to use these abilities while still perpetuating this world, we may find the secret to immortality and the fruit from the tree of life almost impossible to attain. It would be risky to pursue this on our own without first accepting the fact that we must transcend the negative consciousness of this world.

## Tying it all together

We wish to emphasize that just like Napoleon Hill highlights in his publications; this entire book was written with the foundation that nobody has a monopoly over knowledge or understanding. We cannot have a monopoly over science, nor success philosophy. Even the scriptural reference emphasizes that interpretations of it belong to God. But a careful study and research was done to bring to the forefront as many common grounds and denominators that give more comprehension of what the laws of physics say and how the universe works. These principles of knowledge were consistently applied to bring about this information in alignment with truth. This work is certainly not infallible, and thus open to criticism and future integrated new knowledge. There will most likely be, those who will violently disagree and take singled out sentences under their own point of reference to try to discredit this entire work. So like parasitical mentalities, many still do try to demonize the scientific empirical evidence and credit it to the work of the devil. But just like Jesus and Tesla emphasized, it is only time that will ensure and let us know what fruitage will come from all this information. The tree will either produce rotten or fine fruit.

Although there are thousands if not tens of thousands of pieces of data that could add more validation to what has been transcribed through the pages of this book, it was not done so for the sake of time and simplicity. For it is also encouraged to any reader and researcher to gather unbiased conclusions through honest and sincere studies of all fields of knowledge. For it is also a fact that the laws of force and magnetic attraction will help establish empirical evidence in the minds of individuals who choose to do so. This we can be certainly assured that whatever you sow you will also reap, for this will permeate everything we do regardless of whether we believe it or not. We cannot wish the law of gravity away for it is an established fact of science and empirical evidence, so in the same way how could we deny to at least try to do our best to align our lives to the golden laws of the universe.

We also certainly encourage you that you read and reread this publication as well as other suggested material that will add more frames of mind and fresh perspectives to these teachings. We also encourage you that you immerse your self in audio material discussing the same things. In addition, integrated discussions on a regular basis with like minded people who take this information seriously, will help you integrate neural pathways that will unlock your individual potential.

I personally have some suggestions as far as what groups you could join or meet with in a regular basis and thus cause tremendous benefit, for your own personal cognitions and your own experience. I say this in harmony with the very basic principle of life that may be consistently ignored:

> "If a brother or a sister is lacking clothing and enough food for the day, yet one of you says to them, 'Go in peace; keep warm and well fed,' but you do not give them what they need for their body, of what benefit is it? So, too, faith by it self, without works, is dead." (James 2/16,17)

So too myself; what good is it for me to write all these words and sentences without suggesting a system in which you can immediately plug into and create a master mind to perpetuate now your own personal success and desired outcomes?

(This is a preview of the introduction of my next book for you; "Blueprint for Immortality Volume II: Life is a Game)

Chapter 1

The Law of Opposites: "For every action there is an equal and opposite reaction." Isaac Newton

"In the absence of that which you are not, that which you are,… 'is not'" Neale Donald Walsh

In this chapter, some new information will be shared, that at this point of our reading, you may or may not be ready for. Please consider that, if at this place and time you have accepted these concepts that we have now shared with you as factual, or at least as plausible; then know that under the same suggestion please strongly consider the following information.

At first this data may sound ephemeral and too esoteric. But remember all of this information can now be verified and quantified by using the simple techniques such as asking to your accepted authoritative divine source for factual personal experience as to whether these things are so. By this point you may now have accepted that your brain or mind is a powerful transmitter of energetic frequencies, or vibrations imprinted with your intention of transmission. Then, if this is the case for you, please do transmit an intention and do bring about factual personal experience that will validate for you that the previous and following data in this book is in fact true.

Please know and be assured that the following creation stories although used as illustrations to explain our present reality, they do have basis in what will be explained as ultimate reality. In essence where we come from, who we all are and the nature of life, questions that have been asked and begged for, for millennium. The answers for which humanity continues to ache for, have always been answered although maybe not widely spread or accepted, and most of the time hidden and repressed. In essence these answers to life's secrets can be attained by anyone at anytime in the space time continuum. Once asked, it is only a matter of having absolute self awareness to becoming ready to receive the answers.

You will positively become aware that the laws of physics and how they testify to powerful truths, mainly the story of creation. What was created. When it was created. Why it was all created. How it all began.

The story of creation: There is a God but there is no God.

Part 1 of Creation: God becomes self aware

In the beginning; God was all there was. But as God, he could not know he was God since he was all there was. There was nothing else that was not God or love. Therefore in a sense God was nothing, love was nothing, and they did not exist. For how could God, all that was, is and ever will be, know it self, since there was no point of reference outside of self. For even if God is all there is, he is everything and nothing, inside and outside, there and over there and here. God then is everywhere and nowhere, or now-here. Hence a left does not exist in relation to right. Up or down would also not exist. Above and below also non-existent. Cold and Hot and all its varying degrees would also not exist. For how could God know that it was the light if there was no darkness. And how could God know it was love if love was all he was and nothing else but love. For how could God experience loving or being loved if there was no-one else to love or love less or be loved by. And how could God be Joy if there was nothing but joy as the Highest state of happiness one could experience.

Thus absolute bliss became a curse and absolutely meaningless since Paradise was all there was, and thus the Blessed Paradise and absolute joy could not be experienced for there was nothing else. Therefore God was not. And therefore since God was everything, it was also nothing.

Part 2 of Creation:

God the Creator and the re-created

In the beginning God was created. But God could not know it self in experience for he was everything. Since there was no point of reference outside of god self, god was not. Thus in the beginning there was nothing. But nothing was something and it was conscious of it self. Thus this nothingness gave thanks for its consciousness to its God for it realized he was the body of a much higher consciousness, for God had a God. In prayer God asked this higher consciousness, his God, why he was created?

In response God discerned that since he was created to be the body of his God, that he would do the same for himself and create others to be his body and thus recreate itself from the nothingness and all-ness of it all. God discerned that in the realm of the absolute in which he was created, he had to replicate it self but this he could not do outside of him but only through himself for God was everything in his realm of existence. Thus God divided or re-created it self into an infinite amount of smaller parts from his holy body as God, for God was now both whole and the divided, a divine dichotomy. But he made all these separate spirits and sons of God to forget they were God once for they were once before part of the body of God as one. So God finally was ecstatic to be alive for he could not experience life before since it did not know it self. For now God was a single awesome being experienced among an infinite collective of sons, all his holy angels. Now God could experience himself as love for he can now love others. But what could God give to express his love for his creation for it was all a perfect paradise where none of his infinite children experienced anything less than what God is? For all of it was God, love, joy and absolute peace. But this they all did not know.

Part 3 of Creation:

A decisive meeting in heaven

So all the spirits of God assembled themselves before the throne of the most high to give recognition and proper worship for they loved him for his creation. And thus God was asked by one of the many in all creation why they were created? And God said; 'I asked my creator God the same question!', therefore I was inspired to receive the secret of life, for my body as God, is the Temple of my God whom I so dearly love, for I had been given life just the same as my infinite spiritual sons whom received life from I, their creator. You are my holy angels of my life, and my body, for my God self. Thus my spirits sons had been conceived, for they are also the body of my God, so that my God could know it self experientially for there is no point of reference outside of god-self. 'So therefore; I was not, before I conceived you. So what do you think you must do?'— asked God to his son in connection with the rest of creation.

'We must fulfill the will of your God and our God, by creating other bodies to know ourselves experientially so that God may fulfill his will and experience God-self among creation forever and ever, and so it will be.' said this one single spirit sitting before God.

God in his delight explained of his glorious plan, one that was inspired to create from the infinite intelligence of his creators, that he must create that which he was not, for he must become that which he was not, to experience and know what he was; mainly love. For how could the spirits of God help fulfill God his will to know his god-ship and awesome power if he was all there was? For in paradise everything was perfect and complete, there was nothing but love and joy. But this they did not know for love and joy was all there was.

And since they could not come to a solution they prayed to their Father's God and related the matter to God for they could not fulfill his will. And collectively they prayed for the answer to become a reality, and thus God conceived of an answer and began to re-create it self once again. God re-created a second division within his body, for he could not do this outside of itself since God is everything and everywhere. It created a body in which to operate to become that which he was not. But as a matter of fact God is what he is and that which he is not. And a great polarity came into existence, one awesome creation of love for that which all creation applauded. And from the infinite nothingness and all-ness came the physical universe the world of the relative into manifestation as a result of the prayer, the word of God. For through faith we discern that the systems of things in the universe came in existence by the sound of the word of God.

Part 4 of Creation:

God creates the Devil, but there is no Devil.

In the beginning there was nothing, but nothing was something, thus something was everything. Still, everything was not, for even though God knew itself to be nothing but love, he could not know it in experience. So he prayed to his God of this great sadness so that he would conceive of an answer. And thus God in his great wisdom discerned that he must create quite literally what he was 'not'. God understood and comprehended and gave thanks for the revelation from his Creator God.

So God gather all his children, the sons of God before his throne and revealed the matter of the new revelation that he had received from his Father. And the holy angels all with him cried out in joy and applause for God's plan for the ages, for they were in paradise, but this they did not know. For they were nothing but love, joy and peace, but this they did not know. For how could they know what they were being if they could not at least experience their polar opposites. For if God was all love how could he demonstrate his infinite love for there was no means to express it, for its opposite; fear, did not exist. For how could joy be truly experienced as opposed to just known, if there is no sadness. For how could peace be real or mean anything if there was no conflict from which to finally experience peace. How could the oneness of God and all his children really know the fruitage of God's Holy Spirit; love, joy, peace, kindness, goodness, faith, self-control and patience; how could these concepts really mean anything if its polar opposites did not exist; fear, sadness, strife, violence, badness, hate, and lack of self control. How could they mean anything without their opposite. For the children of God could not know it, for it was paradise and perfect joyful ecstasy, but also a curse.

So the great plan of the ages was finally conceived and the infinite physical universe thus was naturally created along all its components and relative terms. The ups and the downs, the lefts and rights, the small and the big, the tall and the short. The hot and the cold, the warm and the cool. The heavens above, and the earth below. Male and female all were created. And so there was a beginning, a middle and an end; the Alpha and the Omega. Past, present and future for God was now in all time and space, for God is also all time and space. For God is everything and everywhere, and he is also nothing and nowhere but always; now-here.

In the beginning before the creation of the great polarity and the physical universe, the sons of God stationed themselves before God to make request for wisdom, or knowledge applied and experienced. Thus one of the angels asked; What is joy? 'It is that which you are always forever and ever,' God said. 'It is that which I am for I am the happy God. 'I know' responded the spirit angel of God before his throne. "But how can I recreate my holy companions and have them share in my joyous light?"

And thus God responded; 'for that to be re-created, one of the spirits of God must become unholy, or not whole. They must resonate so low that they must create the experience of sadness, gloominess, depression and anxiety. Only then could you share your light and joy and then you will know experientially what joy is.' Or you could also decide yourself to become less than joy, and vibrate so low that you become sadness, and I will send one of my holy angels to share in their light and save you from such death. What will you choose?, for everything is Joy and everyone is peace in the paradise of God."

And for infinite amount of time, the holy angels kept stationing themselves before God asking about their same predicament. For all of them desired to know who they were but dared not become less than what they were and fall from the grace of God, they dared not become fallen angels. For some desired to experience forgiveness, but there was none to forgive. And some desired to experience more happiness in giving, but there was none to receive for there was no lack. For some desired to experience the healing of others but there were none to heal. For some desired to share of their peace but there were none who lived in conflict. For some wanted to share their wisdom and love, but there were none whom God had created who were not wise and loving. Since the great polarity; and that which was not God did not exist, mainly fear and hate none of the son's of God could know it in experience. God had created everything perfect for it was paradise. But these things and experiences they did not know.

So the time came to move into motion the plan of all ages, and thus by faith we perceive that the systems of things were put in order by the sound of God's word, so that what is seen has come into existence from things that are not visible. God then decided to quite literally re-create himself into that which he was not, for he loved the world so that he gave himself up in order that everyone exercising faith in him might live through him and not be destroyed forever. God would not allow for one of his children to be lost in the illusion of what they were not, at least not forever. Thus the great polarity; fear, the opposite of love was created. An artificial infinite consciousness was replicated, and exact opposite of his love and joy, a consciousness who desired to create and experience fear and hatred, strife and conflict. Thus God saw that the light was good, and God began to divide the light from the darkness.

God could now look onto itself and see who he really was in experience for he was also experiencing himself as who he was not. For the physical universe in all its relative components allowed God to infuse his essence, in fact wear the physical universe, make it part of his body in complete duality. Thus God became that which he was not, for he is both love and fear that which he is not, but had to re-create for himself and his spirit sons to experience who they really were; absolute love and joy. Thus he was able to inhabit both the positive charge of every particle and the negative charge of every particle of consciousness that is part of the physical universe. Thus the term; God is everywhere, but the Devil opposes him. But because God is everything then the entire negative spectrum of energy is conscious and in fact a god, an artificial construct completed along the positive side of the energetic spectrum of the universe. Duality and oneness, divine dichotomy. The physical universe; the world of relativity came into existence.

Part 5 of Creation:

Life is a game, a massive agreement within an artificial construct.

So now God and all the holy angels, everyone who exists now, has existed and will exist; rejoiced over seeing this great vision. God had now created the opportunity for all his created beings to experience who they truly were. Their love could now be tested, their joy re-experienced, their peace fought for, their mildness tested beyond the limit, they would experience great kindness by giving to those who didn't. They would now know their goodness by seeing evil around them and doing something to heal the good in others. To remind others that they were love and joy. They would move mountains by exercising faith and accomplish great things. They could now truly experience being, doing and having whatsoever they would desire as opposed to knowing these things in concept.

But one of the sons of light, an angel, asked... buy how can we ever truly experience these things when in an instant we could decide to experience who we truly are. God responded; 'Great question! And so in the same manner that you forgot that you are me when I created in your perfection, I will make you forget that you are you as you now stand in perfection in my paradise. You will also forget that we are all one when you decide to come down into the construct. So when you decide to be love, I will be there to give you the opportunity to show your love to those who don't know how. So when they hit you in the chick, you will turn the other and show them who you are. And when they take the things you posses you will give them even more to show your wealth. But not always will you be successful in doing these things for now you can now experience who you are not. And in your anger, sadness and desperation will you say; 'oh why God, father, why have you left me?' And then I will send to you one of my other angels to remind you, that is to bring into your mind the remembrance of who you are so as to recreate your self. This I will also do so that you may know how to bring back others of our one family, and bring back to me all things.'

And great excitement and ecstasy came over all creation over this great game for they could now be anything and everything. And God promised to play the game with them, to set up scenarios of great challenge and opportunity. To create adversaries through people, circumstances and events. So that if some needed saving, a savior could experience being as such. And God said; 'We will create stories of amazing wealth for now there are those who will experience being poor. We will create periods of peace after much turmoil and strife. For there will be a time for everything under the sun, for what has been is what will be, and what has been done will be done again. It already existed from long ago; it already existed before our time. No one will remember those of former times; nor will anyone remember those who come later; nor will they be remembered by those who come still later. And I will make it so, so when you have acquired great wisdom, an abundance of frustration will you experience. So that whoever increases knowledge increases pain. For every action there will be an equal and opposite reaction. This is the coding of the matrix for which the world of the relative will force upon you something else to think of, something else to be, something else to have. But why would God bring upon you such striving for nothing and vain? Then you will remember the time that you were but love and peace but you could not know it, and then you will remember that you are me. And again I will make you forget who you are that you may eventually and finally experience who we know we truly are.

And there will be an appointed time for everything, a time for every activity under the heavens; a time for birth and a time to die, a time to plant and a time to uproot what was planted; a time to kill and time to heal; a time to tear down and a time to build up; a time to weep and a time to laugh; a time to wail and a time to dance; a time to throw stones away and a time to gather stones together; a time to embrace and a time to refrain from embracing; a time to search and a time to give up as lost; a time to keep and time to throw away; a time to rip apart and a time to sew together; a time to be silent and a time to speak; a time to love and a time to hate, and time for war and a time for peace. For in the absence of that which you are not, that which you are, is not.

And my greatest gift will I give by making you forget forever if you choose to do so, for I will make everything beautiful in its own time so as to keep you occupied with what you see, touch and smell. All of the desires of you heart will you be always preoccupied but they will not remind you of who you are. Nor will your happiness result from the things you posses. And as such you will continue to search for me through your outer world and never find me, for the Kingdom of God is within you. And I will even put your desire for eternity into your heart so that you may experience the illusion for all times, until you do not. And although you may live forever in your present avatar of your choice, you will never find out the work that the true God has made from beginning to end.

And you will not know that whatever happens has already happened, and what is to come has already been, until you do. For I am the creator, the alpha and the omega. I am what I am, and I am what I am not, and from the great unseen is where I will always come to you. So if someone says here is God, See! do not believe for another will also come and say; 'No' here is God come and see!' And they will hate, persecute and kill each other for then they will say to each other; 'how could he be God when he does not say the things that my God says, nor did he look like the way I saw him. And they will call each other liars and blasphemers, and apostates. And they will raise their flags in my name and they will cause great destruction.

Flee from them, for they will rob your mind and slave you through fear. Protect your thinking ability for they will hypnotize you with their sweet words and promises of life. And thus you must ask them questions so as to protect your thinking ability. And these are the questions you must ask: Do their words require and demand that you give up your questioning them for fear of angering their God and suffer retribution? Does their teaching tell you to lose faith in yourself by putting faith in them? Do they insist that they hold answers that you could never have? And do they insist that those answers must be accepted without question? For you must always live with knowing that there are unanswered questions than to live with and believe that there are questions which cannot be questioned.

For the closest distance from you to me is here now. So why search for me elsewhere. They cannot have you think for yourself, for you may come up with a different answer from theirs. They will tell you that you are imperfect and broken. For if you cannot accept your own thoughts then how can you accept theirs. Are they really that much different than you? More worthy, more holy that I would only choose them? Flee far from them for they will fill your hearts with fear of God, when you know I am nothing but love. They will make you worry and dread my wrath and my conditional love under a myriad of conditions when you knew that my love is unconditional. Flee far from them for they will make you believe that they themselves are the only ones who truly know God and it is through some one and through only a way in which you can be saved. They will teach you of a God of infinite wealth and power that demands groveling worship, love and adoration, and that this God will go as far as to kill you and your loved ones once you do not. Flee far from them for they will teach you that you are a chosen people separate from all others, that you are above them and as such that it is God's will to war and destroy those who do not think or believe as they do. And they will murder, steal, rape and cause mass genocide in my name.

So when you hear these things call to me and ask me whether these things are so! Has God truly become a Devil? Has God become a self-centered tyrant, an insecure being who demands of you to live in dread of his anger, power and self righteousness? And then I will remind you and say; 'A true Master is not the one with the most students, but one who creates the most Masters. A true leader is not the one with the most followers, but the one who creates the most leaders. A true king is not the one with the most subjects, but one who leads the most to royalty. A true God is not One with the most servants, but One who serves the most, thereby making Gods of all other. For this is both the goal and the glory of God, that his subjects shall be no more, and that all shall know God not as the unattainable, but as the unavoidable.'

For I am God and I am you and you are my body. So my true messengers will remind you we are one. That I am God and I need nothing an therefore require nothing, much less your worship. But I do invite you to share in my workshops for there is much I invite you to be, do and have. For the Devil walks about like roaring lion ready to devour someone. Therefore know the rules of the game and let's play together. Test the inspired utterances and continue to ask me for strong and powerful validation of my love. I will move heaven and earth and always bring you an answer. But do not require others to accept your experience of God as gospel, for each soul has been given the free will to walk their own path and experience their own reality. So do not resist the one who is wicked but refine them by putting hot coils on their head, that their impurities may come up to the surface and remember who they are, for this is the great alchemy of the universe. Do this also that you may not be lost in their ways. For I am the great alchemist and the great refiner, for I will continue to remove great inexorable agents that prevent you from changing. For I am the force of new knowledge and through all time I will progressively modify your thoughts. For this is the secret to your own immortality, beauty and youth. And then you will re-experience a new heaven and a new earth. And my tent will be with you and reside with you. I will wipe every tear from your eyes and death will be no more, neither your mourning nor your outcry nor your pain be anymore. These former things will have passed away. For I will give you access to many trees of life, that you may stretch your hand and eat and live forever, until you do not anymore. For this what means to be God, to be always at choice. So what will you choose?

# RECOMMENDED REFERENCES

Books:

- The Magic of Thinking Big by David Schwartz
- See You at the Top by Zig Ziglar
- The Secret by Rhonda Byrne
- The Power by Rhonda Byrne
- Think & Grow Rich by Napoleon Hill
- The Law of Success in 16 Lesson by Napoleon HIll
- The New Psycho-Cybernetics by Maxwell Maltz
- How to Win Friends and Influence People by Dale Carnegie
- The Magic of Believing by Claude M. Bristol
- The Power of Positive Thinking by Norman Vincent Peale
- As a Man Thinketh by James Allen
- How to Have Confidence and Power in Dealing with People by Les Giblin
- How I Raised Myself from Failure to Success in Selling by Frank Bettger
- The Go Getter by Peter B. Kyne
- Rich Dad, Poor Dad by Robert Kyosaki
- New World Translation of the Holy Scriptures, Reference Bible; Bible & Tract Society of New York Inc.
- Acres of Diamonds by Russell Conwell
- It Works; The Famous Little Red Book That Makes Your Dreams Come True
- Neo Think Universal Secrets by Mark Hamilton
- Neo Think Superpuzzle by Mark Hamilton
- The 5000 Year Leap, A Miracle that Changed the World by W. Clean Skousen

Audios:

"Your Wish Is Your Command, How to Manifest Your Desires" by Kevin Trudeau

*(All audios from the books previously listed)

Movies:

- Matrix Trilogy
- Avatar
- Kung Fu Panda
- Frequencies
- How the Universe Works
- What the 'Bleep' Do We Know
- The Secret
- Ancient Aliens (History Channel)
- Zeitgeist the Movie
- Zeitgeist, Addendum
- Zeitgeist, Moving Forward
- The Universe; Microscopic Universe, (History)
- The Fabric of the Cosmos: Universe or Multiverse? (Nova, PBS)

(OBVIOUSLY THERE ARE A LOT MORE REFERENCES THAT CAN HELP US INTEGRATE THIS INFORMATION BUT FOR SIMPLICITY AND EMPHASIS, THE BASICS LESSONS ON THESE REFERENCES ARE ENCOURAGED. FOR AS WE MASTER THESE PRINCIPLES THROUGH BOTH REPETITION AND MEDITATION, AND AS WE EXAMINE THESE SOURCES HUNDREDS OF TIMES, WE WILL INGRAIN ITS LESSONS MORE DEEPLY.)

JULIAN VALDERRAMA

# INDEX

## A

Abraham (Hebrew patriarch), 166
Adam (first man), 226, 230, 235, 239, 246
*Alchemist, The* (Coelho), 180, 190
aliens, 13, 33, 193
ambassador, 215, 219–21, 240, 242, 272
    duties of, 221
angels, 13, 31, 166, 229, 233–34, 284, 286–87
attraction, law of, 42, 45, 97, 109, 198

## B

behavior, 78, 172, 198, 200, 218–19, 240, 271
bible, xv, xxii, 11–13, 29–30, 33–35, 42, 48, 64, 92, 102, 112, 122, 144, 154, 185, 232
blueprint, i, iii, xv, xix, 78, 172, 192–93, 195, 209, 215, 239
Bryant, Kobe, 5

## C

Carnegie, Andrew, xxii, 9, 22, 85, 134, 140, 150, 159
cells, 78, 145, 225–26
Christ consciousness, 215–17, 219–20, 222, 224, 241–42, 244, 248, 250–51, 257, 259, 269
church, 206, 208–11, 214
Coelho, Paulo, 180, 190
Cold War, 256
competition, 77, 87, 100, 147
congregation, 209–11
consciousness, 72, 129, 131, 133, 175, 184, 187, 213, 216–17, 226–27, 233, 242, 252, 258, 276, 281, 285–86
contentment, 105–9, 111, 114, 118, 139, 143, 145

## D

*Dark Energy, Dark Matter* (NASA), 33
dark matter, 14, 31–34
demons, 13, 87, 234
destiny, 43–45, 53, 66, 75, 112, 181
devil, the, 31, 233–34, 278, 283, 286, 289–90
discontentment, 105–7, 111, 114, 116, 118
DNA, xxi, 80, 102, 111–12, 114, 119, 145, 176–77, 196, 251
double-slit experiment, 15, 17, 20, 26, 36
dream board, 145–46
dream book, 145–46
dreams, 45–46, 49–53, 59, 61–62, 66, 73, 87, 94, 97, 100–101, 125–26, 128, 139, 141–50, 152–53, 158–66, 170–74, 186–87, 190, 263
duality, paradoxical, 15, 18, 31, 35
due diligence, 3, 6–7, 149

## E

Eden, 64, 237, 240–41
education, 85, 87, 100, 118
Egypt, 1–2, 5, 193, 269–70
Egyptians, 6
Einstein, Albert, xvii, 11, 18, 22, 32–33, 65, 91, 97, 99, 131, 134, 213
electromagnetism, 24
Elijah (prophet), 41, 137
elite members of society, 161, 256
energetic field, 45, 68, 232

energy, xxiii, 14–21, 23–26, 31–38, 45, 47, 49–52, 55–56, 65–66, 108, 125–26, 128, 142, 151–52, 163–66, 190, 204–6, 213–14, 225–26, 276–77
  matrix of, 55
  transmission of, 26, 36, 65, 169
epigenetics, 75, 78, 97
eternal beauty and youth, xxi, xxiii, 13, 29, 35, 53, 277
eternity, 55, 58–59, 64, 71, 74, 107, 131, 145, 184, 195, 249, 257, 288
ether, 49–50, 55, 63, 65–66, 68–72, 86, 102, 122, 128, 139, 142, 157, 197, 204, 214, 251, 276
Eve (first woman), 235, 239, 246
evil, 31, 44, 48, 73, 100–101, 103, 113, 143–44, 236–37, 256, 271, 286

**F**

failure, 78, 100, 128–32, 134–35, 139, 151, 154, 157, 167, 234, 246–47, 293
faith, xxi, xxiv, 29, 33, 47–49, 51–52, 61–62, 66, 71–72, 99–100, 120–27, 131, 170, 174, 188, 209–10, 238, 243–44, 283–85, 289
fear, 8–9, 40, 52–53, 59–60, 66, 71–72, 74, 99–100, 115, 119, 123, 143–45, 150–51, 245, 251–52, 265, 270–71, 273, 284–86, 288–89
Ford, Henry, 100
free will, xvii, xxii–xxiii, 34, 181, 193, 238, 248, 253, 290
frequency, xvi, 14, 16, 20–21, 24–26, 31, 35–38, 40, 44, 70, 82, 102, 108–11, 114, 118–19, 154–55, 165–66, 174–75, 199–200, 275–76
  transmission of, 26, 36, 40, 71, 117–18, 139, 157, 174

**G**

Gates, Bill, 149
Georgia Guidestones, 256

Gideon (prophet), 187–88
goals, 10, 22, 46, 49, 52, 60–61, 73, 85, 87, 97, 101, 105, 125–26, 128–29, 134, 139–44, 146–49, 159–64, 171–73, 205
Golden Rule, 198, 200–202, 205–6, 210–11, 213, 244–45
gravity, law of, 4, 17, 23–24, 26, 37, 66, 68, 83, 278
Greene, Brian, 23–24

**H**

happiness, 5, 25, 101–2, 104, 109, 111, 114, 117–18, 136, 138–39, 143–45, 167, 176, 197, 201, 229, 263–64, 266, 281, 285
heaven, 13, 31–32, 41, 51, 91, 122, 124, 135, 148–49, 156, 176, 182, 184, 218, 220, 229, 233, 236, 240–41, 269–70
Hebrews, 1–2, 7, 33, 48, 86, 96, 137
hell/hellfire, 48, 135
Hill, Napoleon, 9, 22, 85, 140, 146, 158, 195–96, 198, 200, 202, 206, 208, 211, 277
Horeb, Mount, 2
humanity, xxi, xxiii, 13, 29, 35, 53, 58, 74, 143, 231, 233–34, 240, 257–58, 268, 277, 280
humankind, xxiii, 53, 60

**I**

ignorance, xvii–xviii, 11, 85, 91, 207
imagination, 65, 73, 98–99, 104, 135, 143, 190, 271, 274–75
immortality, i, iii, xv, xix, xxi, xxiii, 13, 29, 35, 53–54, 63, 65–66, 192–200, 202–3, 205–7, 211, 213–16, 244–45, 257–59, 277
inexorable agents, xxi, xxiii, 13, 29, 35, 50, 53–54, 66, 82, 88, 157, 165, 170–72, 193, 216, 221, 224–25, 244, 258, 268

JULIAN VALDERRAMA

infinity, 39, 58–59, 64, 70–71, 73, 82, 89, 98, 130, 175, 182–84, 195
injustice, xvii, 173
Internet, 39, 85, 93, 161, 256
invention, xxi, xxiii, 13, 29, 35, 53, 257, 268, 277
*Iron Lady, The*, 43
Isaac (Hebrew patriarch), 166
Israel, 1, 96, 131, 137, 168, 187, 261–62
Israelites, 2, 5, 41, 187

# J

Jacob (Hebrew patriarch), 166, 203, 223
Jehovah, 2, 5, 7–8, 33, 84, 115, 137, 151, 167, 169, 178–79, 181, 185, 187–88, 191, 208, 230, 237, 239, 269
Jethro (priest), 2
Johnson, Clifford, 19
Jordan, Michael, 5
Joseph (Jacob's son), 166–70, 173, 186

# K

kindness, 95, 143, 201, 284

# L

law of gravity, xi, 4, 17, 23–24, 26, 37, 66, 68, 83, 278
law of motion, third, 42, 60, 109, 132, 238
*Law of Success* (Hill), 195–96, 209, 293
laws of physics, xi, 22, 39, 44, 54, 60, 64–65, 82–84, 95, 97–98, 103–4, 108, 111, 118, 120, 122, 129–31, 136, 196, 236–37
Lazarus (Jesus's friend), 229–30
love, xix–xx, 6, 46–47, 51, 62, 77, 86, 93, 97, 99–103, 136, 143–44, 152–53, 155, 199–202, 211, 213–14, 256–59, 265–66, 281–90

# M

magnetic attraction, law of, 42

magnetic force, 24–26, 37, 40, 97, 193
magnetism, 23, 25
master mind, 85, 140–41, 159–61, 220, 224, 279
*Matrix, The* (Wachowskis), 50, 67–68, 70, 108, 125, 180, 186, 221, 225, 230
matrix reality, 50, 69, 76, 80–81, 157, 193, 207, 214, 269
messengers, 5–7, 137
Messiah, 219
Midian, 2, 187
minister, 215, 219, 221, 242
money, xix, xxiii, 2, 6–7, 22, 55–58, 60–62, 86, 93, 105, 107–8, 127, 136, 139, 142–46, 152–54, 171, 212, 246, 266
Morpheus (*The Matrix* character), 68–70, 125, 186, 230
Moses (prophet), xxiii–3, 5–10, 41, 52, 67, 76, 262, 269

# N

negative thinking, 44, 109, 139, 147, 150, 251
negative thoughts, 44, 51, 78, 100, 109, 111–13, 238, 255
Neo (*The Matrix* character), 68–70, 125, 186–87, 191, 230
neuroplasticity, 78
new world order, 255–56, 271
Nightingale, Earl, 43, 75
nocebo effect, 53, 79

# P

particles, 14–21, 23–26, 31, 34, 36–40, 50, 52, 54–55, 61, 65, 71, 81, 86, 102, 126, 131–35, 237, 241, 250–51, 286
principles of, 26, 36, 264
passions, 53, 152–53, 155
patience, 35, 95, 100, 131, 143, 284
Paul (spiritual leader), 4, 69, 74, 86, 90, 93

PCES (people, circumstances, events, and situations), 164, 166–68, 171, 185, 189–91, 271
peace, 105–6, 116, 143–44, 156, 170, 193, 195, 201, 203, 205–6, 209, 214, 218, 243, 245, 256–57, 270, 274, 279, 284–88
persistence, 118–19, 127, 131–32, 139, 155, 216, 244, 264, 274
personal legend, 173, 180–87, 189–91
Pharaoh, 2, 8, 170
Pharisees, 87
photons, 15–19, 21–22, 24, 31, 34, 132–33
placebo, 53
Planck time, 45, 193
Plenipotentiary, 215, 217, 220–21, 223, 240, 242, 244, 250, 272, 275
polarity, 25
prayer, 21, 117–18, 174, 176, 179, 184, 246
prejudice, xvii, 202, 232
pride, xvii, 185, 197
principles of life, 27, 154, 196, 198, 235, 255
prospect, 156–57

**Q**

quantum entanglement, 17–18, 20, 26, 35–36
quantum mechanics, xxiv, 12–13, 15, 20, 28–30, 37–38, 42, 231–32, 241, 245, 261
quantum physics, xix, xxi–xxii, xxiv–1, 4–5, 8–9, 12, 14–15, 18, 22, 26, 28, 34–36, 48, 55, 65–66, 84, 91, 121, 189, 193
quantum tunneling, 18–20, 26, 36, 61, 71, 99, 120
quintessence, 78, 221, 225–33, 238, 240–42, 244–45, 248, 250–53, 257, 270, 276

**S**

science, xvi, xxi, xxiii, 11–12, 20–21, 25, 27–28, 30–31, 34–35, 41–42, 49, 64–67, 79, 84, 100, 129, 142, 162–63, 235, 277–78
principles of, 25–37, 49
scientific empirical evidence, 10, 278
scientific method, xvii, xxii–xxiii, 1, 3, 5, 7, 10, 129
self-control, 100, 143, 201, 284
self-determination, 179, 181
sin, 48, 52–53, 235, 243, 245–46
singularity, 24, 127, 276
slaves, 5–7, 41, 68–69, 123, 223, 233, 246–47, 269, 288
Solomon (king), 4, 71, 74, 91, 131, 150, 182–83
sovereignty, 222
spirit science, 28, 30
spirituality, xxi–xxiii, 12, 27–28, 31, 34, 42, 86, 142, 267–68
*Stan Lee's Superhumans*, 89
string theory, 22–24, 26, 35, 37, 42
success, xvii–xviii, xxii, 3, 5–6, 8–10, 13, 22–23, 76–79, 91, 93–96, 100–102, 104–6, 130–31, 134, 141–42, 159–60, 167–69, 188, 195–97, 293
eight-step pattern for, 141
success philosophy, xxi, 12, 195, 258, 268, 277

**T**

Tesla, Nikola, xxiv, 22, 38, 53–54, 58, 65–66, 68–69, 74, 157, 165, 176, 182, 184, 193–94, 196, 199–200, 202, 207, 213, 250
*Think and Grow Rich* (Hill), 9, 43, 196
tree of life, 64, 238–40, 242, 251, 253–54, 270, 272, 275
tree of the knowledge of good and evil, 238
triad of knowledge, xxi, xxiii, 31, 35, 38–40, 142, 203, 257, 259, 277

trilateral commission, 244, 249
Trudeau, Kevin, 4, 21, 87, 90, 92–93

## U

uncertainty principle, 18–19, 26, 36
universe, xvi, 11–37, 44–49, 54–55,
66–67, 73–74, 82–84, 95–98,
122–23, 125–31, 154–55, 162–
68, 173–78, 180–81, 183–85,
198–203, 206–7, 243–45, 248–
49, 270–78

## V

vibration, xvi, 11, 14, 16, 18, 20–21,
24–26, 29, 31, 35–38, 45, 108–9,
111–12, 118–19, 139, 163–64,
200–201, 245–46, 269–70, 276
frequency of, 43, 158

## W

*What the Bleep Do We Know!?*, 15, 21
Woods, Tiger, 5
World War I, 256
World War II, 247, 256

## Y

*Your Wish Is Your Command* (Trudeau),
21, 90, 92

Printed in the United States
By Bookmasters